HTML Mastery: Semantics, Standards, and Styling

Paul Haine

friendsof
DESIGNER TO DESIGNER™
an Apress® company

HTML Mastery: Semantics, Standards, and Styling

Credits

CONTENTS AT A GLANCE

CONTENTS

ABOUT THE AUTHOR

Clawing his way from deepest, darkest Somerset upon his coming of age, **Paul Haine** found himself ironically trapped for a further six years on the opposite side of the country in deepest, darkest Kent, learning about web standards during the spare weeks between history lectures. Now residing in Oxford's famous East Oxford, he spends his days working as a web designer, surrounded by a plethora of Apple-branded hardware, Nintendo kitsch, and a truly massive collection of unusable grunge and pixel fonts.

Paul also runs his personal blog, joeblade.com, alongside his design blog, unfortunatelypaul.com. He attends to both of these approximately every six months during the gap between catching up with his blogroll and refreshing it to begin reading again.

ABOUT THE TECHNICAL REVIEWER

Ian Lloyd runs Accessify.com, a site dedicated to promoting web accessibility and providing tools for web developers. His personal site, Blog Standard Stuff, ironically, has nothing to do with standards for blogs (it's a play on words), although there is an occasional standards-related gem to be found there.

Ian works full-time for Nationwide Building Society, where he tries his hardest to influence standards-based design ("To varying degrees!"). He is a member of the Web Standards Project, contributing to the Accessibility Task Force. Web standards and accessibility aside, he enjoys writing about his trips abroad and recently took a year off from work and all things Web but then ended up writing more in his year off than he ever had before. He finds most of his time being taken up by a demanding old lady (relax, it's only his old Volkswagen camper van).

Ian is married to Manda and lives in the oft-mocked town of Swindon (where the "boring lot" in the UK version of *The Office* are from) next to a canal that the locals like to throw shopping carts into for fun.

Ian is the author of *Build Your Own Website the Right Way with HTML & CSS* (SitePoint, 2006), which teaches web standards–based design to the complete beginner. He has also been technical editor on a number of other books published by Apress, friends of ED, and SitePoint.

ACKNOWLEDGMENTS

Thanks to everybody who's put up with me during the last eight months of writing: Vikki, Emma, Thom, Verity, my parents, the entire Britpack, and many others whom I'm no doubt offending by not mentioning them specifically. Thanks to everyone at Apress and friends of ED involved with this book, to Chris Mills for taking the project on in the first place, and to Ian Lloyd for his technical review.

Special thanks to Leon, Ian, Helen, and gv for keeping my website running when I was too busy writing.

INTRODUCTION TO HTML FOR WEB DESIGNERS: SEMANTICS AND STANDARDS COMPLIANCE

In the beginning, there was HTML, and it was good. Then, after some time had passed, there was a *lot* of HTML, and it was not very good at all. Then, after some more time had passed, there was XHTML, and it was better, though often not as good as it could have been.

A few years ago, being a web designer didn't require an understanding of HTML or CSS, or if it did, it didn't need to be a *comprehensive* understanding. A basic awareness would be enough, and proficiency in software such as Photoshop and Dreamweaver was far more important. Websites could be generated directly from images without ever viewing the markup behind them, and the state of that markup—was it well written, was it lean, was it efficient, was it meaningful—was not considered. In fairness, there wasn't much of an alternative a few years ago; you made your websites with tables and spacer images for layout and avoided semantic markup because support for web standards in browsers was simply not there yet.

The result of this was that websites could often be heavy and slow, usually only worked properly in one browser, were complicated to update and maintain, required duplication of content for "print-friendly" versions, and search engines had a hard time indexing, making sense of, and ranking them. This, in turn, led to a proliferation of shady search-engine-optimization tricks, <meta> elements overstuffed with keywords, and per–search-engine entry pages. Presentation (the look and feel) and behavior (usually JavaScript) were both mixed in with content, and pages had no meaning or logical structure—the concern of the day was how pages *looked*, not what they *meant*.

It was not a happy time to be a web designer.

Nowadays, the budding web designer needs to know a lot more about the building blocks of his or her trade—needs to know how to write (X)HTML, needs to know how to write CSS, and needs to know how to solve a layout bug in three versions of Internet Explorer plus Firefox, Opera, *and* Safari (or better still, he or she needs to know enough to avoid those layout bugs in the first place). Web designers have once again begun to learn how to write (X)HTML by hand, but the transition from building table-based sites in Dreamweaver's design view to hand-coding (X)HTML sites in Dreamweaver's code view can be fraught with complications.

This book is aimed at web designers who may have just learned enough (X)HTML and CSS to create a basic two-column layout, may have spent a lot of time in FrontPage or Dreamweaver and now wish to learn more about the technology their sites are built upon, or may otherwise consider themselves as being beyond the level of beginner and want to take their markup skills further. The intention of this book is not to teach you (X)HTML from the ground up; it is assumed that you have a basic knowledge already. The intention is also not to focus on designing an entire site with CSS, though there will be several examples throughout of applying CSS and JavaScript to your newly written, standards-based markup.

Rather, its intention is to explore (X)HTML in depth, to examine how to take full advantage of the variety of different elements on offer, to help you in creating semantically rich and structurally sound websites that you, your visitors, and passing search engines will all appreciate. Along the way, you will examine how best to improve your text with phrase elements, make judicious and informed use of presentational elements, create informative and useful tables and forms, and discover how there can be so much more to enhancing your content than simply hitting the I or B buttons in your design editor of choice.

Conventions

If I refer to HTML or XHTML, it means the reference is specific to HTML 4.01 or XHTML 1.0, respectively. If the reference is relevant to both, I will write (X)HTML.

When referring to "modern browsers," this means browsers that are standards compliant (or as near as they can be). At the time of writing, this includes Opera, Firefox (and other browsers, such as Camino or Mozilla, that use the same rendering engine), Safari, and Internet Explorer 7.[1] It is assumed that modern browsers will continue to be standards compliant as future versions are released.

Important words or concepts are normally highlighted on the first appearance in **bold type**.

Code is presented in fixed-width font.

Sometimes code won't fit on a single line in a book. Where this happens, I use an arrow like this: ➡.

```
This is a very, very long section of code that should be written all ➡
on the same line without a break.
```

So, on with the show.

---

1. Internet Explorer 7 is included tentatively, as at the time of writing the final release has only just been made public. Although its standards support has increased, it doesn't appear to be at quite the same level as Opera or Firefox.

1 GETTING STARTED

Lorem ipsum dolor sit am[et] ... it. Mauris vitae nisi ut ... olor sit amet, consectetuer a[c] ...
sem aliquam fringilla. Pr[ui]s. Vestibulum arcu ... ngilla. Proin pellentesque tin ...
mauris, pharetra sed, rut[um] llentesque mauris sem, ... sed, rutrum nec, congue ve ...
ullamcorper ut, rutrum i[d] ... rutrum id, vulputate at, aug ...

Suspendisse justo. Done[c] [cing], mi ut malesuada ... to. Donec lacinia ...
vestibulum, massa ipsum [in] [in] massa neque quis ... bulum, massa ipsum ...
eros. Pellentesque ut mi. [ecenas] vitae dui. Nam ... is eros. Pellentesque ut mi. ...
nulla dolor, faucibus sed [, lectus]. Ut in justo. ... vitae dui. Nam nulla dolor ...
[us]. Ut in justo.

Mastering HTML isn't just about knowing every tag that's available and what it means. Equally important is knowing *about* HTML—that is, understanding what tags and attributes are and how to use them, grasping the differences between HTML and XHTML, knowing what a doctype is and how to read it, and so on. Knowing about HTML will not only help you to understand it, but also help others understand you when you're discussing it.

This chapter consists of three main sections. The first section covers the terminology to use when talking or writing about HTML. The second section examines the differences between HTML and XHTML, two versions of the same language, and investigates some common misconceptions about both. Finally, the last section breaks a typical XHTML and HTML document into pieces, and looks at what each piece means and what it does.

If you're already familiar with these topics, then you can skip to the next chapter. However, I do strongly recommend reading this chapter as a refresher—it won't take too long to get through, and it's full of useful information. Also, knowing more about HTML than your peers will make you look stylish and cool, and who doesn't want that?

(X)HTML terminology

If you want to create expert (X)HTML and impress your friends and colleagues, it isn't enough to only walk the walk; you must also talk the talk. Using the correct terminology is important both to avoid confusion and to aid your own and others' understanding. For instance, if someone refers to the "title tag," is he or she referring to the title of the document that displays in the browser title bar, or to a tooltip of information (the title attribute) that displays when the mouse cursor hovers over an element (an image or link, usually)? Or perhaps the person is referring to a text heading that appears on the page, most likely in an <h1> element. There are tags, there are elements, and there are attributes; and each is an entirely different affair.

To make sure that we all have the same level of understanding before moving ahead, in this section I explain what each of the terms you'll frequently encounter when discussing (X)HTML refers to. I also discuss some other common terms that can cause confusion, including div, span, id, class, block, and inline.

Elements and tags

An **element** is a construct consisting (usually) of an opening tag, some optional attributes, some content, and a closing tag. Elements can contain any number of further elements, which are, in turn, made up of tags, attributes, and content. The following example shows two elements: the <p> element, which is everything from the first opening angle bracket (<) to the very last closing angle bracket (>), and the <em> element, which encompasses the opening <em> tag, the closing </em> tag, and the content in between.

```
<p class="example">Here is some text, some of which is
<em>emphasized</em></p>
```

A **tag** indicates the start and end of an element. The opening tag can contain multiple attributes, but it cannot contain other elements or tags, while the closing tag cannot contain anything but itself. In the preceding example, there are four tags: an opening `<p>`, an opening `<em>`, a closing `</em>`, and a closing `</p>`.

Not all elements have closing tags. For example, `<img>`, `<br>`, `<meta>`, and `<hr>` are referred to as **self-closing elements**, **empty elements**, or **replaced elements**. Such elements are not container tags—that is, you would not write `<hr>some content</hr>` or `<br>some content</br>`—and any content or formatting[1] is dealt with via attribute values (see the next section for more information). In HTML, a self-closing element is written simply as `<img>`, `<br>`, `<meta>`, or `<hr>`. In XHTML, a self-closing element requires a space and a trailing slash, such as `<img />`, `<br />`, `<meta />`, or `<hr />`.

> *Watch out for the `<script>` element: it is a container, so it has a required closing tag, even though it can remain empty of content and uses the `src` attribute to reference external scripts. This issue is made more complex by the fact that Opera (version 9 and above) and Safari both support a self-closed `<script>`, so the element will work, but it will remain invalid, and unsupported in other browsers.*

Attributes

Attributes appear within tags, and they can only contain the value of the attribute, for instance:

```
<p class="example">Here is some text, some of which is
<em>emphasized</em></p>
```

This example shows the `class` attribute. An attribute can contain multiple, space-separated values, which is useful if you need to apply different classes to one element. For instance, if you have two styles, one named example and another named `reference`, you can apply them both to a paragraph like so:

```
<p class="example reference">
```

Other attributes you may have already encountered might include `alt`, `src`, and `title`, but there are many more attributes, some element-specific (like the `selected` attribute used with the `<option>` tag) and some not (like the `class` and `id` attributes). If there is one thing I want people to take away from this book, it is this: **there is no such thing as an** `alt` **tag**.

Other terms you should know

With the descriptions of elements, tags, and attributes safely behind us, let's turn our attention to a few other terms you should know when writing (X)HTML: div, span, id, class, block, and inline. Like elements, tags, and attributes, you will often encounter these items

---

1. Excluding formatting with CSS.

in your work as a web designer, and it's just as important to have a good understanding of what they are and how they function.

People are often confused by these terms because they misunderstand their purpose or make mistakes when associating them (e.g., associate the id attribute only with the <div> tag and the class attribute only with the <span> tag).

Divs and spans

Divs and spans are two tags that, when used well, can help give your page a logical structure and some extra hooks to apply any CSS or DOM scripting that you might need later. When used badly, they can litter your document unnecessarily and make your markup, styling, and scripting needlessly complicated. I cover these two tags again in more depth in Chapter 6, but in this section I simply outline the main differences between and uses of them.

A **div** (short for "division") is used for marking out a block of content, such as the main content block of your document, the main navigation, the header, or the footer. As such, it is a **block** element. It can contain further elements, including more divs if required, but it cannot be contained within an inline element. For example, a simple website may have a header, a main column of content, a secondary column of content, and a footer. The (X)HTML for this could look like the following:

```
<div id="header">
    ...
</div>
<div id="mainContent">
    ...
</div>
<div id="secondaryContent">
    ...
</div>
<div id="footer">
    ...
</div>
```

These content blocks can then be positioned and displayed as required using CSS.

A **span** is used for marking out sections *within* a block element and sometimes inside another inline element. It is an **inline** element, just the same as <em>, <strong>, or <a>, except without any semantic meaning—it is simply a generic container. It can itself contain further inline elements, including more spans. For example, say you wish to color the first two words of a paragraph red, keeping the rest of the paragraph black. You can use a <span> for this:

```
<p><span class="leadingWords">The first</span> two words of this ➥
paragraph can now be styled differently.</p>
```

A span *cannot* contain a block element—that is, you cannot place a <div> within a <span> and expect it to work the way you want.

Divs and spans are also used extensively in microformats, which I cover later in Chapter 5.

Block and inline elements

To oversimplify things a little, every element in (X)HTML is contained within a box, and that box is either a block-level box or an inline-level box. You can see where the box exists by applying a border or outline with CSS. Visually, the difference between the two is as shown in Figure 1-1.

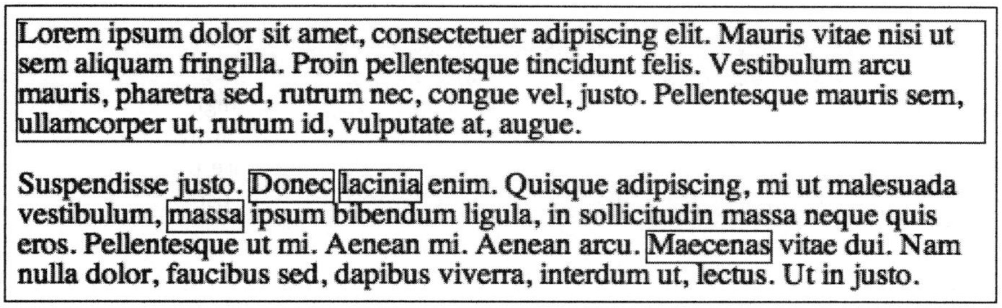

Lorem ipsum dolor sit amet, consectetuer adipiscing elit. Mauris vitae nisi ut sem aliquam fringilla. Proin pellentesque tincidunt felis. Vestibulum arcu mauris, pharetra sed, rutrum nec, congue vel, justo. Pellentesque mauris sem, ullamcorper ut, rutrum id, vulputate at, augue.

Suspendisse justo. Donec lacinia enim. Quisque adipiscing, mi ut malesuada vestibulum, massa ipsum bibendum ligula, in sollicitudin massa neque quis eros. Pellentesque ut mi. Aenean mi. Aenean arcu. Maecenas vitae dui. Nam nulla dolor, faucibus sed, dapibus viverra, interdum ut, lectus. Ut in justo.

Figure 1-1. The box model, applied to block and inline boxes

A **block-level box**, such as a div, a paragraph, or a heading, begins rendering on a new line in the document and forces a subsequent element to start rendering on a new line below. This means that in an unstyled document, block elements stack vertically and line up along the left side of their containing element. They also expand to fill the width of their containing element. It is not possible to place two block elements alongside each other without using CSS.

An **inline-level box**, such as a <span> or an <em>, begins rendering wherever you place it within the document and does not force any line breaks. Inline elements run horizontally rather than vertically, and they do so unless you indicate otherwise in your CSS or until they are separated by a new block element. They take up only as much space as the content contained within them. It is not possible to stack two adjacent inline elements one on top of the other without using CSS. Furthermore, when an element is inline, if you apply margin-top/bottom or padding-top/bottom to it, then the value will be ignored—only margins and padding on the left and right have an effect. Figure 1-2 shows what happens to the outline when I apply 20 pixels (px) of padding to the spans in this example.

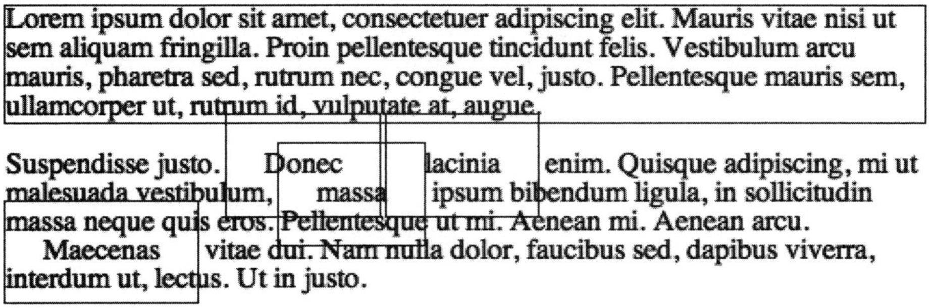

Lorem ipsum dolor sit amet, consectetuer adipiscing elit. Mauris vitae nisi ut sem aliquam fringilla. Proin pellentesque tincidunt felis. Vestibulum arcu mauris, pharetra sed, rutrum nec, congue vel, justo. Pellentesque mauris sem, ullamcorper ut, rutrum id, vulputate at, augue.

Suspendisse justo. Donec lacinia enim. Quisque adipiscing, mi ut malesuada vestibulum, massa ipsum bibendum ligula, in sollicitudin massa neque quis eros. Pellentesque ut mi. Aenean mi. Aenean arcu. Maecenas vitae dui. Nam nulla dolor, faucibus sed, dapibus viverra, interdum ut, lectus. Ut in justo.

Figure 1-2. Inline elements with extra padding

As you can see, although the box itself has expanded 20px in all directions, the top and bottom padding does not affect any surrounding element.

Although you can use CSS to display a block element as inline and vice versa, be aware that this does not change the *meaning* of each element; you will still be unable to place a div within a span.[2]

> There's a lot more to say about the differences between block and inline elements and their respective structures and operations. For a more detailed discussion on this subject, I recommend reading the excellent "Block vs. Inline" article series by Tommy Olsson (www.autisticcuckoo.net/archive.php?id=2005/01/11/block-vs-inline-1), and for a visual explanation of where the padding, margins, and borders of a box lie, have a look at Jon Hicks's 3D CSS Box Model (www.hicksdesign.co.uk/boxmodel).

id and class attributes

The id attribute is used to identify elements and mark up specific functional areas of a website, and the class attribute is used to classify one or more elements. These important attributes help you target elements when it comes to styling or scripting. I refer to both of these attributes throughout the book, but for now all you need to know is that a specific id attribute value can be used just once per page, whereas a class attribute value can be used multiple times (the attributes themselves can be used multiple times per page). For example, say you begin a document with this:

```
<body id="homepage">
```

You would then not be able to use an id attribute value of homepage anywhere else on the same page. However, if you do this:

```
<body class="homepage">
```

then you are free to use the class attribute value of homepage as many times as you like throughout the same page, but bear in mind that it still applies the same CSS, no matter what tag you apply it to.

When using class and id attributes, it can be very tempting to assign values based on how you want the element to look, rather than what it is, but it is best to avoid doing so. For example, instead of values such as

```
<div id="rightColumn">
<strong class="redText">
<p class="big">
```

---

2. The ins and del elements are either block or inline depending on context. If you place a block within either element, they will act as block elements, but if you place them within an inline element or a block element, they will act as inline elements. I talk about these two elements again in the next chapter.

you should instead use values such as

```
<div id="secondaryContent">
<strong class="important">
<p class="introduction">
```

Why? Simply because one day you may find you need that `<strong>` element to be blue instead of red, or you may want to move your secondary content from the right column to the left—and when that happens, your class or id value will make no sense.

> Note that in XHTML, you cannot begin an id attribute with a number, so something like `<body id="3columns">` fails validation, but `<body id="columns3">` is OK.

You can also apply an id *and* a class to one element:

```
<body id="homepage" class="page">
```

To reference these attribute values in your CSS, you type the value and then prefix an id with a hash mark (#) and classes with a period (.), like this:

```
#homepage {
    background: blue;
}

.page {
    color: white;
}
```

These two attributes are not tied to a specific tag; any tag whatsoever can be given either or both attributes.

XHTML vs. HTML

The question of whether to use XHTML or HTML will often not even come up in an average web project; most web designers these days will naturally gravitate toward XHTML, as it is perceived as being new, advanced, and the "X" makes it sound cool. The truth is, XHTML isn't as different from HTML as people think, and the purpose of this section of the chapter is to discuss exactly how XHTML differs from earlier versions of HTML, debunk some myths and misconceptions about XHTML and HTML, examine the issues behind MIME types, and cover when it is (and isn't) appropriate to use XHTML over HTML.

Differences between XHTML and HTML

There are several rules that apply to XHTML that do not apply to HTML. These are fairly straightforward and you may know some (or all) of them already, but to reiterate:

- The <html>, <head>, and <body> tags are all required in XHTML.
- The <html> tag must have an xmlns attribute with a value of http://www.w3.org/ 1999/xhtml.
- All elements must be closed. I touched upon this earlier, but just remember that an opening tag must have either an equal closing tag (if it's a container tag) or a self-closing space-plus-slash.
- All tags must be written in lowercase.
- All attribute values must be quoted with either single quotes or double quotes. Thus, class=page is invalid but class="page" and class='page' are both fine.
- All attributes must have values. Some attributes, such as the selected attribute used with the <option> tag, could be written in a shortened form in HTML—that is, <option selected>data</option> would be valid. In XHTML, however, you must write <option selected="selected">data</option>.
- Ampersands should be encoded. That is, you should write & instead of just &. This is true wherever the ampersand is: in your content or in a URL.

Myths and misconceptions about XHTML and HTML

When XHTML first gained prominence some years ago, it was seen by many the "savior" of the Web—something that could take us away from the tag soup of old-style, table-based HTML markup. Bringing with it more formality and a strict set of rules, XHTML was expected to be easier to write, easier to maintain, and in all ways *better* than HTML.

In fact, aside from the differences mentioned in the preceding section, XHTML is not so very different from HTML, and what matters more than which version you use is *how you write it*. The sections that follow present some myths and misconceptions you may have heard and the truth behind them.

XHTML has a greater/fewer number of elements than HTML

Yes—XHTML has both a greater number *and* a fewer number of elements than HTML, depending on what doctype you're writing to. If we're just comparing HTML 4.01 Strict to XHTML 1.0 Strict, then there are *fewer* elements in the latter than in the former, as elements that were *deprecated* in HTML 4.01 Strict have been *removed* from XHTML 1.0 Strict: <dir>, <menu>, <center>, <isindex>, <applet>, <font>, <basefont>, <s>, <strike>, <u>, <iframe>, and <noframes>. With the possible exception of <iframe> (which is often used to include advertisements on a page), you're unlikely to need any of these elements anyway, as they all have better alternatives in the form of either a more meaningful element (e.g., using <del> in place of <s> and <strike>, which I talk more about in the next chapter) or CSS (e.g., using the CSS font property in place of the <font> element). So, comparing Strict to Strict, the answer is there are fewer elements in XHTML 1.0, but because they were all deprecated in HTML 4.01 anyway, it shouldn't make any difference in your coding practices.

> *All of the elements just mentioned are permitted in Transitional doctypes, along with some attributes such as the* target *attribute used on <a> elements.*

There's also a difference when you look at XHTML 1.1, which introduces the Ruby elements[3] typically used in East Asian typography. It drops the name attribute altogether and replaces the lang attribute with xml:lang. XHTML 1.1 must also be served with a MIME type of application/xhtml+xml—more on that later.

XHTML has better error-checking/is stricter/is more robust than HTML

Yes and no—the answer depends on what you're doing. If you're serving your XHTML pages with a MIME type of text/html, then your markup is no more robust than HTML is, and browsers will often try to correct any errors in your markup for you and attempt to display what they assume you mean. If you're serving your XHTML with a MIME type of application/xhtml+xml, then the slightest error will cause your pages to break and usually only display an XML parsing error. I cover more about MIME types later in the chapter.

XHTML is more semantic/structural than HTML

No. As mentioned earlier, it's not the technology you use, but how you use it that counts. You can create the worst mess of markup imaginable with as many nested layout tables, line break tags, and semantically meaningless elements as you like, and it can still be a valid XHTML document. Similarly, you can create the purest, cleanest, most semantic page you've ever seen, and it can still be written in HTML 4.01.

XHTML is leaner/lighter than HTML

Not so. Because a valid XHTML document requires quoted attribute values, closing tags for every element, and a whole bunch of tags and attributes in the head of the page, an XHTML page actually ends up being "heavier" than an equivalent HTML page. For instance, Anne van Kesteren's home page (http://annevankesteren.nl) begins like this:

```
<!DOCTYPE html PUBLIC "-//W3C//DTD HTML 4.01//EN">
<!-- It's valid, sure. -->
<title>Anne's Weblog</title>
```

Immediately after the title are some linked-in style sheets and scripts, and then it's on with the document—no <html> tag, no <head> tag, and no <body> tag, either open or closed. To write the same markup in XHTML would require all of these. It *is* true that an XHTML document written with web standards in mind will use less overhead than an old-style, tag-soup HTML document, but that's a difference in the web author's methodology, rather than a difference in the version of HTML used.

---

3. See www.w3.org/TR/ruby for more information.

XHTML is required for web standards compliance

False. As (I hope) I've made clear by now, writing XHTML in itself is not necessarily enough. Whether you write HTML or write XHTML, the important part is that you write it *well*.

What's all this noise about MIME types?

Ah, the MIME types. I'll warn you now that this is the sort of incendiary subject that can cause a lot of upset when you start discussing it, and words such as "evil" and "harmful" start being thrown around. Nevertheless, I attempt to sum up the issue in this section dispassionately, sensibly, and with a minimum of fuss. Before I continue, here are just two things to bear in mind:

- For the average web author (or manager of web authors), the topic of MIME types will rarely, if ever, directly affect either them or the visitors to their website.
- Nonetheless, it is worth knowing about.

So, here we go.

Although they share a common vocabulary, XHTML has several advantages over HTML, including the following:

- XHTML has the capability to incorporate other XML-based technologies, such as MathML, into your document.
- XHTML that is not well-formed will be immediately spotted, because browsers will refuse to display the page and will display an error instead.
- XHTML provides a guarantee of a well-formed[4] document.

None of the preceding points are true, however, unless you are serving XHTML with a MIME type of application/xhtml+xml. If your web server is serving your web pages with a MIME type of text/html (practically all web servers will do so), then you will not be taking full advantage of XHTML.

So, this being the case, you may choose to simply configure your server to serve your XHTML pages with the correct MIME type. However, it's not that easy, for two reasons:

- Internet Explorer does not support pages served in such a way, and it will attempt to download them instead of displaying them.
- Your pages may no longer work.

The first problem can be solved through **content negotiation**[5]—that is, serving one MIME type to modern browsers and another to Internet Explorer. The second problem can be caused by a number of reasons. An invalid XHTML document will now no longer display at

---

4. I should point out that "well-formed" does not mean the same as "valid." For instance, a tag with an attribute mymadeupattribute="true" is well-formed, but still invalid.

5. For a detailed explanation of content negotiation, see the article "MIME Types and Content Negotiation" by Gez Lemon at http://juicystudio.com/article/content-negotiation.php.

all, resulting in an error message. Even if your document is valid, though, that's not the only problem you may run into:

- Comments in <style> and <script> tags of the <!-- --> form that you may have been using to hide your CSS or scripts from old browsers will now be treated literally as comments, so your CSS or scripts will appear not to exist.
- Scripts that use document.write() will no longer work.
- Your CSS can be interpreted differently, depending upon how you wrote it in the first place.

The smallest validation error will cause your pages to break and become unusable, with the error visible for the entire world to see. This is particularly a cause for concern if you have an open comments system or are using a content management system (CMS) that doesn't always generate correct markup. All it takes is for one unencoded ampersand to slip through and your pages will break completely.

So, that's the issue of MIME types in a nutshell. To some people it doesn't matter; to others it matters a lot. Essentially, though, it's like this: your XHTML pages *should* be served with the application/xhtml+xml MIME type, doing so *may* cause unforeseen complications, and continuing to serve your pages with a text/html MIME type will *probably* be OK for the foreseeable future, but just be aware that you're not taking full advantage of all of XHTML's features when you do so.

My personal preference is to write XHTML served as text/html, despite the issues just noted. This is for a number of reasons, not least being that employers and clients have a tendency to insist upon it for marketing purposes. I also prefer the structure, knowing that I *must* close all of my tags and that I *must* quote all of my attribute values. I can do all of this in HTML if I choose, but with XHTML there's the element of compulsion that I believe helps me write better markup.

Deciding between HTML and XHTML

So which should you use, HTML or XHTML? It depends. The World Wide Web Consortium (W3C) recommends writing XHTML over HTML[6] to better enable you to convert your documents to XHTML 2 (covered in Appendix A) when it arrives, so if this is something you plan to do, write XHTML now. If you find yourself having to take into consideration other factors, such as legacy applications or CMSs that are producing HTML 4 (unquoted attributes, uppercase tags, etc.), then it makes little sense to wrap that output in a template with an XHTML doctype and you should use HTML 4 in this case. If you need to save on bandwidth, use HTML 4. If you need to use XML, use XHTML . . . and so on.

Ultimately, it's a judgment call entirely dependent on your own circumstances. Just don't make the mistake of thinking that by writing XHTML you've done all you need to do to create a professional, well-structured, semantically meaningful document.

---

6. See the article "HTML Versus XHTML" at www.webstandards.org/learn/articles/askw3c/oct2003.

Anatomy of an XHTML document

Finally, let's look at how a strict XHTML 1.0 document is laid out:

```
<!DOCTYPE html PUBLIC "-//W3C//DTD XHTML 1.0 Strict//EN"
    "http://www.w3.org/TR/xhtml1/DTD/xhtml1-strict.dtd">
<html xmlns="http://www.w3.org/1999/xhtml">
  <head>
    <title>Our title</title>
  </head>
  <body>
    <p>Our content</p>
  </body>
</html>
```

Let's now go through this markup one line at a time.

Doctype declaration

First we see a doctype declaration. A **doctype declaration** provides an indication as to what **Document Type Definition** (**DTD**) you're going to be writing your markup to. A DTD is basically a page detailing the rules and grammar of the markup. It can look a little daunting, but let's break it down and examine each piece. The doctype starts off like this:

```
<!DOCTYPE
```

Nothing much more to say here; this is just how a doctype begins. The root element of the document that will appear after the doctype declaration—the <html> element—needs to be specified immediately after the opening of the declaration:

```
<!DOCTYPE html
```

Note that we can use html or HTML, depending on the version of (X)HTML we're writing to and how we're writing it. For all XHTML doctypes, the root element should be in lowercase, but for HTML doctypes the root element *may* be uppercase if the rest of your tags are written so.

Following that, we have the word PUBLIC:

```
<!DOCTYPE html PUBLIC
```

This indicates that the DTD we're about to reference is publicly available. If the DTD was private, then we would use SYSTEM instead (as in "a system resource," probably a locally held resource somewhere on your network).

Next we have the **Formal Public Identifier** (**FPI**), which describes details about both the DTD and the organization behind the DTD. The FPI is enclosed in quotes and uses two forward slashes as a separator:

```
"-//W3C//DTD XHTML 1.0 Strict//EN"
```

These four fields have the following meanings:

- The opening – character means that the owner of the DTD isn't an organization registered by the International Organization for Standardization (ISO); the W3C is not. If the owner was registered by ISO, you would use + in place of -.
- W3C indicates that the owner of the DTD is the W3C.
- DTD XHTML 1.0 Strict is a type or class (DTD) followed by a description (XHTML 1.0 Strict), which is broken down into two further sections: a label (XHTML) and a document type definition (1.0 Strict). The class and description are known respectively as the **Public Text Class (PTC)** and the **Public Text Description (PTD)**.
- The language of the DTD is EN, which is the two-character language code for English.

Finally, we have a URL that points to the location of the DTD. This URL is, like the FPI, declared within double quotes:

```
"http://www.w3.org/TR/xhtml1/DTD/xhtml1-strict.dtd"
```

And that, basically, is the anatomy of a doctype.

Available doctypes

There are three XHTML 1.0 doctypes available, plus one XHTML 1.1 doctype. The XHTML 1.0 doctypes are Strict, Transitional, and Frameset (to be used only when you are using frames to lay out your documents), and they differ only in the FPI and URL:

```
<!DOCTYPE html PUBLIC "-//W3C//DTD XHTML 1.0 Strict//EN"
    "http://www.w3.org/TR/xhtml1/DTD/xhtml1-strict.dtd">

<!DOCTYPE html PUBLIC "-//W3C//DTD XHTML 1.0 Transitional//EN"
    "http://www.w3.org/TR/xhtml1/DTD/xhtml1-transitional.dtd">

<!DOCTYPE html PUBLIC "-//W3C//DTD XHTML 1.0 Frameset//EN"
    "http://www.w3.org/TR/xhtml1/DTD/xhtml1-frameset.dtd">
```

The XHTML 1.1 doctype also differs only in the FPI and URL, and it comes in only one variant rather than Strict and Transitional versions:

```
<!DOCTYPE html PUBLIC "-//W3C//DTD XHTML 1.1//EN"
"http://www.w3.org/TR/xhtml11/DTD/xhtml11.dtd">
```

There is also a doctype for XHTML Basic, a stripped-down version of XHTML used (mostly theoretically at the time of this writing) for pages designed for mobile devices such as mobile phones:

```
<!DOCTYPE html PUBLIC "-//W3C//DTD XHTML Basic 1.0//EN"
"http://www.w3.org/TR/xhtml-basic/xhtml-basic10.dtd">
```

Purposes of doctypes

Doctypes in (X)HTML serve two important purposes. First, they inform user agents and validators what DTD the document is written to. This action is passive—that is, your browser isn't going and downloading the DTD every time a page loads to check that your markup is valid; it's only when you manually validate a page that it kicks in.

The second and, for practical purposes, most important purpose is that doctypes inform browsers to render documents in **standards mode** rather than **quirks mode**. This is known as **doctype switching**, and it was included in browsers as a way of determining how to render a document, the assumption being that if an author has included a doctype, then that author knows what he or she is doing, and the browser tries to interpret the strict markup in a strict way (i.e., standards mode). The absence of a doctype triggers quirks mode, which renders the markup in old and incorrect ways, the assumption here being that if the author *hasn't* included a doctype, then he or she probably is not writing standard markup, and therefore the markup will be treated as if it has been written in the past for buggier browsers.

The <html>, <head>, and <body> elements

Following the doctype is the opening <html> tag with an xmlns attribute. This attribute is used to declare an **XML namespace**, which describes which markup language is being used. The value used in this example is http://www.w3.org/1999/xhtml, and it should be present in any XHTML document.

> *Note that it's possible to style the <html> element in your CSS as you would style any other element; however, this can yield sometimes unpredictable results. For instance, you'll encounter problems if you try to give both the <html> and <body> elements a background image, because Internet Explorer includes the browser scrollbars as part of the web page (to allow for CSS-styled scrollbars) and you may find background images or colors dipping underneath the scrollbar and appearing on the other side. Furthermore, styling the <html> element can cause browsers to treat the body element differently—as a <div>, rather than as the <body>.*

After the root <html> element is open, we have the <head> of the document, which contains a <title> and can also contain <style>, <script>, <meta>, and <link> elements. <title> is the only compulsory element within the head, and it will be displayed in your browser's **title bar**. The document title is an oft-neglected area of the document; you've surely seen pages with the title "Untitled Document" before. This is unfortunate, as given proper care and attention, the document title can provide you and your users with many benefits: a better search engine ranking for you and greater usability for users.

> *For example, try opening several* Untitled Document *windows and then switching between them after minimizing them—can you tell which is which? A similar problem can occur when a company or website name is placed before the actual page title.*

Following the closing <head> tag is the opening <body> tag, which can contain any non-head-specific markup: paragraphs, lists, images, and so on. The <body> tag has several presentational attributes: background, text, link, vlink, and alink, which are used to set the document's background color, text color, link color, visited link color, and active link color, respectively. All of these attributes have been deprecated, and their effects should be created with CSS instead. The background-color, color, a:link, a:visited, and a:active properties and pseudo-classes are appropriate.

The closing <body> tag is followed immediately by the closing <html> tag. That's an XHTML document in its entirety.

The XML declaration

Before I go on, any purists reading this section will have noticed that I've left out a line that looks something like this:

```
<?xml version="1.0" encoding="utf-8"?>
```

If in use, this line would appear directly before the opening doctype line. It is known as an **XML declaration**,[7] and its purpose is to declare that the document is an XML document, the version of XML, and also (optionally) the character set the document has been encoded in. While the W3C recommends including this declaration (but that it is optional), doing so will have a number of adverse effects, the worst of which is causing Internet Explorer to switch to quirks mode—anything appearing before the doctype apart from whitespace will cause this to happen. Therefore, it's best to leave this line out.

Anatomy of an HTML document

Now let's look at the same template, but written in HTML 4.01 Strict instead of XHTML 1.0 Strict:

```
<!DOCTYPE html PUBLIC "-//W3C//DTD HTML 4.01//EN"
    "http://www.w3.org/TR/html4/strict.dtd">
<title>Our title</title>
<p>Our content</p>
```

That's not a misprint—the preceding code is actually all you need for a document written in HTML. The <html>, <head>, and <body> tags do not need to be explicitly created, but you must still write your markup as if they are there—because they are. You can look at such a document in a JavaScript DOM inspector, or write some CSS rules for the <body> element, and you'll see that the elements are there even though you haven't written them in, so you must ensure that any head-specific markup such as <meta> or <link> tags appear before any of your <body> markup begins. Thus, the following markup is valid because the head and body areas can be inferred by the context:

---

7. The XML declaration and the doctype are collectively known as an **XML prolog**.

```
<!DOCTYPE html PUBLIC "-//W3C//DTD HTML 4.01//EN"
    "http://www.w3.org/TR/html4/strict.dtd">
<title>Our title</title>
<meta http-equiv="Content-Type" content="text/html; charset=UTF-8">
<p>Our content</p>
```

But the following markup is not valid, because the <meta> element has been included after the <p> element has already indicated that the head area has ended and the body area has begun:

```
<!DOCTYPE html PUBLIC "-//W3C//DTD HTML 4.01//EN"
    "http://www.w3.org/TR/html4/strict.dtd">
<title>Our title</title>
<p>Our content</p>
<meta http-equiv="Content-Type" content="text/html; charset=UTF-8">
```

Summary

Hopefully, this chapter has helped you gain an understanding of the vocabulary used to describe the markup and general structure of (X)HTML, and cleared up any misconceptions you may have held about it. It also provided you with a breakdown of a basic (X)HTML document, so you can now recognize the constituent parts. Knowing all of this isn't enough to master the language, but it will certainly help you.

2 USING THE RIGHT TAG FOR THE RIGHT JOB

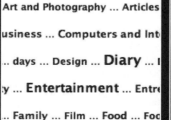

When building websites, it's very easy to get by on only a few tags: a heading here and there, some paragraphs and lists, and a sprinkling of <em> and <strong> and a few divs and spans to add some body to the <body>. However, this approach ignores the many other tags available that can allow you to enhance your pages with scripts and styles without needing to clog up the works with classes and semantically meaningless <span> tags. In this chapter, we'll examine a number of these additional tags and how to use them.

I've divided this chapter into four loosely related sections:

- **Document markup**: This catchall section covers paragraphs, headers, lists, links, addresses, deletions and insertions, and quotes.
- **Presentational elements**: This section covers elements that do not have any semantic meaning, such as <i> and <tt>.
- **Phrase elements**: In this section, we'll look at inline elements that convey semantic meaning, such as <cite>, <kbd>, and <acronym>.
- **Images and other media**: The <img> and <object> tags, image maps, CSS background images, and embedded media are examined here.

Throughout the chapter you'll find examples of how you can take advantage of these semantics and structures to add functionality and styling to your web pages using unobtrusive DOM Scripting and CSS.

> *Due to their complexity, tables and forms (and all related markup) are covered in their own chapters later in the book.*

Document markup

First, let's look at the general category of document markup elements, including paragraphs, line breaks, and headings; how to display contact information, quotes, lists, and links; and how to mark up changes to your documents.

Paragraphs, line breaks, and headings

Perhaps the markup you've used most often when writing web pages is <p>. There isn't much to be said about <p>: it is simply used to mark up a paragraph. Yet this humble element is often abused by WYSIWYG software as a quick and dirty spacer. You have likely seen markup such as the following before, where an author has pressed the Enter key a few times:

```
<p> </p>
<p> </p>
<p> </p>
<p> </p>
```

This is a prime example of (X)HTML being co-opted into acting in a presentational manner. We find here multiple, pointless paragraphs, with a nonbreaking space entity inside due to some browsers not displaying empty elements, but the effect should really be achieved with CSS. A quick way of adding some space beneath your content is to enclose the content in a <div>, like this:

```
<div id="maincontent">
  <p>Your content here.</p>
</div>
```

Then add some padding to the bottom of the #maincontent section with CSS:

```
#maincontent { padding-bottom: 3em; }
```

I use em as a unit of measurement here rather than px, so that the spacing beneath the paragraphs of content will scale appropriately when users change the text size in their browsers.

Similarly, the <br /> tag for line breaks is often used to add a few lines of space here and there when it should be used simply to insert a single carriage return (e.g., when formatting a poem or code samples—but then perhaps you should be using <pre>, which is discussed further in the section "The <hr>, <pre>, <sup>, and <sub> elements").

Heading tags are used to denote different sections of your web page or document, and they allow various user agents (such as screen reading software or some web browsers such as Opera) to easily jump between those sections. There are six heading levels, <h1> through to <h6>, with <h1> being considered the most important heading and <h6> the least important (see Figure 2-1). Having six heading levels available to you means that you should never need to write <div id="heading"> or <p><strong>heading</strong></p>.

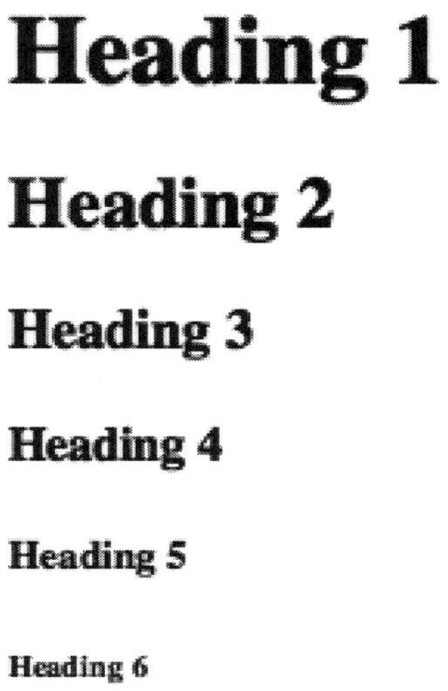

Heading 1

Heading 2

Heading 3

Heading 4

Heading 5

Figure 2-1.
The six heading levels,
in all their unstyled glory

Heading 6

So, with all these exciting different headings to choose from, where should you start and what should you consider the "most important" heading? This largely depends on the content of your site. If you are building a blog or a similar article-based website, then the title of each blog entry or article could be your <h1>. Alternatively, you may decide that your website brand (e.g., eBay, Amazon.com, etc.) should be considered the most important heading, and set that to be your <h1>.

It's possible to automatically generate a rudimentary table of contents (TOC) for a single document by using JavaScript to pull out the headers in a page, as described by JavaScript guru Peter-Paul Koch at www.quirksmode.org/dom/toc.html. Although this rudimentary TOC lacks the permanence and scope of a TOC for a collection of documents, it does have the advantage of dynamically updating when you insert or remove a header.

Contact information

The <address> tag is used for marking up contact information—nothing more, nothing less. The HTML specification is very specific about the <address> tag's use: it is not for displaying contact information for just anybody or anything; rather, it is used to display contact information related to the document itself. For example, say you are maintaining a list of contact details for a society membership directory. In this case, use of the <address> tag—once per each member—would not be appropriate. However, if you also had on that page the webmaster's contact details, or the contact details of whoever maintains the directory, then the <address> tag *would* be appropriate to use for just that person. It doesn't have to specifically describe a physical, brick-and-mortar location—the example in the HTML specification, for instance, contains links to personal pages and a date:

```
<address>
  <a href="../People/Raggett/">Dave Raggett</a>,
  <a href="../People/Arnaud/">Arnaud Le Hors</a>,
  contact persons for the <a href="Activity.html">➡
W3C HTML Activity</a><br />
  Date: 1999/12/24 23:37:50
</address>
```

The <address> element is a block-level element, and as such it can contain only inline elements—no paragraphs, lists, or divs. This element is also of use when using the hCard microformat, which I discuss in Chapter 5.

Quotes

HTML provides you, the web author, with two distinct ways of marking up quotations, one for block-level quotes and the other for inline quotes. However, I only recommend the use of the former method: the <blockquote> element.

Block quotes

<blockquote> is another tag that has historically been used for its presentational effect rather than its semantic meaning or structural relevance. Indeed, this misuse is even referenced in the HTML specification:[1]

> *"We recommend that style sheet implementations provide a mechanism for inserting quotation marks before and after a quotation delimited by* BLOCKQUOTE *in a manner appropriate to the current language context and the degree of nesting of quotations.*
>
> *"However, as some authors have used* BLOCKQUOTE *merely as a mechanism to indent text, in order to preserve the intention of the authors, user agents should **not** insert quotation marks in the default style.*
>
> *"The usage of* BLOCKQUOTE *to indent text is deprecated in favor of style sheets."*

As you can see, the <blockquote> tag has been so commonly used to indent text instead of acting as a container for quotes that the W3C recommends against user agents automatically including quote marks and has taken the unusual step of actually *deprecating* this misuse. How this can be enforced I can only guess.

The <blockquote> tag also allows for a cite attribute to allow the author to reference the source of the quote (usually in the form of a URL, but it can be any form of citation, such as the name of another author or the title of a movie). User agent support for utilizing this hidden information is currently poor. While Firefox will allow you to right-click a <blockquote> element, select Properties, and see the citation information in a pop-up alert box (see Figure 2-2), most other user agents simply ignore it.

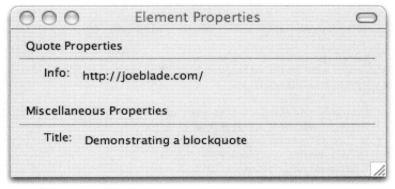

Figure 2-2. Firefox displays the cite and title attributes of a blockquote. It's not an intuitive method of displaying the information, but at least it's there.

---

1. See www.w3.org/TR/html4/struct/text.html#h-9.2.2.

We can retrieve the citation information and display it on the client side in at least two ways. The first is with CSS, and the second is with some DOM Scripting.

Here's a CSS way:

```
blockquote[cite]:after {
    content: "Source: " attr(cite);
}
```

This is an example of an **attribute selector**, part of the CSS2 specification. It means that if a <blockquote> element with a cite attribute is found, the value of that attribute should be displayed after the contents of the quote. There are some fairly severe downsides to this method, though. First, it will work only in modern browsers. It won't work in Internet Explorer 6 or below, and while Internet Explorer 7 *will* support attribute selectors, it *won't* support the :after and :before pseudo-elements or the content property, so again this method will fail. Second, Firefox and other Mozilla browsers will not allow you to select, click on, or otherwise engage with the content (see Figure 2-3). As far as these browsers are concerned, this generated content is much like the bullet character in an unordered list—it doesn't exist in any meaningful fashion. This may not be a problem if your citation is a name, but if it's a URL, then ideally it ought to be clickable or at the very least selectable.

This is a blockquote with *joeblade.com* as the cite attribute value.
Source: http://joeblade.com

Figure 2-3. Mozilla browsers can display the source with CSS, but you can't click or select the link.

The second method uses DOM Scripting, which has the advantage of working in a wider range of browsers, but the disadvantage of only working where JavaScript is present. So, for example, someone reading the text in a newsfeed (via RSS, Atom, etc.) might not see the JavaScript-generated content. (But it will degrade gracefully, at least; users without JavaScript will just see the quote.) The script to achieve this could look something like this:

```
function betterBlockquotes()
{
    if (document.getElementsByTagName) {
    quotes = document.getElementsByTagName("blockquote");
    for(i=0; i<quotes.length; i++)
    {
        citation = quotes[i]getAttribute('cite');
        citeLink = document.createElement('a');
        citeLink.setAttribute('href', citation);
        citeLink.appendChild(document.createTextNode('Source: '));
        p = document.createElement('p');
        p.appendChild(citeLink);
        quotes[i].appendChild(p)'
    }
    }
}
window.onload = betterBlockquotes;
```

> *The preceding script is fairly minimal. It could be enhanced by pulling out the* title
> *attribute value of the block quote and using that for the link text, or it could include*
> class *attributes on the generated elements to allow for specific styling.*

This method loops through a document, picking out all the blockquotes, and then it sifts
through them to find those with cite attributes. When it finds a blockquote with a cite
attribute, the script creates a new <a> element and drops the cite attribute value into the
a's href attribute value. It creates the required 'Source: ' text fragment (it's generated
by the script, as we don't want that showing up if there isn't any citation), and then finally
creates a new <p> element and inserts it into the document just after the blockquote itself.
The result looks exactly the same as the preceding CSS example, and despite not appearing in the original (X)HTML markup, it can still be styled as desired (see Figure 2-4).

This is a blockquote with *joeblade.com* as the cite attribute value.

Source

Figure 2-4. Using JavaScript allows us to create a clickable link.

Inline quotes

While the <blockquote> tag should be used for block-level quotes, there also exists a <q>
tag for inline quotes. I'll warn you now: I'm going to conclude by recommending you *don't*
use the <q> tag, so if you want to save yourself a bit of time, you can skip the next few
paragraphs and pick up again where I start discussing lists. If, however, you like to know
the details anyway, read on.

What is *supposed* to happen when you use the <q> tag is that the browser automatically
includes typographically correct quote marks at the beginning and end of the quote, meaning that you, the author, should *not* include them. Furthermore, with judicious use of the
lang attribute, those quotes should be displayed in the style appropriate to the specified language (e.g., some European languages will use chevrons or *guillemets*: « and » instead of
" and "). Also, browsers should display an awareness of nested quotes (in English, if a quote
begins with the double-quote character, then quotes within that quote should use the single-
quote character and vice versa). So, for example, the following fragment of HTML:

```
<p><q>This is a quote that has a <q>nested quote</q>➥
as part of it.</q></p>
```

should display as follows:

"This is a quote that has a 'nested quote' as part of it."

While this may all sound very exciting, the reality is more humdrum. Not only is modern browser support inconsistent—for instance, Firefox (and other Mozilla browsers) will correctly nest double and single quotes, while Safari will not—but Internet Explorer does not generate any quotes at all, which makes things even more problematic.[2] Do you add the quotes yourself and end up with two sets of quotes in modern browsers? Do you leave the quotes out and allow modern browsers to get on with things, but ignore the most popular browser in the world? The question of what to do about Internet Explorer's poor standards support is a question that you will face often. In the case of <q>, I suggest simply not using it at all. The inconsistent support for <q> features has essentially rendered it useless—you can't even use the CSS2 quotes property (as in q {quotes: none}) to remove generated quotes, because Safari doesn't support that property, and although there are various other solutions involving JavaScript, CSS, or a combination of the two, they all fail in one situation or another.[3] Urgh.

So, to summarize how best to use <q>: just don't. Let's move on.

Lists

Three list types are available in current (X)HTML versions: unordered lists <ul>, ordered lists <ol>, and definition lists <dl>.

> *Two other forms of lists, <menu> and <dir>, have been deprecated, and the W3C recommends using an unordered list in their place.*

The differences between the list types are fairly minimal and straightforward:

- An **unordered list** should be used when your content is (as you would expect) not in any particular order.
- An **ordered list** should be used when your content *is* in an order of some kind: alphabetical, numerical, and so on.
- A **definition list** is designed for associating names or terms with values or other data—any items that have a direct relationship with one another, such as a glossary of terms. Though it is a *definition* list, the W3C also suggests using such a list to mark up dialogue,[4] with each definition term as a speaker and the definition description as the spoken words, so we can consider allowed usage of this element to be fairly liberal.

---

2. I'm referring to the Windows version of Internet Explorer, by the way. Internet Explorer on the Mac deserves a special mention for being the only browser—even now—that gets almost all of the <q> display properties correct. It even changes the quote character depending on the value of the lang attribute. Say what you like about the browser, but it was ahead of its time.

3. See www.alistapart.com/articles/qtag.

4. See www.w3.org/TR/REC-html40/struct/lists.html#h-10.3.

Unordered and ordered lists

Unordered and ordered lists consist of an opening <ul> or <ol>, respectively, followed by any number of list item—<li>—elements, and then finally a closing </ul> or </ol>. The opening and closing tags can contain only list items, but list items can contain anything, including paragraphs, divs, headers, and yet more lists. So long as they're all contained within a single list item, it's perfectly valid and well-formed markup. As far as differences between (X)HTML versions go, in HTML you don't have to close list items with </li>, but in XHTML you do. Figure 2-5 shows the default styling of both list types.

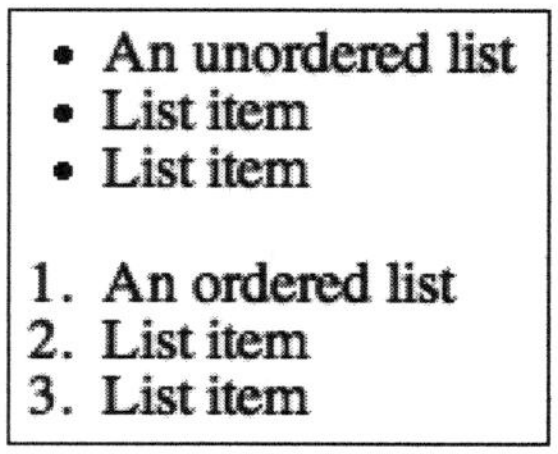

Sadly, lists do not have any interesting or obscure attributes that have not been deprecated in strict doctypes. The start and value attributes used to be available to us. start allowed authors to start the numbering of an ordered list at a number other than 1, which was useful if you needed to interrupt an ordered list, such as in the case of a list of search results split over several pages. value allowed authors to give a specific list item an out-of-sequence number. It may be possible to reproduce the functions of these attributes with CSS in the future using CSS counters,[5] but as yet very few browsers will support this. If you need to use these attributes, consider using a Transitional doctype, otherwise your document(s) will fail validation tests. There also existed a compact attribute, intended to inform browsers that the list was a brief, compact list and should be rendered with that in consideration, but with no browser support, this attribute has also fallen by the wayside.

- An unordered list
- List item
- List item

1. An ordered list
2. List item
3. List item

Figure 2-5.
An unordered list and an ordered list with their default styling

Thankfully, though the markup may not be exciting, it is at least flexible, and with CSS you can display a list in a wide variety of ways: horizontally, vertically, expanding/collapsing, or as an image map (see the section "Image maps" later in the chapter). For instance, take the following navigation menu:

```
<ul>
    <li><a href="/">Home</a></li>
    <li><a href="/contact/">Contact</a></li>
    <li><a href="/about/">About</a></li>
    <li><a href="/archive/">Archive</a> </li>
</ul>
```

We can turn this into a horizontal menu very easily:

```
li {
    float: left;
}
```

We can achieve the same effect by turning the <li> from a block into an inline container with use of display: inline; but a block-level container will offer us more styling options in the future. Floating the list items left will cause the list to look as shown in Figure 2-6.

---

5. See www.w3.org/TR/REC-CSS2/generate.html#counters.

Figure 2-6. An unordered list with the list items floated left

Simple! But clearly quite ugly and a bit unusable at this stage, so let's tidy things up a little:

```
li {
    border: 1px solid;
    float: left;
    list-style-type: none;
    padding: 0.2em 1em;
}
```

By adding a border, removing the list bullet and adding a touch of padding, we get the list shown in Figure 2-7.

Home	Contact	About	Archive

Figure 2-7. An unordered list with the list items floated left, bordered, and padded

As you can see, we already have a very serviceable horizontal menu. We could jazz this up even more with some styling of the anchor tags, giving them a background-color, using display: block to allow them to fill the whole list item area, changing their background with :hover, and so on.

> *Russ Weakley, a co-chair of the Web Standards Group, has created a huge collection of different list styles (more than 70 at the current count) available at* http://css.maxdesign.com.au, *and the article titled "CSS Design: Taming Lists" by Mark Newhouse at* www.alistapart.com/articles/taminglists *is also well worth a look. To help take some of the pain out of creating lists of links, it's also worth trying out Accessify's List-O-Matic (*http://accessify.com/ tools-and-wizards/developer-tools/list-o-matic*), an online list-builder that lets you select from a variety of prebuilt styles.*

So, already you can see that a simple list can be displayed in a different way from its default style. It's possible to use CSS to create some quite dynamic behavior with lists (though in most cases JavaScript is also required for compatibility with Internet Explorer). As documented by Eric Meyer (http://meyerweb.com/eric/css/edge/menus/demo.html), browsers that supported the :hover pseudo-class on any element (Firefox et al.) could use that to display nested lists as pop-out menus. The CSS to accomplish this is very simple:

```
li ul {display: none;}
li:hover > ul {display: block;}
```

This means that any <ul> that is a descendent element of an <li>—that is, a nested list—should not be displayed. The second line says that any <ul> that is a child element of an

<li> that is being hovered over should display as normal. In compliant browsers, the end result looks like Figure 2-8.

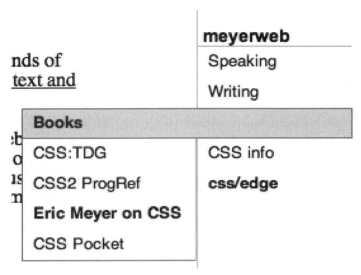

Figure 2-8. A pure CSS nested menu

All very neat. As mentioned, though, Internet Explorer 6 and below won't have a clue what to make of your li:hover,[6] so JavaScript is required. Patrick Griffiths's Suckerfish Dropdowns script (www.htmldog.com/articles/suckerfish/dropdowns) provides both a CSS solution and a JavaScript solution that are pretty robust (multiple nested menus are catered for) and very easy to implement, requiring only the inclusion of a small script and the addition of a class selector to your CSS file.

The definition (is this)

The definition list consists of an opening <dl>, followed by a definition term (<dt>), and then any number of definition descriptions (<dd>). A typical definition list looks like this:

```
<dl>
    <dt>Bottle</dt>
    <dd>A receptacle having a narrow neck, usually no handles, ➡
and a mouth that can be plugged, corked, or capped.</dd>
    <dd>To hold in; restrain: "bottled up my emotions."</dd>
    <dt>Rocket</dt>
    <dd>A vehicle or device propelled by one or more rocket engines,➡
 especially such a vehicle designed to travel through space.</dd>
</dl>
```

---

6. Internet Explorer 7 will support :hover on all elements, so it is likely that these pure CSS menus will work without scripting.

Most browsers would display the preceding code in a similar way to that shown in Figure 2-9.

Bottle
> A receptacle having a narrow neck, usually no handles, and a mouth that can be plugged, corked, or capped.
> To hold in; restrain: *bottled up my emotions*.

Rocket
> A vehicle or device propelled by one or more rocket engines, especially such a vehicle designed to travel through space.

Figure 2-9. A definition list, with the definition terms on the left and the definition descriptions indented

Definition lists are, as noted, fairly flexible. As long as there is a direct relationship between the term and the definition(s), many constructs can be represented using this list. For instance, a photograph as the term could have descriptions including information about both the photographer and the camera. In addition, a definition list could be used to display a schedule for a series of presentations at a conference, with the title of the presentation as the definition term and the descriptions including details of the presenting author and the date and time. A definition list could also be used in an online shopping application to describe product details, and so on.

Although definition lists are flexible in use, you should bear the following caveat in mind: a definition term cannot contain any block-level elements—no paragraphs, headers, or lists—which means that terms cannot be given differing levels of importance in the same way that headings can (<h1>, <h2>, etc.). A definition description, however, can contain any element or series of elements, so long as they're well-formed.

Links

Links are most likely up there alongside paragraphs and headers as among the first pieces of HTML you ever learned, but we can still plumb the depths of obscurity and poke around at a few unused and potentially useful attributes. Strictly speaking, the <a> tag is not a link; it's an **anchor**, which can either link to a new file, point to a named anchor elsewhere (either on the same page or on a different page), or point to any element that has an id attribute. There's also the <link> tag, which is used solely in the head of a document. You may have used it already for linking style sheets to your pages, but it can also be used to provide extra navigational information, as you'll see shortly.

First, let's go through a quick refresher of the basics. An anchor tag linking to another document will use the href attribute, like so:

```
<a href="newpage.html">link</a>
```

To link to another anchor tag, you target the **fragment identifier**, which is set in the linked anchor tag via the name or id attribute. The linking is done like so:

```
<a href="newpage.html#parttwo">link</a>
```

If you want to link to an anchor tag or other identified element on the same page, there is no need to include the filename:

```
<a href="#parttwo">link</a>
```

Linking to an anchor or an identified element on the same page can have multiple uses. A common use is for a table of contents for a lengthy document with anchors scattered throughout, and sometimes a "back to the top of the page" link: `<a href="#top">back to top</a>`.[7] Another common use is to create **skip links**, which are links that allow people to skip past long blocks of navigation links to get at the content. Skip links are usually included for users who navigate with a keyboard, or a mobile or screen-reading device, but sometimes also present visually as well for users who are zooming in and may not enjoy scrolling around. A typical skip link looks like this:

```
<!-- present near the top of the page -->
<a href="#maincontent">Skip Navigation</a>
<ul>
  <li><a href="/about/">About</a></li>
  <li><a href="/contact/">Contact</a></li>
  <li><a href="/help/">Help</a></li>
  and so on...
</ul>
<a name="maincontent" id="maincontent"></a>
<!-- beginning of your actual content -->
```

Use of these sorts of links can dramatically increase the usability of your website for certain groups of users, but there are several browser bugs and usability issues to consider.

> *A useful article that summarizes good use of skip links is Jim Thatcher's "Skip Navigation"* (www.jimthatcher.com/skipnav.htm).

An anchor tag that isn't linking anywhere and is literally just an anchor point will include its fragment identifier as a value of either the name attribute or the id attribute, like so:

```
<h3><a name="parttwo">Part Two</a></h3>
```

> *It is valid to have an empty anchor tag of the form* `<a name="parttwo"></a>`, *but the HTML specification warns that some browsers may not recognize it.*

So, what's the difference between using the name and the id attribute? Well, the name attribute can only be applied to anchor tags for link-targeting purposes, whereas you can use the id attribute in any tag. So, if you give each of your heading tags a unique identifier, you can point your links directly to those instead of having to include an extra anchor. For instance, the preceding example can be simplified like this:

---

7. It's a good idea to explicitly include an anchor or identified element with a name/id of top—some browsers will infer such location, but not all will do that.

```
<h3 id="parttwo">Part Two</h3>
```

If you *are* using an anchor, then bear in mind that if you give it an ID *and* a name, they must be identical. Furthermore, you cannot have an identical name and ID in separate elements on the same page.

You also have the option of using the hreflang attribute to specify the language of the resource designated by the href attribute, and the charset attribute to specify the character encoding, but it is unlikely that you will ever need to use these attributes.

Relationship issues

You can specify the relationship *type* of the link by using the rel attribute, and the reverse relationship with the rev attribute, both of which can be used in either <a> links or <link> links. The nature of these two attributes can be a little tricky to grasp, so let's consider an example. You may have encountered rel before when using the <link> tag to reference an RSS feed in the head of your web page, like this:

```
<link rel="alternate" type="application/rss+xml" ➥
href="http://example.com/feed/" />
```

The preceding code means that "an alternative version of this document exists at http://example.com/feed/," and user agents can spot that and find the RSS feed—most modern browsers will display a feed icon in the browser address bar, allowing the user to select, view, and subscribe to the feed. The rev attribute works the same way, but in reverse. So, using the preceding example, the document at the feed URL could have a rev attribute value of alternate, but this time it would mean "this document is an alternative version of the document located at http://example.com/."

The rev and rel attributes can take any value, but the HTML specification lists several predefined types:

- alternate: As mentioned earlier, this value designates alternate versions of the document in which the link occurs. It can be used with the lang and hreflang attributes if the alternate version is a translation, and with the media attribute if the alternate version is designed for a different medium. For instance, if you were linking to a print style sheet, you would use the attribute/value media="print".[8]

- stylesheet: A rel attribute value of stylesheet informs the user agent that the linked document is a style sheet (rather obviously). You can use it in conjunction with alternate (as in rel="alternate stylesheet") to specify a range of alternative style sheets that the user agent can allow the user to select from (both Firefox and Opera have this functionality built in).

---

8. The media attribute has a number of valid values, but only a few are widely supported. The values available are screen, tty, tv, projection, handheld, print, Braille, aural, and all, which are aimed respectively at computer screens, terminals, televisions, projectors, handheld devices, printed pages, Braille tactile feedback devices, speech synthesizers, and all of the above. Of these, you are most likely to use screen and print, and possibly handheld (which has limited support among handheld browsers). Opera uses projection when in full-screen mode, so if you have specified a screen type for your main style sheet, you may wish to consider including projection: <link media="screen, projection" ... />.

- start: In a collection of documents, a rel attribute value of start indicates to user agents and search engines which document should be considered the starting point for the collection.

- next: This value indicates that the linked document is the next document in a collection of documents.

- prev: This value is similar to next, except it indicates the previous document rather than the next. If you're a completist, you could have links with both rev/prev and rev/next in them, but it would probably be enough to just have the revs.

- contents: This value refers to a document serving as a table of contents.

- index: This value refers to a document providing an index for the current document.

- glossary: This value refers to a document providing a glossary for the current document.

- copyright: This value refers to a document providing a copyright statement for the current document.

- chapter: This value refers to a document serving as a chapter in a collection of documents.

- section: This value refers to a document serving as a section in a chapter.

- subsection: This value refers to a document serving as a subsection in a section.

- appendix: This value refers to a document serving as an appendix in a collection of documents.

- help: This value refers to a help document that should relate to the website or web page—for instance, a collection of "further reading" links or an explanatory document listing FAQs.

- bookmark: This value refers to a bookmark (i.e., a starting point within a document or collection of documents).

These are just the link types predefined by the W3C; you can also define additional types of your own. For instance, you could label any links that point to external sources with a rel="external" attribute, and in his weblog Joe Clark advocates using the rev attribute to indicate that a zoom layout is available (http://axxlog.wordpress.net/archives/2005/01/14/zoom-hack).

> A **zoom layout** is a CSS layout specially formatted for low-vision users. It usually features large, light text on a dark background and a single-column design. See Joe Clark's article "Big, Stark & Chunky" at www.alistapart.com/articles/lowvision for more information.

Some user agents already take advantage of these attributes. For example, Opera features a navigation bar that displays links with rel attributes in a fixed toolbar (see Figure 2-10) and will allow you to select alternate style sheets from a drop-down menu (as does Firefox).

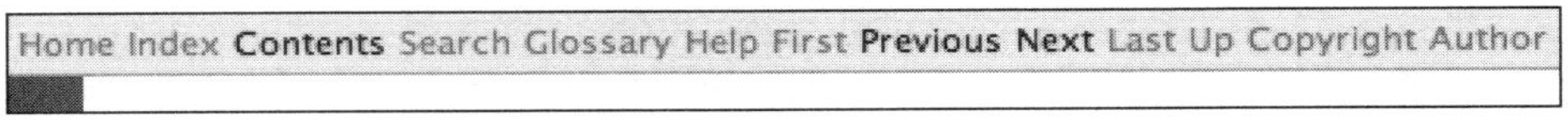

Home Index Contents Search Glossary Help First Previous Next Last Up Copyright Author

Figure 2-10. Opera's rel-based navigation bar. The page here has a Contents link, as well as Previous and Next links.

Both Opera and Firefox rely on the alternate style sheet link to also have a `title` attribute, which is used to display the options to the user (see Figure 2-11). The attributes also provide web authors with extra hooks for CSS and JavaScript, as you will see later on.

Edit
View
Go
Bookmarks
Tools
Window
Help
Toolbars
Status Bar
Sidebar
Stop ⌘.
Reload ⌘R
Text Size
Page Style
Character Encoding
Page Source ⌘U
No Style
Default Theme
Clutter Free
Big and Zoomed
Handheld Devices
The Printed Page
Imagination: Dustin Diaz
Sitemap
accessibility by Dustin Diaz

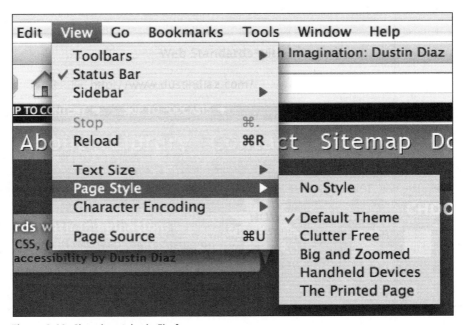

Figure 2-11. Changing styles in Firefox

Technorati (`http://technorati.com`), a weblog search and tracking engine, utilizes the `rel` attribute to help generate its tag-based navigation (see Figure 2-12).

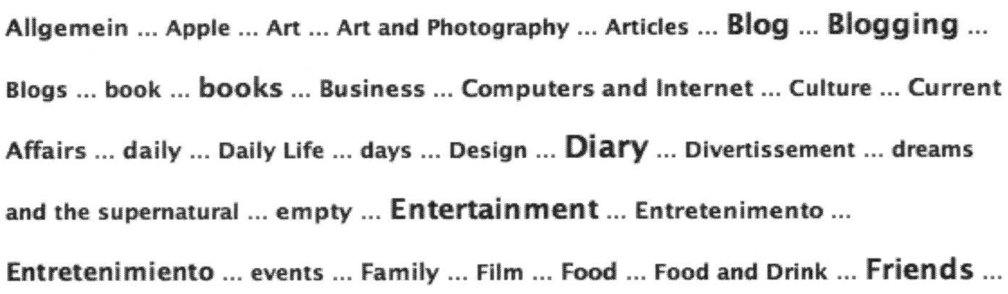

Allgemein ... Apple ... Art ... Art and Photography ... Articles ... Blog ... Blogging ...
Blogs ... book ... books ... Business ... Computers and Internet ... Culture ... Current
Affairs ... daily ... Daily Life ... days ... Design ... Diary ... Divertissement ... dreams
and the supernatural ... empty ... Entertainment ... Entretenimento ...
Entretenimiento ... events ... Family ... Film ... Food ... Food and Drink ... Friends ...

Figure 2-12. A Technorati tag cloud, with the more popular tags appearing in a larger font

By adding rel="tag" to a link within a blog post, you are indicating that the resource indicated by the href of the link can be used as a general category page for the specific topic. For instance, if you are writing an article on Apple's iPod for your blog, you could include a link such as the following somewhere in the body of your article:

```
<a href="http://technorati.com/tag/ipod/" rel="tag">iPod</a>
```

When you do this, Technorati and other tag-aware services and aggregators can determine that your article belongs in the category of "ipod," and that the resource indicated can be considered as a collection of related articles. Your article can then be included in future collections of related articles.

We'll take a closer look at the use of rel="tag" in Chapter 5, so don't worry about it too much at this stage.

Targeting links

Something worth noting is that the target attribute, which is used on anchor tags to direct a link into either a new browser window or an alternative frame within the window, has been deprecated, so if you are writing strict XHTML, you must use JavaScript to replicate this behavior. This is where you can take advantage of the rel attribute: by using a simple bit of JavaScript, it is possible to pick up any links with a rel value of external and cause them to open in new windows.[9] Here's a short script that does just that:

```
function popup()
{
    if (document.getElementsByTagName) {
    a = document.getElementsByTagName("a");
    for(i=0; i<a.length; i++)
    {
        if(a[i].getAttribute("rel") ➥
&& a[i].getAttribute("rel") == "external")
        {
            a[i].onclick = function()
            {
                window.open(this.getAttribute('href'));
                return false;
            }
        }
    }
    }
    else return false;
}
window.onload = popup;
```

---

9. If you want to style your external links in a different fashion from your regular links, then you would still need to add a class. Although you can use CSS attribute selectors to target links with a specific rel value (using a[rel=external]), these will not work in Internet Explorer.

What's happening here? Well, it's a JavaScript function that will collect all `<a>` tags in the (X)HTML document, and then loop through that collection picking out each `<a>` with a `rel` attribute value of external, set its onclick action to open in a new window, and finally instruct the user agent to not follow the link again in the existing window (with `return false`). This allows you to maintain a valid, XHTML Strict document without muddying up your markup with inline `onclick` attributes, and if you change your mind in the future, you only have to change (or remove) this script, instead of having to change every link.

> *The preceding script is by no means the only way to do achieve this effect. For a comprehensive, all-singing, all-dancing new window script, I suggest Roger Johnanson's script, available at* www.456bereastreet.com/archive/200610/opening_new_windows_with_javascript_version_12/. *It covers a wider range of situations and includes support for progamatically including a warning to users about the new window.*

Also worth noting is the CSS `:target` pseudo-class, introduced as part of the as-yet incomplete CSS 3 specification (see www.w3.org/TR/css3-selectors), but supported already in Firefox and Safari (and likely to soon be supported in Opera version 9 and above). This pseudo-class allows you to style a targeted anchor or identified element. Though it's not supported in any version of Internet Explorer,[10] it never hurts to include this type of extra treat for users of modern browsers. To see it in action, you should create a file containing a number of links, like so:

```
<p><a href="#one">link to paragraph one</a> | ➠
<a href="#two">link to paragraph two</a> | ➠
<a href="#three">link to paragraph three</a></p>
```

Then, underneath, create three paragraphs, each with a unique id matching those in your links:

```
<p id="one">paragraph one</p>
<p id="two">paragraph two</p>
<p id="three">paragraph three</p>
```

Finally, include the following line in the head of your document:

```
<style type="text/css">:target { background: yellow;}</style>
```

Now, in either Firefox or Safari, start clicking those links. The targeted paragraph gains a yellow background, which is useful to indicate to users where they should be looking if they've followed a link from a separate page or a list of contents at the start of a long document, and it saves them from having to hunt around for what they want.

---

10. You can replicate the :target functionality in Internet Explorer with JavaScript. See Patrick Griffiths and Dan Webb's "Suckerfish :target" article (www.htmldog.com/articles/suckerfish/target) for more information.

Accessible linking

You can enhance the accessibility and usability of your website with judicious use of the tabindex and accesskey attributes (on the <a> tags, but not the <link> tags) and the title attribute (available to use on all elements).

The title attribute gives extra information about the related element. In the case of anchor links, it should be used to give a description about what the link is about, but only if the link text does not already provide enough information. For instance, there's no need to write <a href="/contacts.html" title="Contacts">Contacts</a>, as a screen-reading device is likely to read out both the title and the link text redundantly. A better title in this case might be "E-mail, telephone, and postal contact information for the board of directors," as this title allows you to have a short link (one that would fit in a narrow navigation list or similar) but still provide a detailed explanation. Some browsers display the title value as a tooltip, visible when users hover over the element with their mouse, while other browsers display the value in the status bar in lieu of the URL. In the case of <link> links, the title value is usually what is used to generate a menu of alternative style sheets and such to users.

The tabindex and accesskey attributes both only apply to elements that can take keyboard focus: anchor links and form fields (I discuss these attributes' use with form fields in Chapter 4). tabindex allows you to create a specific tabbing order for users who are using a keyboard instead of a mouse to navigate your site. You do this by giving an attribute value of a number, such as tabindex="1", which would make that element the first element focused when the user presses the Tab key. A tabindexed element with a higher value would be the next, and so on.

The tabindex attribute has its uses, but you should use it with care. If you have built your site well, with your navigational elements in a logical order in the source markup, then you are unlikely to even need to apply tabindexes to your links, as the browser will be able to work out the logical tab order automatically. You also run the risk of confusing users if your tabindex structure is radically different from what they're used to, and you may encounter maintenance problems if you find you need to insert a new link in the middle of your list, leading to a renumbering of all the subsequent tabindexes.

The accesskey attribute comes with a similar "use with caution" warning. This attribute allows you to specify a character to be used as a keyboard shortcut, such as accesskey="s", which would result in that element gaining focus when the user activates that shortcut. Depending on the browser, this shortcut could be with Ctrl+S, Alt+S, or even Ctrl+Alt+S (plus the Mac equivalents).

It sounds nice enough, but there are strong arguments for avoiding accesskeys altogether.[11] To start with, there is no standard accesskey scheme, which results in many sites having different shortcut keys. Most browsers do not come with any ability to display what the accesskeys actually are to the user, which means the user must either find an accessibility statement and refer to it or view the source markup. Also, conflicts between accesskeys and hard-wired browser shortcuts can upset user expectations, and with so many different

---

11. To hear what various web standards notables have said about accesskeys, I suggest starting with Dave Shea's blog entry titled "I Do Not Use Accesskeys" (www.mezzoblue.com/archives/2003/12/29/i_do_not_use) and going from there.

browsers available, it was discovered by Web Accessibility Technical Services that / \ and] were the only characters not already used by a browser.[12]

Opera, which provides keyboard shortcuts for everything but the kitchen sink, deals with this problem by including a keyboard shortcut that "enables" accesskeys—pressing Shift+Esc will then allow you to use the accesskeys without needing any modifier key (so to jump to a form field that had an accesskey value of s, you would just need to press S instead of Shift+S or Ctrl+S). However, this does not address the problem of discovering exactly what accesskeys are in use on any given website, and Opera doesn't even provide a notification to let you know whether you're in an enabled mode or not—or let you know, without delving into the help files, that such a system exists at all.

A system in use at Accessify attempts to get around this problem by allowing users to set their own accesskeys (http://accessify.com/preferences/accesskeys), but this solution is unlikely to become widespread: it's site-specific; it can't be shared easily between sites, as cookies cannot be read from across different domains for security reasons; and users would still have problems on sites that did not implement this method.

There is a place for both tabindex and accesskey attributes, such as in web-based applications that need to mimic a desktop application, or in complex forms where the source order of the form elements may differ from the desired layout.

Marking up changes to your document

The <del> and <ins> tags are both used for marking up changes to a document, most commonly for changes within the text (e.g., correcting details within a blog post after newer, more accurate information has been acquired). They can be used to note changes in document structure as well (e.g., wrapping whole sections of your website). They're versatile, as they can be either block or inline, depending on the context. Both of the following examples are valid:

```
<p> Lorem ipsum dolor sit amet, ➡
<del>consectetuer adipiscing elit</del>.</p>
<del><p> Lorem ipsum dolor sit amet,➡
 consectetuer adipiscing elit.</p></del>
```

If you have these tags within a block element—that is, a block element that doesn't allow nested block elements, such as a paragraph or a heading—then they can be considered as inline elements, like <span> or <strong>. However, if you use these tags to *contain* a block element, then they can be considered as block elements themselves (though you may need to apply display: block in your CSS to take advantage of block-style margins, paddings, and borders).

These tags do have some limitations, though. For instance, you can't use <del> to mark the removal of an <li>, like this:

```
<ul><del><li>list item</li></del></ul>
```

---

12. Web Accessibility Technical Services, "Using Accesskeys - Is it worth it?", www.wats.ca/show.php?contentid=32, January 2005.

because the only valid tag you can place directly within a <ul> is the <li>. The same is true for removing table rows (<tr>) from tables—it would be invalid markup, even though it makes logical sense.

Visually, the <del> tag will usually default to drawing a line through its content, while the <ins> tag will draw an underline, as shown in Figure 2-13. I generally remove the underline with CSS (ins {text-decoration: none;}), because if something is underlined on a web page, people tend to try and click it, but it may be OK if your actual links are distinctive enough.[13]

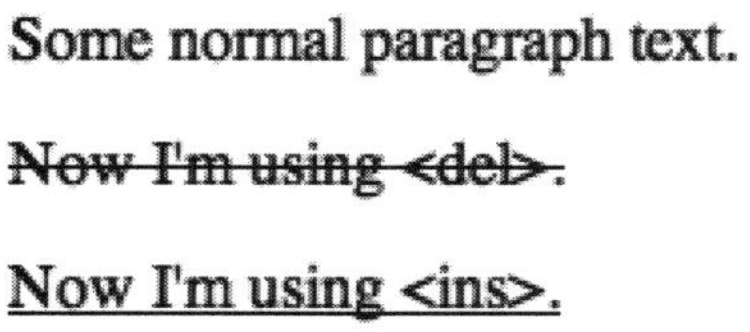

Some normal paragraph text.

~~Now I'm using <del>.~~

<u>Now I'm using <ins>.</u>

Figure 2-13. A paragraph with some deleted and inserted content

Two attributes are specific to <del> and <ins>: datetime and cite. The former allows you to set a date for when the correction took place, and the latter is for you to provide a link to a page explaining the reason behind the correction:

```
<p> Lorem ipsum dolor sit amet, <del datetime="20060509" ➥
cite="http://example.com/errata.html">consectetuer ➥
adipiscing elit</del>.</p>
```

As is often the case with these kinds of attributes, their information is hidden from most users, so if you want to display it, you will need to use JavaScript, as discussed earlier when we examined how to retrieve the cite attribute value from a <blockquote>. You can also use JavaScript to control the display of your deletions and insertions. This could be in the form of a simple display/hide toggle link, or you could go a bit further.

> *Jonathan Snook experimented with using JavaScript to create a <div> containing both the* datetime *and* cite *values for each <del> or <ins>, and then displaying that <div> alongside the containing paragraph. See his article "An experiment with INS and DEL" at* www.snook.ca/archives/html_and_css/an_experiment_w *for more information.*

Presentational elements

A **presentational element** says nothing about the content it describes, but instead says everything about how it *appears*. A range of these elements are still in the HTML specification, some of which we can still use and others of which have more appropriate

---

13. The W3C uses <ins> and <del> for its working drafts of specifications. For instance, at www.w3.org/Style/css21-updates/WD-CSS21-20050613-20040225-diff/cover.html the W3C has really gone to town with them.

alternatives. The HTML specification doesn't explicitly list elements as being presentational *per se*, so I'm going to go over elements that are commonly held to *be* presentational: <hr>, <pre>, <sup>, <sub>, <i>, <b>, <strike> and <s>, <u>, <tt>, <big>, and <small>.

When considering using any of these elements, the acid test should be this: are you using the element purely for the visual effect? If the answer is no, then you're probably OK; if the answer is yes, a more suitable alternative may be out there. A further test is if you can remove the style sheet from your document and have the document still make sense. If this isn't possible, then you may find a presentational element is exactly what you need.

Font style elements

A **font style element** is defined by the W3C as an element that simply specifies font information, and thus has no semantic meaning or value. Although they have not all been deprecated, their use is generally discouraged in favor of style sheets. The font style elements as defined by the W3C are <i>, <b>, <tt>, <big>, <small>, <strike>, <s>, and <u>. There are also two **font modifier elements**, <font> and <basefont>, but both have been deprecated and are no longer of any use to us. Font style elements go against what I've been saying about considering what your content *means*, rather than what it *looks like*—these elements say a lot about appearances and nothing about meaning. Nevertheless, some of them can still be useful to us, particularly when (X)HTML does not provide us with a meaningful alternative.

The <i> and <b> elements are the two most obvious presentational elements, and in the drive toward increased accessibility and a standards-based design methodology they have often been eschewed in favor of <em> and <strong>, respectively, because the former tags convey purely visual information while the latter tags convey meaning as well—emphasis. However, people can go too far and use <em> and <strong> as standard replacements, using them constantly for any instance where they require italic and bold text. This error has been perpetuated by numerous WYSIWYG tools that keep the common I and B buttons but change their function, adding an <em> or <strong> element to the markup instead. This would be fine if web designers and authors actually meant, every time, to emphasize, but that isn't always the case.

Both of these elements still have their uses, and neither has been deprecated or removed from any (X)HTML specification. For instance, <i> can be used when italicizing text in a foreign language (i.e., <i lang="it">Molte grazie</i>). Using a span for this purpose would require an additional class name,[14] such as <span class="foreign" lang="it">, so with <i> and <span> both as semantically meaningless as each other, I recommend simply using the <i> element, because it already does what you want and will take up less space in your markup.

The <tt> element renders text in a teletype or monospaced font. Again, this element is semantically meaningless, and you may find other elements such as <code>, <pre>, or

---

14. If you're only concerned about CSS2-supporting browsers, then you can use an attribute selector in your CSS to achieve the italic effect: span[lang] { font-style: italic;}. This means that you don't need the extra class name, but it also means you lose the effect in Internet Explorer, content aggregators, and other non-CSS user agents.

<samp> more suitable to describe your content (discussed further in the next section). Nevertheless, it remains part of current (X)HTML specifications, so it is there for you if required.

<big> and <small> both affect the font size of their contained content, and nested <big> or <small> elements will cause the contents to be even bigger or smaller. It's purely presentational, and you may find that the CSS font-size property is more appropriate for your needs, though some, such as accessibility advocate Joe Clark, have suggested using nested <big> and <small> elements in tag clouds[15] to achieve the "weighted by importance" visual effect. Others, such as Tantek Çelik, suggest using nested <em> elements instead,[16] which has the benefit of being more meaningful but loses the visual effect in non-CSS user agents—you pays your money and you makes your choice.

The only font style elements that have been deprecated in both HTML 4 and XHTML 1 are <strike>, <s>, and <u>. <strike> and <s> have an identical function: they draw a horizontal line through their content, and this function can be visually replicated by using the CSS text-decoration property. If you wish to indicate that some content has been deleted, then use the <del> element (discussed previously). <u> is used for underlining content, and again this function can be replicated with text-decoration. It is also advisable to not underline anything that isn't a link—links and underlines are so commonly associated with one another that anything on the Web that's underlined now looks like a link to users.

As far as styling these elements goes, there's not much point beyond specifying further font information (such as specifying a range of specific typewriter-style fonts for <tt>, or increasing the size variation between different levels of <big> and <small>). However, don't be put off using any of these elements just because they're presentational. With the exceptions of <strike>, <s>, and <u>, all of these elements are part of current and future (X)HTML specifications, and if you find yourself writing <span class="typewriter">...</span> or <span class="foreign" lang="fr">...</span> a lot, then consider using <tt> or <i> instead; they're as semantically meaningless as a span, but they already do what you want and take up less space in your markup. You can always restyle these elements, just as you would a span if required, but if you think you might wish to do this in the future, then bear in mind that you might end up with an <i> styled as a <b>, and vice versa.

It is also worth considering these elements when designing WYSIWYG interfaces for average users, because having incorrect semantics is worse than having no semantics at all. For example, if you think your users may want to italicize a citation, don't give them the chance to do so with the <em> element; the <i> element is a safer choice because it isn't going to confuse any tool or browser trying to utilize your semantic information.

The <hr>, <pre>, <sup>, and <sub> elements

The <hr>, <pre>, <sup> and <sub> elements are all technically presentational elements, but they *also* convey meaning that cannot (or should not) be replicated with CSS. Take the

---

15. See http://blog.fawny.org/2005/01/23/weighted.

16. See http://tantek.com/log/2005/02.html#d02t0800.

<hr> element, for instance: it's a straightforward horizontal rule. In many cases, this can (and should) be reproduced by simply adding a CSS border to the top or bottom of a block element, but you should only do this if you're using an <hr> element to apply a border. If you're using an <hr> element specifically as a *separator* of the sort you might find separating sections of a book chapter, then your rule does have a structural purpose and should be used instead of the CSS border.[17]

The <hr> tag comes with several attributes—size, width, noshade, and align—but all have been deprecated, so we must use CSS for style, which can be a little quirky, as Internet Explorer essentially treats <hr> as an inline element, whereas Firefox *et al.* treat it as a block element. For instance, if you want to color your horizontal rule red, you must set both the color property *and* the background-color property. If you want to align the rule to the left or right, you must set the text-align property for Internet Explorer and use margin: 0 auto for other browsers.

For an even more interesting rule, you can use the background-image property—but this won't work in Internet Explorer. There are two solutions at the time of this writing. The first is to wrap your <hr> in a <div>, give your <div> the background image, and then use display: none to remove the <hr> from view. Non-CSS user agents will then see the <hr>, but CSS user agents will see your background image instead. The second solution, for the markup purists, is to dynamically include a <div> with JavaScript. You could then style the <div> and hide the <hr> with CSS.

For example, the following script notes where all of the <hr> elements are, and then creates a <div> with a class name of rule and inserts it just before each <hr>. Your markup remains free of extraneous <div> tags, but you can still style those that are being dynamically inserted.

```
function lovelyrules() {
    if (!document.getElementsByTagName || ➡
!document.createElement || !document.insertBefore) return;
    var rules = document.getElementsByTagName("hr");
    for (var i=0; i<rules.length; i++) {
        var div = document.createElement("div");
        div.className = "rule";
        rules[i].parentNode.insertBefore(div, rules[i]);
    }
}
window.onload = lovelyrules;
```

Now, what about <pre>? The visual effect caused by the <pre> tag is to preserve the whitespace (i.e., the tabs, spaces, and line breaks) in your markup, so if that whitespace is important in understanding the content, such as code samples, then use <pre> (see Figure 2-14). The effect can be replicated with the CSS white-space property, but using this property in place of <pre> means you'll lose the effect in non-CSS user agents.

---

17. This is exactly the sort of thinking that has led the W3C to suggest a <separator> element in XHTML 2.0 (see Appendix A).

What follows is some pre-formatted text:

```
h1 {
            background-color: white;
            color: blue;
            font-size: 3em;
            font-style: italic;
}
```

Figure 2-14. A comparison of `<pre>` in both source code and rendered in a browser. The whitespace (tabs and carriage returns) that I inserted in the source code have been retained.

Similarly, the `<sup>` and `<sub>` (superscript and subscript) elements can convey important meaning via presentation. Consider the two following equations:

- $e=mc^2$
- e=mc2

Although they look alike, only one of the preceding equations is Einstein's; spelled out, the former equation is "e equals m times c squared," while the latter is "e equals m times c times 2." Or how about this:

- H_2O
- H2O

The first is chemical equation for water—two hydrogen atoms and one oxygen atom—and the second is simply the letter "H" followed by the number 2, then the letter "O", and is meaningless. So, the placing and styling of the "2" is therefore important, and if you removed its styling and positioning and placed it in a style sheet, some browsers could lose the meaning.

The W3C also notes that some languages (other than English) require the use of subscripted and superscripted text. Here's an example in French:

- Mlle Dupont

Stylistically, you can also use superscripts and subscripts in English. You'll most likely have seen them in dates, or to indicate the presence of footnotes/endnotes:

- The 14th of September
- The committee report stated that the minister had acted in good faith.[ii]

Phrase elements

A **phrase element** adds meaning to a fragment of text. It's likely that you've already encountered phrase elements without even knowing it; <em> and <strong> are two such elements, but there are several other, underused phrase elements that can help to make your document more structurally and semantically meaningful while still maintaining your desired visual style. The full list of phrase elements is as follows: <em>, <strong>, <cite>, <dfn>, <code>, <samp>, <kbd>, <var>, <abbr>, and <acronym>.

Emphasis

As mentioned previously, <em> and <strong> should be used not to italicize or bold text; rather, they indicate emphasis, with <strong> being more emphatic than <em>, and the combination of the two more emphatic still. Where visual browsers will usually display an <em> and <strong> with italic and bold text, respectively, screen readers may change volume, pitch, and rate when encountering these elements.

Here's an example usage:

```
<p>I was a <em>little</em> bit angry, then I was ➡
<strong>very</strong> angry, then I was ➡
<em><strong>extremely</strong></em> angry!</p>
```

The preceding code would render in most user agents as follows:

I was a *little* bit angry, then I was **very** angry, then I was ***extremely*** angry!

You may not want your emphasis displayed in such a way. Remember that you can always restyle <em> and <strong> elements to display however you like, while still retaining their semantic meaning. For instance, if the text of your document was in Japanese ideographic text, then you would be unlikely to need an italic version for emphasis, and a change in background color may be more appropriate.

> *This preceding issue of* internationalization *is discussed in more detail in Molly E. Holzschlag's article "World Grows Small: Open Standards for the Global Web"* (www.alistapart.com/articles/worldgrowssmall)*.*

Citations and definitions

We've already encountered the cite attribute, used within <blockquote> tags to attribute a source to the quote, and within <del> and <ins> tags to refer to an explanatory document, but there also exists a <cite> *tag* to contain stand-alone references not associated with any particular element, or citations of other material. You would use this tag for referring to other sources, such as book or movie titles. Most user agents will display a citation in italic font, a typographic convention you'll often see in the print world as well.

Also usually italicized by default is the <dfn> element, which indicates the first usage of a term that will be used repeatedly throughout a document (i.e., its defining instance), for example:

```
<p>You can keep your CSS rules in a file separate from your HTML.
This file is known as a <dfn>style sheet</dfn>. You can also have a
separate style sheet that determines how your web page looks when it is
being printed...</p>
```

The preceding code would render as follows:

"You can keep your CSS rules in a file separate from your HTML. This file is known as a *style sheet*. You can also have a separate style sheet that determines how your web page looks when it is being printed . . ."

It's worth considering adding unique id attributes to your definitions, as this enables you to link directly to them from a glossary if you have one (which could be constructed using a definition list).

Coding

Four phrase elements are particularly useful for describing programming or other computing-related tasks, such as describing user input: <code>, <var>, <samp>, and <kbd>. The former two are used to display raw computer code, (X)HTML markup, CSS, and so on. <code> will usually display in user agents in a monospaced font, while <var> will display in an italic font (see Figure 2-15).

```
<code>
    #!/usr/local/bin/perl<br />
    print "<var>Content-type: text/html\n</var>";<br />
    print "<var>Hello World</var>\n";<br />
</code>
```

```
#!/usr/local/bin/perl
print "Content-type: text/html\n";
print "Hello World\n";
```

Figure 2-15. <code> and <var> in use. The content within <var> tags is italicized by default.

As noted earlier, you may wish to lose the line breaks in such an example and wrap the code in <pre> tags, to preserve any breaks and tabs and other whitespace formatting. If you're displaying long lines of code, though, eschewing <pre> and using breaks instead will better prevent those long lines from breaking out of your layout.

While <code> and <var> are used for displaying code, <samp> (as in "sample") describes the output of that code. It is used simply, and it will also usually display in a monospaced font:

```
<p><samp> [paul@localhost ~]$ perl hello.cgi</samp></p>
<p><samp>Content-type:  text/html<br />➥
&lt;H1&gt;Hello World&lt;/H1&gt; </samp></p>
```

With all these monospaced fonts now in your document, it's probably worth considering using CSS to mix things up a little. For instance, you could display <samp> as the output of a command prompt window, as shown in Figure 2-16.

```
Content-type: text/html
<h1>Hello World</h1>
```

Figure 2-16. <samp> displays in a monospaced font by default, and as such it can look a bit too much like <code>. Using CSS to style it differently can help distinguish the two.

The CSS for this is straightforward enough:

```
samp {
background: #000;
border: 3px groove #ccc;
color: #ccc;
display: block;
padding: 5px;
width: 300px;
}
```

Finally, there is <kbd>, which is used to indicate keyboard input by the user, like so:

```
<p>Press <kbd>A</kbd>, then <kbd>B</kbd>, then ➥
<kbd>C</kbd>. Finally, press the <kbd>Enter</kbd> key to continue.</p>
```

I think that the obvious thing to do with a <kbd> element is to style it to look vaguely keyboardlike:

```
kbd {
background-color: #F1E7DD;
border: 1px outset #333;
color: #333;
padding: 2px 5px;
}
```

The preceding CSS yields a result like that shown in Figure 2-17.

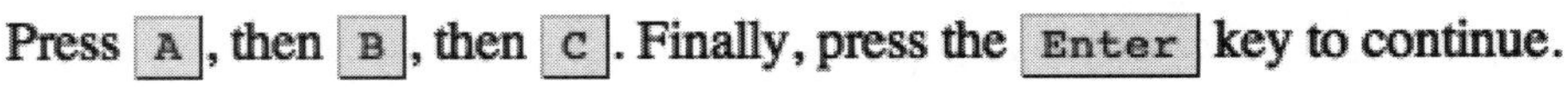

Press A , then B , then C . Finally, press the Enter key to continue.

Figure 2-17. Several <kbd> elements styled to look like actual keys

Abbreviations

For displaying abbreviated text, you have two options available: <abbr> and <acronym>. The <abbr> element indicates abbreviated text, with the full, unabbreviated text often contained within a title attribute, while <acronym> is used for acronyms (and possibly initialisms as well) instead of abbreviations. What's the difference? Well, the W3C is a little hazy on the issue, but the *Oxford English Dictionary* defines the three terms as follows:

- **Abbreviation**: A shortened form of a word or phrase.
- **Acronym**: A word formed from the initial letters of other words (e.g., *laser*, which is an acronym of Light Amplification by Stimulated Emission of Radiation).
- **Initialism**: An abbreviation consisting of initial letters pronounced separately (e.g., *BBC*).

Or in other words, *all acronyms and initialisms are abbreviations, but not all abbreviations are acronyms or initialisms*. So when in doubt, using <abbr> to describe your content will be correct. Unfortunately (did you see this coming?), Internet Explorer 6 and below do not support the <abbr> element, which has led to many people using <acronym> instead (which Internet Explorer does support), even though not all abbreviations are acronyms. Typical. The question of whether you use <acronym> incorrectly or use <abbr> correctly and forget about Internet Explorer is one you will have to answer yourself, but my preference is for the former—I'd rather use the right semantics for the situation than use the wrong ones.

> *Dean Edwards has come up with a way of tricking Internet Explorer into sort of supporting* <abbr>, *detailed in his article "abbr-cadabra" (*http://dean.edwards.name/my/abbr-cadabra.html*). Internet Explorer 7 includes native support for* <abbr>.

Another factor to take into consideration is how screen readers and other aural devices treat abbreviations. An abbreviation that is an acronym or a truncation should be pronounced as if it's a regular word; an abbreviation that is an initialism should be spelled out rather than pronounced. We can control this with a specific aural style sheet and, due to the lack of a specific initialism tag, a couple of extra class names:

```
<abbr>Mr</abbr>
<acronym>NATO</acronym>
<abbr class="initialism">BBC</abbr>
```

The aural styling of these elements using CSS is as follows:

```
@media aural {
abbr , acronym {speak : normal;}
abbr.initialism {speak : spell-out;}
}
```

Alternatively, you can include an aural style sheet separately in the head of your document like this:

```
<link rel="stylesheet=" media="aural" href="aural.css" />
```

Images and other media

Without images, the Web would be far less interesting to look at, though on the other hand we'd also never have to run across any animated construction-worker GIFs on an unfinished page. You can always find a silver lining if you look hard enough.

Using images within your website is something you are likely very familiar with, but this topic is still worth discussing, due to the different ways images can be included: inline, via CSS background images, via image maps, and through the <object> element. Each method has pros and cons, as described in the sections that follow.

Inline images

The simplest method of including an image is directly within the markup, using the self-closing <img> element:

```
<img src="image.jpg" />
```

There are some things to consider here. First, let's look at alt attributes. In both XHTML and HTML, all images should have alt attributes regardless of whether the attribute contains a value. An alt attribute's one and only purpose in life is to provide an *alternative* to the image, which means that the value of the attribute must duplicate any meaningful content within the image. If your image has no meaningful content, then leave the alt attribute in, but leave it empty: alt="". (Also consider whether you can remove the image entirely and place it within your CSS as a decorative background image, as discussed in the next section.)

The alt attribute is not there to provide any additional information or a descriptive caption—this is the purpose of the title attribute. The content of an alt attribute should only be displayed if the image is unavailable for whatever reason; it is an alternative (either display the image or the alternative text, not both). Unfortunately, due to Internet Explorer's (incorrect) behavior of displaying the content of an alt attribute as a tooltip,[18] it's been frequently misused for that very purpose when, in fact, a title attribute might be more appropriate.

Also available is the longdesc attribute, which provides a link to a page containing a more elaborate supplement to the alt attribute value. Browser support for this attribute is historically very poor, though, so you should use with caution, if at all.

---

18. If a title attribute is present as well, then Internet Explorer will display that value in the tooltip rather than the alt attribute value. If both attributes are present but the title attribute is empty, then no tooltip will display.

The img element allows you to specify an image width and height value in pixels, in the form of width="150". These attributes are optional, but an advantage of using them is that a web browser can accurately display textual content in the correct space before the images have loaded, avoiding the problem of text jumping around to make way for images as they arrive. A disadvantage is that they are presentational attributes, and ideally these sorts of values would be set in the CSS to make it easier to change if the image dimensions ever changed. Furthermore, the presence of size attributes will cause the alt attribute value to display in a box sized to the same dimensions, which may not be desirable if the text is larger than the space allowed.

CSS background images

Images can also be included via the CSS background-image property. You should use this property to place decorative images within your pages to help keep your markup as clean as possible, allowing you to make significant changes to the look and feel of your website by changing only your style sheet (and also allowing you to specify different images for printed, mobile, and projected versions of your site). A disadvantage is that when images are not available but CSS is, alternative content will not be displayed—so using a CSS background image for navigation button text or similar is not advised.

So long as you're not reproducing textual content, background images can be very useful to help us achieve certain visual effects. In his article "Faux Columns" (www.alistapart.com/articles/fauxcolumns), Dan Cederholm documented the concept of **faux columns**, where using a single tiled background image on the <body> of your web page creates the illusion of two equal-height columns, irrespective of which column contains the most content. Or see Doug Bowman's article "Sliding Doors of CSS" (www.alistapart.com/articles/slidingdoors), where he details a technique in which using an oversized background image in a navigation menu allows the text to be resized and the background image scaled with it. Also worth a look is Tim Murtaugh's article "CSS Design: Mo' Betta Rollovers" (www.alistapart.com/stories/rollovers), where he describes how judicious use of the background-image property and the :hover pseudo-class allows you to create CSS-based image rollovers without recourse to JavaScript.

Image maps

Image maps come in two varieties: client side and server side. A client-side image map consists of an image with a series of predetermined hotspot areas of varying shapes and sizes that represent links. A server-side image map is a similar construct, but the pixel coordinates of the mouse click are sent to the server, which calculates the subsequent action. Client-side image maps are preferable as they can be made accessible to people browsing with images disabled or unavailable, and they offer immediate feedback as to whether users are clicking an active region.

The muddy markup required for an image map is anathema to the mantra of separating presentation from content. There are two distinct parts: the map element (<map>) and the image element (<img>), neither of which is nested within the other. The map element is a container tag with a name attribute, and the tag contains any number of self-closing <area> tags. These <area> tags use the shape attribute to determine the shape of the area (circle, rect, poly, or default), a coords attribute to stake out the dimensions of the shape, and either an href attribute to determine where users should be taken to after they've clicked or a nohref attribute if no link is in use.

In the meantime, the <img> element gains a usemap attribute, the value of which should be the same as the value of the map's name attribute. It also needs an ismap attribute to say that the image is a map. Phew.

Here's an example (following XHTML rules) that will—hopefully—clarify the preceding explanation:

```
<map name="Map">
    <area shape="rect" coords="118,192,203,249" ➡
href="http://joeblade.com" alt="Home" />
    <area shape="circle" coords="52,76,39" ➡
href="http://joeblade.com" alt="About" />
    <area shape="poly" ➡
coords="159,145,115,96,115,39,160,21,205,40,206,103" ➡
href="http://joeblade.com" alt="Contact" />
</map>
<img src="imagemap.jpg" alt="" width="300" ➡
height="272" usemap="#Map" ismap="ismap" />
```

This image map contains three clickable areas: a rectangle, a circle, and a six-sided polygon. As you can imagine, hand-coding image maps this way is fairly laborious, but most WYSIWYG software comes with the ability to create areas just by pointing, clicking, and dragging. Figure 2-18 shows an example of an image map created in Dreamweaver.

Figure 2-18. An image map created in Dreamweaver. Creating clickable areas this way is a simple matter.

While it is not possible to re-create circular or polygonal areas with a pure CSS solution, you can create rectangular areas by styling a simple unordered or ordered list of links. The steps to do this are as follows:

1. Create a list of links with standard (X)HTML.

2. Give each link a unique id attribute.

3. In the CSS, give the list a background image, width, and height, and add position: relative; to make sure your links (that you will position absolutely) are placed in relation to the top left of the list and not the browser window.

4. Also in the CSS, give each link the required width, height, and background image or color.

5. Using position: absolute; and the top, left, right, and bottom CSS properties, position each link within the list as appropriate.

6. Hide the link text with text-indent: -9999px;.[19]

Let's go through that process again, this time with examples. The (X)HTML is simple enough:

```
<ul>
<li><a href="/" id="homelink">Home</a></li>
<li><a href="/about/" id="aboutlink">About</a></li>
<li><a href="/contact/" id="contactlink">Contact</a></li>
</ul>
```

The CSS is slightly less simple, but it shouldn't give you much of a headache. You'll most likely need a graphical editor of some kind to help you work out the coordinates, though. First of all, you style the list:

```
ul {
background: url(imagemap.gif) top left no-repeat;
height: 272px;
position: relative;
width: 300px;
}
```

Next, reset the margins and padding of both the list and the list items to 0. This may not always be necessary, but it will help when trying to position elements, and it also aids in cross-browser consistency.

```
ul, li {
margin: 0; padding: 0;
}
```

---

19. The negative text-indent value will shunt the text content of the link way off to the left side of the screen, making it effectively invisible. When doing this on a link, however, Firefox (and possibly some other modern browsers) will draw its "active" link outline around the entire space, leading to a large outline box stretching off to the left. To overcome this, just add overflow: hidden; and the outline box will only surround the visible, clickable area instead.

Then you deal with the links. Each one needs to be positioned separately, by referencing the id attribute set in the markup, but shared values can be dealt with in one try. I'm going to give these links background colors of green to demonstrate where the clickable areas will lie—in the real world, you would blend them in better with their backgrounds.

```
a {
background: green;
display: block;
overflow: hidden;
position: absolute;
text-indent: -9999px;
}
```

Finally, position each link and give them all a width and height:

```
#homelink {
top: 15px;
left: 50px;
width: 75px;
height: 75px;
}

#aboutlink {
top: 20px;
left: 110px;
width: 100px;
height: 125px;
}

#contactlink {
top: 190px;
left: 120px;
width: 75px;
height: 50px;
}
```

If all has gone well, your CSS-based image map should look a little like Figure 2-19.

The advantage of creating a maplike structure in this way is that the (X)HTML is just a plain old list of links, making life easier for users of text browsers and the like. The disadvantage is as mentioned earlier: background images set via CSS will not provide any alternative text if images are disabled but CSS is enabled, so the map becomes inaccessible in this scenario.

Figure 2-19. A CSS-based image map, as seen in the browser

Being objective

<object> is designed to include *objects* such as images, videos, and Java applets in a web page. It was intended to replace the more specific <img> and <applet> tags, as well as the proprietary <embed> and <bgsound> tags. It comes with a fallback mechanism, whereby you can nest <object>s, allowing the user agent to display alternative content if it cannot render the preferred choice. For instance, you can nest a video, an image, and finally some text like so:

```
<object data="myVideo.mpg" type="application/mpeg">
    <object data="myPicture.gif" type="image/gif">
        Some descriptive text, and <a href="link.htm">a link</a>.
    </object>
</object>
```

The user agent should first try to display the video, but if it can't, it should then try to display the image, and if it can't do that, it displays the text—no need for alt attributes here. Unfortunately, poor browser support has made <object> very hard to use as it was intended, and the tag itself is overloaded, with 17 element-specific attributes.[20] Internet Explorer treats any <object> content as if it were an ActiveX control, prompting the user

---

20. A trimmed-down <object> is likely to appear in XHTML 2.0, as detailed in Appendix A.

with a security warning if the user's security settings are set to do this, even if the tag is just displaying a static image. There can also be problems with scrollbars appearing around the image, as if you were including a web page within an <iframe>[21]—this behavior is clearly undesirable.

But <object> isn't just about including images: it is also used to embed rich media players such as Windows Media Player, RealPlayer, QuickTime,[22] and Flash Player,[23] along with the <param> element, which passes various parameters to the media player in question. It's unlikely that you'll ever be hand-coding these embedded objects by hand, unless you're comfortable writing markup like classid='CLSID:22d6f312-b0f6-11d0-94ab-0080c74c7e95', so I don't cover this sort of usage in great detail here. Simply be aware that when embedding media, the <object> tag is what you usually need to use.

Summary

This chapter covered a substantial number of (X)HTML tags available to you, with the exception of table- and form-related markup, which will follow in their own dedicated chapters. As you've seen, you have a wide range of options when it comes to structuring, describing, and displaying your content, and although you may only ever use a fraction of the available tags, knowing the tags you are able to use in the first place and how to correctly use them are important parts of mastering HTML.

---

21. An <iframe> is frame that can contain other content, including other web pages. It can be treated the same as any other frame, except it can also be positioned anywhere on a page and given fixed dimensions.

22. Apple recommends that you use JavaScript to embed QuickTime movies, due to Internet Explorer now requiring any embedded ActiveX control to be manually activated by the user due to a patent dispute between Microsoft and Eolas. You can find more details at www.apple.com/quicktime/tutorials/embed.html.

23. Anyone interested in embedding Flash without invalidating their document should read the article "Flash Satay: Embedding Flash While Supporting Standards" by Drew McLellan (www.alistapart.com/articles/flashsatay).

3 TABLE MASTERY

In the olden days, when the Internet was made of wood and powered by steam, table markup, created by Netscape and implemented in version 2.0 of its browser, represented the only way you could lay out your pages in anything other than a vertical document structure. Table markup became standardized in HTML 3.2,[1] and using tables to lay out pages was perfectly acceptable, though it was noted even then in the W3C Recommendation that doing so "typically causes problems when rending to speech or to text only user agents."[2]

The only caveat was that if you were using tables for layout, you didn't use any non-necessary markup; you were limited to the basics: the <table>, <tr>, and <td> tags. Essentially, a layout table had to be made as invisible as possible to all user agents, which means any advice you may have heard about adding a title or summary attribute to a layout table reading "This is a layout table" is just plain wrong.

If I had written this book three or four years ago, I would probably have said that it was still OK to use tables for layout. Indeed, in the first edition of Jeffrey Zeldman's landmark book *Designing with Web Standards* (New Riders Press, 2003), he advocated a "hybrid" approach, where you use CSS as much as possible but use tables for the basic structure, giving you a website that would at least have the desired layout in browsers not advanced enough to understand your CSS.[3] The presence of legacy browsers and the limited CSS support in the modern browsers of the day meant that web designers really had little choice.

But obviously I'm not writing this book three or four years ago—I'm writing it now, and now, in 2006, the situation is different. The HTML 4 specification no longer suggests using tables for layout purposes. Remember, we're aiming to separate our presentation from our content, and laying out a website in a table would be the complete opposite of this. In fact, I will go so far as to say that you will *never* need to use tables for layout purposes—browser support for CSS is now capable enough to reproduce almost all of the effects that we would previously have used tables for.

Even though there is no longer any serious need to use tables for layout (though you'll be tempted to use them sometimes, believe me), there's still a need for tables for displaying *tabular data*—calendars, schedules, exam results, product pages, and so forth—and the available markup can be as simple or as complicated as required.

So, this little history lesson brings us to the markup itself. I'll be frank: table markup is possibly the *most* exciting markup you'll ever encounter. Seriously, if you thought that (X)HTML was fun before this stage, you're in for a *real* treat now![4] I've split this chapter into three sections. In the first, I'll cover the table markup itself so you know what we're talking about. In the second section, I'll cover the styling of tables, and finally I'll discuss some ways to enhance a well-made table with JavaScript.

To begin with, then, let's look at the basics of table markup in a section I imaginatively call "Table basics."

---

1. You may hear people claim that table markup was introduced in HTML 2.0—this is not the case.

2. See www.w3.org/TR/REC-html32#table.

3. At the time of this writing, a second edition of *Designing with Web Standards* is due out soon, where I expect this advice to have been amended or removed.

4. Sadly, there is no <sarcasm> element, but if there was one, this would probably be an appropriate place to use it.

Table basics

It's reasonably straightforward to create a simple table when hand-coding markup. The bare essentials of a single table is an opening <table> tag, followed by at least one table row (a <tr>), followed by at least one table cell (a <td>, meaning "table data"). Here's an example:

```
<table>
    <tr>
        <td>Some data</td>
    </tr>
</table>
```

That's about as minimalist as you can get when it comes to creating tables, but you're unlikely to create a table with only one item of data, so let's make things a touch more interesting. The following markup is for a two-column table with four rows of data (the presentational border attribute is just here as a visual aid to better distinguish the layout of the table, and its effect should be replicated with CSS in a production environment):

```
<table border="1">
  <tr>
    <td>Name</td>
    <td>Place of residence</td>
  </tr>
  <tr>
    <td>Paul Haine</td>
    <td>Oxford</td>
  </tr>
  <tr>
    <td>Vikki Roberts</td>
    <td>Bracknell</td>
  </tr>
  <tr>
    <td>Leon Boardman</td>
    <td>London</td>
  </tr>
  <tr>
    <td>Emma Sax</td>
    <td>Peaslake</td>
  </tr>
</table>
```

Figure 3-1 shows how the preceding markup would normally render in a browser.

Name	Place of residence
Paul Haine	Oxford
Vikki Roberts	Bracknell
Leon Boardman	London
Emma Sax	Peaslake

Figure 3-1.
A basic table

Beautiful, I'm sure you'll agree. Those table data cells, the <td> tags, can contain most other (X)HTML tags, including other tables—something we all relied on heavily when using tables for layout in the past.

You can make this table a bit clearer and easier to read by marking out the headers at the top of the table, to indicate columns. While you can do this easily by adding a class name to each table cell and then styling it with CSS, a far better way is to turn those uppermost table cells into bona fide table headers with the <th> tag used in place of <td>.

```
<table border="1">
  <tr>
    <th>Name</th>
    <th>Place of residence</th>
  </tr>
  ...
</table>
```

The preceding markup renders as shown in Figure 3-2.

Name	**Place of residence**
Paul Haine	Oxford
Vikki Roberts	Bracknell
Leon Boardman	London
Emma Sax	Peaslake

Figure 3-2.
A basic table using <th> for header cells

There are several benefits to this approach. To begin with, it's a great aid to accessibility. While a screen-reading device may, in the hands of a competent user, read the first table example as "Name, Place of residence, Paul Haine, Oxford, Vikki Roberts, Bracknell . . .," with table headers available it can understand how the headers relate to the data and read it out as "Name, Paul Haine, Place of residence, Oxford, Name, Vikki Roberts, Place of residence, Bracknell . . ."[5] Of course, in this simple example it would be easy enough to infer the table

5. The W3C provides a tool to help understand how your tables could be read by assistive devices at www.w3.org/WAI/References/Tablin.

structure. It's not hard to work out that "Name, Place of residence, Paul Haine, Oxford, Vikki Roberts, Bracknell . . ." is a person's name followed by a place name, but when tables get more complex (by having more rows and columns), this becomes much more of an issue.

> You can also use the `speak-header` CSS property to control whether table header cells are read out once or always, in an aural style sheet.

Besides making the table more accessible to users of screen readers, using proper table headers also provides sighted users with a useful visual cue as to the structure of the table and makes life marginally easier for the web author, who doesn't have to include an extra class name for every header. In addition, gives the designer another extra hook for CSS and scripting.

Now that you've headed up the table, you can make things even better by including a table caption, in the form of the `<caption>` element. This element needs to be placed directly after the opening `<table>` tag:

```
<table border="1">
  <caption>Personal details</caption
  <tr>
    <th>Name</th>
    <th>Place of residence</th>
  </tr>
  ...
</table>
```

Most user agents will render the caption as shown in Figure 3-3.

Personal details

Name	Place of residence
Paul Haine	Oxford
Vikki Roberts	Bracknell
Leon Boardman	London
Emma Sax	Peaslake

Figure 3-3.
A basic table using a
`<caption>`

If you want the caption to appear below the table (as is common in academic publications), then don't move the `<caption>` tag—it needs to stay under the initial `<table>` tag no matter what you want to do. Instead, you could use the `align` attribute with a value of `bottom` (it also accepts `top`, `left`, and `right`, which position the caption on top, or aligned to the left or right, respectively). But doing this presents a problem: the `align` attribute has been deprecated in XHTML, which means that if you're writing to a strict XHTML doctype you must use CSS (discussed later in the chapter).

You may also include various inline elements within the <caption>, such as <em> and
—even <img /> is valid—but you may not include block elements, such as <p> or <h1>.

Finally, you can add a summary attribute to the opening table tag (<table summary="">). This attribute is of no use to sighted users and will not be displayed onscreen[6]—it's there purely to aid in accessibility. Its purpose is to announce to nonsighted users the purpose of the table, if that purpose is not clear already from the surrounding content or the caption text. It's *not* meant to be a complete description of all rows, columns, and data, so don't overdo it.

Adding structure

If your table looks like it's getting a bit long and unwieldy, you can add some further structure with <thead>, <tfoot>, and <tbody> to help your browser make sense of things. These tags allow you to group rows into a header section, a footer section, and a body section, which has several advantages. When printing a long table, a browser can print the header and footer section on every page to aid in readability—there's no need to keep checking back on the first page to find out what column you're looking at. When a page is displayed onscreen, a browser can keep the header and footer area static and allow the body to scroll, enabling the web designer to place a long table in a restricted space. Also, much like the <th> tags, these three tags give you another hook for CSS and scripting without out extra classes.

Like <caption>, these tags must be placed within the table markup in a very specific order and location. First, you must include <thead>. This tag can go anywhere you like, but it's good practice to place it directly under the opening <table> tag—unless you've included a <caption>, in which case the <thead> tag must go directly underneath that. You can place it underneath your <tfoot> and <tbody> if you like, and it would still be valid markup, but only do this if you want a bit of a brain ache when you come back to your markup a few months down the line and wonder what on earth you were thinking.

The <tfoot> tag, however, *must* come before the <tbody> tag. Why does the footer come before the body? It's so that a user agent can render the top and bottom of the table before starting on the middle, which is useful if you plan to have your table body scroll and you have many rows.

Finally, you add the <tbody> tag. This tag is actually implicit in your table regardless. For example, try adding tbody {font-style: italic} to your CSS and apply it to a basic table, and you'll see that it styles the text in your table in an italic font. Even though its existence is implied, you *must* explicitly include the <tbody> tag if you're using <thead> and <tfoot>. So, once these tags are added, your markup should look a little like this:

---

6. Unless you're pulling it out with JavaScript. Arguably, though, you shouldn't be doing this, as the attribute was never designed to be seen by sighted users.

```
<table border="1">
  <thead>
    <tr>
      <th>Name</th>
      <th>Place of residence</th>
    </tr>
  </thead>
  <tfoot>
    <tr>
      <th>Name</th>
      <th>Place of residence</th>
    </tr>
  </tfoot>
  <tbody>
    <tr>
      <td>Paul Haine</td>
      <td>Oxford</td>
    </tr>
    <tr>
      <td>Vikki Roberts</td>
      <td>Bracknell</td>
    </tr>
    <tr>
      <td>Leon Boardman</td>
      <td>London</td>
    </tr>
    <tr>
      <td>Emma Sax</td>
      <td>Peaslake</td>
    </tr>
  </tbody>
</table>
```

3

With the exception of the headers now repeated at the foot of the table, there's no visual difference between a table that has these elements and one that doesn't, but it's good to include them as they provide extra, useful information about the structure of your table that can be exploited when printing or when viewing onscreen.

> *Be careful when using the `<tfoot>` tag. Because this element may repeat itself over several pages, it's best used as a duplication of the `<thead>` content (as in the preceding example), rather than the literal conclusion of a long table, such as a final total beneath a column of prices (which would make little sense if it appeared before the table had been completed).*

Adding even more structure

If you need a table to span more than one row or column, you can achieve this effect with the rowspan and colspan attributes, each of which takes a numerical value indicating how many cells a particular cell should stretch across. This is all quite straightforward. For example, let's imagine that in addition to residing in Oxford, I have a second residence in Barcelona (hey, I can dream). Adding this data to the table requires an additional row, but rather than leaving an empty table cell next to the new place of residence, I'll insert a rowspan attribute so that the cell containing my name pairs up with both places of residence:

```
<tr>
  <td rowspan="2">Paul Haine</td>
  <td>Oxford</td>
</tr>
<tr>
  <td>Barcelona</td>
</tr>
<tr>
  <td>Vikki Roberts</td>
  ...
```

The table now renders as shown in Figure 3-4.

Personal details

Name	Place of residence
Paul Haine	Oxford
	Barcelona
Vikki Roberts	Bracknell
Leon Boardman	London
Emma Sax	Peaslake

Figure 3-4.
A basic table using the
rowspan attribute

A table cell can span both rows and columns if necessary. You just need make sure your cells and spans add up. For instance, if your table has two rows, one containing five <td> elements, then the second row can only span up to five cells—any more than that and the table will not be valid and will render unpredictably, and any fewer than that and the slack must be taken up by remaining cells.

I've heard it suggested in the past that rowspan and colspan are presentational and should be avoided, but this is incorrect. There's no way of replicating this table structure in CSS, and you're using the attributes to define structure, not presentation, so you should keep that information in the markup.

As you may have noticed by now, most of the table markup presented so far relates only to rows and individual cells within those rows—there is no `<tc>` tag. Instead, we have two tags that can define columns and groups of columns, and both are optional: `<col>` and `<colgroup>`.

The `<colgroup>` tag allows you to specify how many groups of columns will exist in the table (so one `<colgroup>` per group of columns, and a group can contain just one column), and how many columns are contained within each group with the use of a span attribute and a numerical value. This tag is placed directly after the opening `<table>` tag (but after the `<caption>`, `<thead>`, and `<tfoot>` sections, if these exist), and it does not contain any markup other than optional `<col>` tags, described further shortly.

Consider, for example, the table shown in Figure 3-5.

Personal details

Name	Place of residence	Date of birth		
		dd	mm	yyyy
Paul Haine	Oxford	14	06	1978
Vikki Roberts	Bracknell	12	01	1985
Leon Boardman	London	01	03	1956
Emma Sax	Peaslake	28	02	1979

Figure 3-5. A table with multiple columns: there are three column groups here, headed by Name, Place of residence, and Date of birth.

Reading along the uppermost headers, you can see that this table has three groups of columns, with the final column spanning the width of three cells. Using `<colgroup>`, you can define that structure at the start of the table like so:

```
<table border="1">
  <colgroup></colgroup>
  <colgroup></colgroup>
  <colgroup span="3"></colgroup>
  <tr>
  ...
```

With this markup, you're saying that this table contains three groups of columns, the first two of which contain a single column (a single column is implied; you don't need to add a span="1" attribute in this case), and the third group contains three columns.

There also exists a `<col>` element, a self-closing element that also has a span attribute and that's used for specifying the existence of columns within a `<colgroup>`. Functionally and semantically, it's practically the same as `<colgroup>`, but unfortunately the HTML specifications do not allow for nested `<colgroup>` elements, so you must use `<col>` instead. Using the preceding example, you can specify the final set of three columns in two different ways, either with one `<col>` per column, like this:

```
<table border="1">
  <colgroup></colgroup>
  <colgroup></colgroup>
  <colgroup><col /><col /><col /></colgroup>
  <tr>
  ...
```

or with a single `<col>` and a span attribute, like this:

```
<table border="1">
  <colgroup></colgroup>
  <colgroup></colgroup>
  <colgroup><col span="3"></colgroup>
  <tr>
  ...
```

This is starting to look like a lot of work—why would anybody bother with this at all? It's true that at first glance it might appear that you're supplying redundant information, but this markup does have its uses. There are some side benefits, but the main reason for the existence of `<colgroup>` and `<col>` is to allow browsers to render the table even if all of the table row data has yet to arrive. Without the information provided by these two tags, a browser must first parse the entire table to find the row with the largest number of cells in it. Next, the browser must calculate the width of that row, and only then will it know the width of the table and allow it to be rendered. When you let the browser know up front about the column structure of the table, the browser can render the data as it arrives.

Perhaps of more interest to the visual design is styling columns with CSS. Without any `<colgroup>` or `<col>` in your markup, styling a single column differently from all the rest would require you to add extra attributes to every table data cell within that column. I'll talk more about styling these columns later in the chapter—admittedly, there isn't a great deal you can do that will work across the major browsers, but it's always nice to have the option.

Associating data with headers

When your table becomes more complicated, it can be harder to clearly associate your data with your table headers for the vision impaired. For instance, in Figure 3-6, each data cell has two headers.

	Staff	Managers
Bitbyte	20	1
UltraHyperMegaCorp	3000	1000

Figure 3-6. A table with multiple headers on both rows and columns

Visually, it's clear how the data relates to the different headers, but this information may be less clear to a screen reader. You can help clarify matters by using the scope attribute on the <th> or <td> tags, which accept four values: col, row, colgroup (yes, it's both an attribute and an element), and rowgroup.

The scope attribute is straightforward enough to use:

```
<table border="1">
  <tr>
    <td></td>
    <th scope="col">Staff</th>
    <th scope="col">Managers</th>
  </tr>
  <tr>
    <th scope="row">Bitbyte</th>
    <td>20</td>
    <td>1</td>
  </tr>
  <tr>
    <th scope="row">UltraHyperMegaCorp</th>
    <td>3000</td>
    <td>1000</td>
  </tr>
</table>
```

It's now clearer to assistive devices that the headers that begin a column are actually columns, and the headers that begin a row are actually rows. Similarly, if the scope of a header cell covers multiple rows or columns, use the value colgroup or rowgroup instead of col or row.

Another way of associating data with headers is by using the id and headers attributes. Each data cell receives a headers attribute, which contains a space-separated list of the id attribute value of every header cell that applies to that data cell. Clear? Perhaps not, so here's an example. Take a look at the table in Figure 3-7, which is the same as the one shown in Figure 3-6 except (for some reason) whoever made it decided to divide the staff numbers into short and tall groups.

	Staff		Managers
	Short	Tall	
Bitbyte	11	9	1
UltraHyperMegaCorp	2100	900	1000

Figure 3-7. A table with multiple headers and columns

It's a little more complex than the previous table, but it's not *really* complex. Here's the markup behind it, complete with id and header attributes:

```
<table border="1">
  <tr>
    <td rowspan="2"></td>
    <th colspan="2" id="staff">Staff</th>
    <th rowspan="2" id="managers">Managers</th>
  </tr>
  <tr>
    <th id="short">Short</th>
    <th id="tall">Tall</th>
  </tr>
  <tr>
    <th id="bitbyte">Bitbyte</th>
    <td headers="staff short bitbyte">11</td>
    <td headers="staff tall bitbyte">9</td>
    <td headers="managers bitbyte">1</td>
  </tr>
  <tr>
    <th id="ultrahypermegacorp">UltraHyperMegaCorp</th>
    <td headers="staff short ultrahypermegacorp">2100</td>
    <td headers="staff tall ultrahypermegacorp">900</td>
    <td headers="managers ultrahypermegacorp">1000</td>
  </tr>
</table>
```

As you can imagine, the technique shown in this markup can quickly become very unwieldy the larger your table becomes. This coupled with the fact that you'll almost certainly have to write these attributes in makes the scope attribute all the more appealing. Alternatively, you could take a look at the Accessible Table Builder (http://accessify.com/ tools-and-wizards/accessibility-tools/table-builder), which allows you to create a table via a web-based interface with either scope or headers and id.

Finally, there exists an axis attribute. axis is a little-known and little-used attribute, and that's essentially because it has never been any use to us, is absolutely no use to us now, and is unlikely to be of any use to us in the future (so feel free to skip the next couple of paragraphs). The attribute was created in the event that browsers would, at an unspecified point in the future, incorporate query-language capabilities to retrieve data from a table, similar to the way that the SQL language can be used to access data from a database. The attribute would be used to group table header cells into categories, like so:

```
<th axis="personal-data">Name</th>
<th axis="location">Place of residence</th>
<th axis="location">Place of birth</th>
<th axis="favorites">Favorite food</th>
<th axis="favorites">Favorite color</th>
```

Then, using a browser's built-in querying language, a user would be able to pull out all data related to those categories as well as the table header data. However, the W3C provided no recommendations or suggestions as to how browsers would access axis data, and no browser has ever implemented any system to do so or has any public plans to do so. So, for both today and the foreseeable future, this attribute is pretty useless (though it has not been deprecated, so it is still valid to use). Although you can use CSS2 selectors or JavaScript to target table cells that contain axis, you may as well just use a class instead and trade in a bit of semantic markup for the added convenience and wider browser support.

Abbreviating headers

Although there exists an <abbr> element, discussed in the previous chapter, there also exists an abbr *attribute* that can be used within a <th> tag and provides an abbreviated version of the contents of the <th>. It is used like this:

```
<th abbr="Name">First name and last name</th>
<th abbr="Residence">Place of residence</th>
<th abbr="Birthplace">Place of birth</th>
```

The idea behind the abbr attribute is to allow screen readers to read out the abbreviated version instead of the full version each time, saving valuable seconds. However, I'm skeptical about how useful this attribute actually is, as in my experience—particularly with tables with many columns—there's a need to use the abbreviated version at *all* times, to help the table fit within the page layout. Generally, if we *could* abbreviate the header while retaining the meaning, we would do so. In such cases where an abbreviation is absolutely necessary, it is as likely to be needed for visual users as for the vision impaired, and so the abbr attribute should not be used. Instead, use the <abbr> element with a title attribute used within the <th> tags, like so:

```
<th><abbr title="First name and last name">Name</abbr></th>
<th><abbr title="Place of residence">Res.</abbr></th>
```

As discussed in the previous chapter, Internet Explorer 6 and below versions do not support the <abbr> tag, so use it with caution.

Almost-standards mode

The existence of a doctype in your website has a very noticeable effect on the way your page is rendered. The presence of a doctype will cause a browser to render the (X)HTML in what is known as **standards mode**, the assumption being that if you have included a doctype, then you know what you're doing and the browser will try and interpret your strict markup in a strict way. The absence of a doctype triggers **quirks mode**, which will render your markup in old and incorrect ways, the assumption here being that if you *haven't* included a doctype, you're probably not writing standard markup either, therefore your markup will be treated as if it has been written in the past for buggier browsers.

While Internet Explorer has just these two modes, a further mode exists in Mozilla-based browsers: **almost-standards mode**. This mode is triggered when a *Transitional* doctype is used. It's not generally worth worrying about, but the difference between standards and almost-standards modes is related to tables, so it's worth mentioning here.

When in standards mode, extra line-height is applied to the contents of a table cell, with the result being that a table cell containing an image will gain a bit of extra space. This is the correct behavior according to the CSS1/2 specifications.

3

This behavior caused a problem for websites that had been designed using the old "slice-and-dice" method of construction: slicing up an image and using a table to put it all back together again. The extra whitespace caused by the line-height was breaking these designs, usually only by a few pixels, but enough to be noticeable. To aid in backward compatibility (after all, we try not to design sites with these techniques any more), almost-standards mode was created, which did not implement this line-height part of the specification. That's the *only* difference, so it's unlikely to ever be a problem for you, but if you find yourself running into the whitespace problem and don't want to switch to a Transitional doctype, another solution is to add img {display: block;} to your CSS.

> *See* http://developer.mozilla.org/en/docs/Gecko%27s_Almost_Standards_Mode *for more information about almost-standards mode.*

Table markup summary

The preceding sections sum up most of the table-related markup, aside from some presentational attributes that I cover in the next section. As you've seen, you have several ways in which you can create a more accessible, semantically rich construct with plenty of hooks for styling and scripting. As you've also seen, tables can easily become bloated maintenance nightmares, especially if you start using the id and headers pair of attributes.

Part of the aim of this book is to encourage you to code by hand, to slave away over your markup and learn its quirks and nuances to a near-pedantic degree. I'll confess, though, that when it comes to building tables, I rarely code them by hand. It's possible to do so, of course, but this is where WYSIWYG software such as Dreamweaver really comes into its own. Creating large data tables with a few clicks of the mouse is comparative bliss, and options such as where to place the <th> tags and whether to include a <caption> and/or a summary attribute are built in—even scope attributes can be included automatically. Creating rowspans and colspans is a breeze in such software; doing so usually just involves selecting the cells you want to merge and then merging them. It's often only the column groupings, id, and headers that you ever need to hand-code.

So don't fear WYSIWYG software when it's actually being helpful; just keep an eye on the markup it's creating, in case it slips and falls.

Styling tables

Styling tables consistently across browsers can, unfortunately, be a bit of a black art. This difficulty often relates to Internet Explorer's support of various table-related CSS properties such as border-collapse being either absent or incorrect—or simply just different from Firefox, Safari, and Opera—but it's not always Internet Explorer at fault. I try to note significant differences among the various browsers throughout this section, but consider yourself warned: this process can often be a little unpredictable.

For general table-styling inspiration, it's worth having a look at the CSS Table Gallery (http://icant.co.uk/csstablegallery), a Zen garden–style website where a single table is restyled with user-submitted style sheets.

Presentational attributes

When it comes to presenting a table, you have many presentational attributes available to use. These attributes can generally now be replicated (more or less) with CSS, however, so there's little need for them unless it's particularly important to you that a user agent lacking CSS support gets a table bordered only, for instance, on the left side. Before I go into more complex styling (such as alternating table row background colors and using the :hover pseudo-class), I'll list those presentational attributes and explain how they can now be achieved with CSS.

First, quite straightforwardly, here are the attributes that have been deprecated or removed from the HTML and XHTML specifications: align, valign, width, and height. Each of these has an equivalent in CSS. The width and height attributes are both reproduced in the width and height CSS properties. The two alignment attributes, align and valign, are reproduced in CSS with text-align (accepting values of left, right, center, and justify) and vertical-align (accepting values of baseline, bottom, middle, sub, super, text-bottom, text-top, and top).

As mentioned earlier, the align attribute is also used to position the <caption> element, with a value of top, left, right, or bottom. To position it in CSS, we don't use the align property; instead, we use the caption-side property, which accepts a value of top or bottom, or we use the text-align property to align the caption left or right. Unfortunately, Internet Explorer 7 and below do not support this property, so if it's particularly important to you that your caption appears beneath the table instead of above in all browsers, you'll need to continue using the deprecated align attribute. Otherwise, use CSS.

You may have run into the bordercolor *attribute in the past, alongside* bordercolordark *and* bordercolorlight, *which could be used to achieve a pseudo-3D effect. These attributes are all proprietary Microsoft extensions, so they were never valid in the first place, but now they can be avoided entirely with CSS. The* bordercolor *attribute, as you might expect, sets the color of the border of the table cell if a* border *attribute has been set on the opening table tag. This can be replaced with the* border-color *CSS property. A shaded, pseudo-3D border can be re-created with the* border-style *property, with a value of* outset, inset, ridge, *or* groove.

There are also three bordering attributes available that have related effects: border, frame, and rules. The border attribute is simple: it accepts a numerical value that defines the width in pixels of any border appearing within the table, and it needs to be set to a value greater than 0 for any border-related attribute to have an effect. The frame attribute specifies which sides of the border surrounding a table will be visible. It accepts a wide range of values—void, above, below, hsides, lhs, rhs, vsides, box, and border—but all of these effects can be achieved with the border property in CSS (border-top, border-left, etc.). Finally, the rules attribute defines where horizontal and vertical rules appear within the table and accepts values of none, groups, rows, cols, and all. As with the frame attribute, the effect of rules can more or less be reproduced with CSS borders.

Spaced out

cellspacing and cellpadding are two attributes you're most likely familiar with; they control the spacing between cells and the padding inside cells, respectively. The cellpadding effect can be easily reproduced in CSS by applying padding to the <td>, like so: td {padding: 3px;}. All very simple and straightforward.

The cellspacing effect can also be reproduced with CSS, but the CSS to do this is not supported by Internet Explorer—not even in version 7—so if this effect is particularly important to you, and you have a large Internet Explorer user base, then you'll need to continue using the cellspacing attribute (it hasn't been deprecated, so you can use it even if your doctype is XHTML Strict). If it's not so important to you, then read on to see the CSS, which should work fine in all other modern browsers.[7]

To start with, you need to understand the CSS border-collapse property. This property specifies which border model a table uses and accepts a value of either collapse or separate. The **collapsing borders** model means that adjacent table cells will share their borders with each other, as shown in Figure 3-8.

Name	Place of residence
Paul Haine	Oxford
Vikki Roberts	Bracknell
Leon Boardman	London
Emma Sax	Peaslake

Figure 3-8.
A basic table using the collapsing borders model

The **separated borders** model means that adjacent table cells will maintain their own borders, as shown in Figure 3-9.

Name	Place of residence
Paul Haine	Oxford
Vikki Roberts	Bracknell
Leon Boardman	London
Emma Sax	Peaslake

Figure 3-9.
A basic table using the separated borders model

---

7. Table cells do not have margins, so trying to use the CSS margin property to affect cell spacing will not be effective.

To replicate the cellspacing effect, you can see that first of all, `table {border-collapse: separate;}` needs to be in your CSS. Then, you can control that spacing with the `border-spacing` property applied to the `<table>` element: `border-spacing: 3px;`.

This process is a little more involved than simply setting the attribute directly in the markup, but if you want to remove as much presentational markup from your website as possible, that's how it's done. This method also allows you more control, as the `border-spacing` property is not limited to just one value; it can take up to two values, the first for the horizontal spacing and the second for the vertical. Also, it is not limited to values set in pixels. For instance, you could write `border-spacing: 4em 0.25em`, which would apply 4ems of spacing to the left and ride sides of a row, cell, or the table itself, and 0.25ems of spacing to the top and bottom sides.

There's another CSS property, `empty-cells`, that does not replicate any presentational attribute, but I'm mentioning it here because it also requires `table {border-collapse: separate;}` to have been set. This property accepts a value of either hide or show, and, as you might expect, it controls how empty table cells are displayed—either hiding them from view or showing them. You can apply `empty-cells` to an entire table or drill down to a specific table cell. Its effect is shown in Figure 3-10, where the first table cell has been hidden.[8] Internet Explorer does not support this property, so the usual caveats apply.

	Staff		Managers
	Short	Tall	
Bitbyte	11	9	1
UltraHyperMegaCorp	2100	900	1000

Figure 3-10. A table with an empty, invisible cell

Border conflicts

When you use the collapsed border model, and the borders are being shared between cells, there is a possibility that styles may begin competing for a particular border, as there are a variety of elements all rubbing shoulders: cells, rows, row groups, columns, column groups, and the edges of the table itself. The general rule is that at each edge the most eye-catching border style gains precedence, unless the border style is a value of hidden, which removes the border no matter what else is specified.

Therefore, border conflicts are resolved like this:

1. A hidden border takes precedence over all other border style declarations.
2. A border with a style of none has the lowest priority. Although this may sound the same as a hidden border, there is a difference: none is the default state for all elements, whereas hidden overrides any visual style.

---

8. If your table was created in Dreamweaver or a similar program, then your table cells will probably all contain a nonbreaking space entity (` `), which will not be considered as empty cells (even though they will appear empty in your browser). If you want to make use of the `empty-cells` property, you'll need to ensure your table cells are literally empty: `<td></td>`.

3. Narrow borders are discarded in favor of wider borders. If two competing borders have the same width, then the style of the border comes into play, with the order of preference being double, solid, dashed, dotted, ridge, outset, groove, and finally inset.

4. If the competing borders differ only in color, then precedence depends on what element the border is being applied to, with the order of precedence being first a cell, then a row, followed by a row group, column, column group, and the root table element. When two elements of the same type are in conflict, then the left-most element takes precedence (unless the document is in a right-to-left reading environment, in which case the rightmost element wins).

There is no rule as to how to deal with conflicting colors, so this is left up to whoever codes the browser itself. Expect each browser you test to do something different in this case.

> *Internet Explorer, the crazy rebel, does not follow these rules exactly, giving precedence to the table border over all other elements. It tends to treat border styles of* hidden *as* none, *so all visual borders gain precedence over hidden borders.*

Styling columns

As mentioned earlier, use of the <colgroup> and <col> elements allows you to apply some style to individual columns. There are some limitations, though. Only four CSS properties are permitted—border, background, width, and visibility—and even so, the cross-browser support for these is inconsistent.

To understand why only four properties are available here, you have to think about where those <colgroup> and <col> elements lie in the markup. Remember, they take place before all the table rows and cells. So this bit of CSS means "take the content of a <col> and align its content to the right":

```
col { text-align: right; }
```

The inheritance aspect of CSS means that any child elements will also inherit this value, unless they are told otherwise. But the <col> doesn't have any content, and it doesn't have any child elements! Because they exist outside the <tr><td> structure, elements contained within that structure cannot inherit properties from either the <colgroup> or the <col>. As there is nothing visible within a <col>, a value of text-align, color, or similar will not have a visible effect.

Except in one browser. Yes, of course, Internet Explorer is once again doing its own thing. In some cases, Internet Explorer will allow uninheritable properties to be inherited. It seems to make a best guess at what you're trying to do, and allows you to do it, so the previous text-align example will actually cause a column of text to align to the right. But it *shouldn't*, and doesn't in browsers that understand inheritance, so don't rely on this technique.

If you do use this method for Internet Explorer, then you can fudge the issue in modern browsers by using attribute selectors in combination with the id and headers attributes. With a style of td[headers=yourValueHere] { your styles here}, *you can apply styles to a particular column, but remember that it will involve considerably more markup and more maintenance on your part.*

Returning to those properties that *are* allowed, we find further difficulties, not the least of which is Internet Explorer not allowing some of the allowed properties. Brain melted yet?

- Technically, you should be able to apply a border to either a <colgroup> or a <col>, and this should work in Opera, Firefox, and Safari, but not Internet Explorer.

- You should be able to apply a background color or image in all browsers to either a <colgroup> or a <col>.

- The width property should also work across most browsers when applied to either a <colgroup> or a <col>. When applying it to a <colgroup>, be aware that the value specified will apply to each <col> within that group—thus, a <colgroup> with a width of 100px, containing three <col> tags, will actually be 300px wide in total.

- The visibility property, accepting a value only of collapse when applied to a column, does not currently work in any browser, but if it did, it would cause that column to disappear.

So much for styling columns, eh? It seems that at best, you can apply a background color (as shown in Figure 3-11) or image and a fixed width to a column, and that's about all you can expect to work reliably across multiple browsers. But hey, it's better than nothing, and it's certainly better than applying a class on each table cell in a given column.

Personal details

Name	Place of residence	Date of birth		
		dd	mm	yyyy
Paul Haine	Oxford	14	06	1978
Vikki Roberts	Bracknell	12	01	1985
Leon Boardman	London	01	03	1956
Emma Sax	Peaslake	28	02	1979

Figure 3-11. A table with one <colgroup> styled to have an alternate background color

I'm starting to feel that this discussion is turning a bit negative, so let's move on to some more interesting uses of CSS.

Striping table rows

When a table has more than a few rows, it can be helpful to your readers to implement what is commonly known as **zebra striping**, as shown in Figure 3-12.

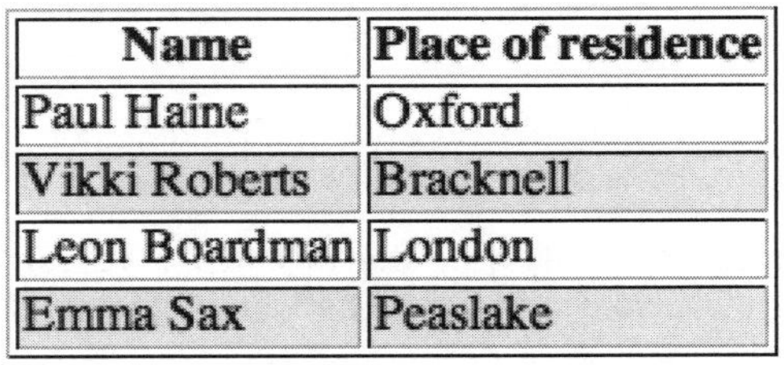

Name	Place of residence
Paul Haine	Oxford
Vikki Roberts	Bracknell
Leon Boardman	London
Emma Sax	Peaslake

Figure 3-12.
A zebra-striped table

Aside from being aesthetically pleasing, zebra striping a table is a valuable aid to usability, providing readers with a visual guide to help them keep track of the associations between data in different columns.

This effect is very easy to achieve with CSS. First, you need to add a class name to every alternate row in the table, like this:

```
<table border="1">
  <tr>
    <th>Name</th>
    <th>Place of residence</th>
  </tr>
  <tr>
    <td>Paul Haine</td>
    <td>Oxford</td>
  </tr>
  <tr>
    <td class="alt">Vikki Roberts</td>
    <td class="alt">Bracknell</td>
  </tr>
  <tr>
    <td>Leon Boardman</td>
    <td>London</td>
  </tr>
  <tr>
    <td class="alt">Emma Sax</td>
    <td class="alt">Peaslake</td>
  </tr>
</table>
```

There's no need to add a class to every row. Because only two colors are going to be in use, you can simply style all rows with a single background-color and then override that property for the alternate rows, like this:

```
tr { background-color: white; }
tr.alt { background-color: yellow; }
```

That's all there is to it. Zebra striping has some downsides, one being the addition of the class attribute. This is not a big problem if your table is small, but manually adding the attribute to larger tables could prove to be quite laborious, though it shouldn't be an issue if your table is generated by some server-side code such as PHP or ASP—then you can make sure alternate rows get the attribute set on the server. If you don't want to hand-code these attributes *and* your table isn't being generated on the server side, you can use JavaScript instead (see the section "Scripting tables" for details on how this is done).

Something else to bear in mind is that you must make sure that if you start moving your table rows around, you keep track of which ones have the class attribute, or else you may find your stripes bumping up against each other.

It will also be possible in the future to use CSS3 to automatically style alternate table rows using the :nth-child pseudo-class, which targets an element that has a certain number of siblings before it. For example, if you have a number of <div> containers, each containing a number of paragraphs, then this CSS

```
p:nth-child(2) {background-color: red;}
```

will target the second paragraph in each <div>. How does this relate to zebra striping? Well, this pseudo-class also accepts odd and even keywords, so the stripe effect could be achieved with this CSS:

```
tr:nth-child(odd) {background-color: red;}
```

This particular bit of CSS3 is not currently supported by any browser, however, but as Mozilla-based browsers and Safari have already begun implementing parts of the CSS3 specification (i.e., the :target pseudo-class, as mentioned earlier), it's possible that support for :nth-child will be with us by the time this book is published.

Remaining with these stripy notions, another useful feature that is quick and easy to implement makes use of the :hover pseudo-class applied to the table row:

```
tr:hover {background-color: pink;}
```

The effect is simple but effective, as shown in Figure 3-13.

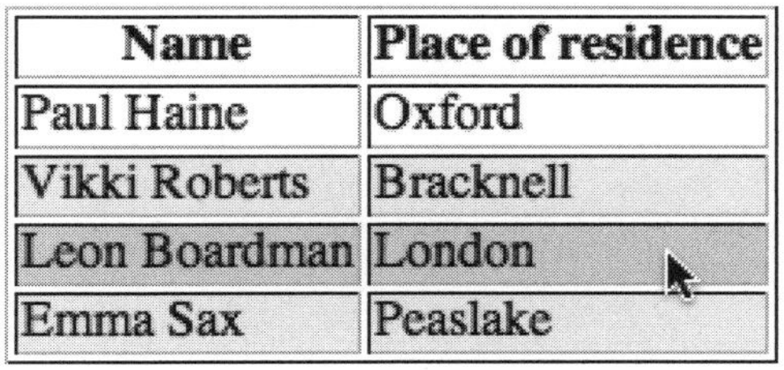

Name	Place of residence
Paul Haine	Oxford
Vikki Roberts	Bracknell
Leon Boardman	London
Emma Sax	Peaslake

Figure 3-13.
A table with a
highlighted row

This highlighting helps a user remain focused on a specific row. If you wanted to, you could enhance this feature further by adding a hover effect on the table cell as well:

```
td:hover {background-color: red;}
```

Figure 3-14 shows the result.

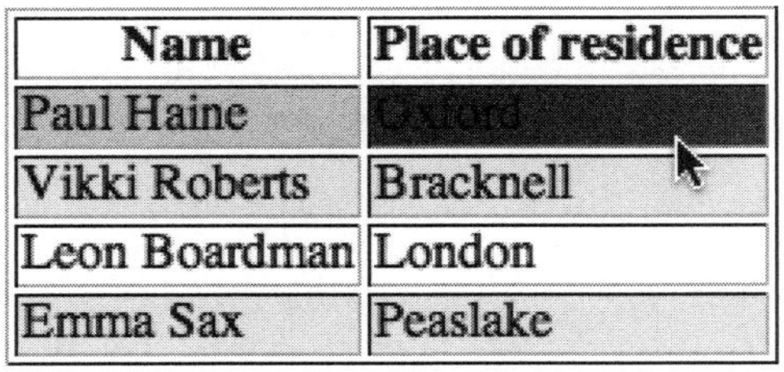

Name	Place of residence
Paul Haine	Oxford
Vikki Roberts	Bracknell
Leon Boardman	London
Emma Sax	Peaslake

Figure 3-14. A basic table with an alternating background color on the rows, another color on the hover row, and a fourth color on the hover cell

All well and good, but there's a predictable downside: Internet Explorer 6 and below only support the `:hover` pseudo-class when it's used on the <a> tag (but version 7 will support this technique). It's possible to use JavaScript to allow older versions of Internet Explorer to have the same enhancement (see the section "Hovering with scripts"), but as this is an enhancement rather than required functionality, you might consider providing it just in the CSS so that modern browsers get to see it, and those browsers lacking sufficient support are simply left with an unenhanced table.

Scrollable tables

As mentioned earlier, including a <thead> and <tfoot> in your table would be beneficial when printing, as the header and footer information could be printed on both pages automatically. If the table spanned many pages, then you wouldn't need to keep checking back to the first page to remind yourself of the column names. But why should the printers get all the benefits? Using CSS, it's possible to create a table of fixed height, with a static header and footer and a scrollable middle area, as shown in Figure 3-15.

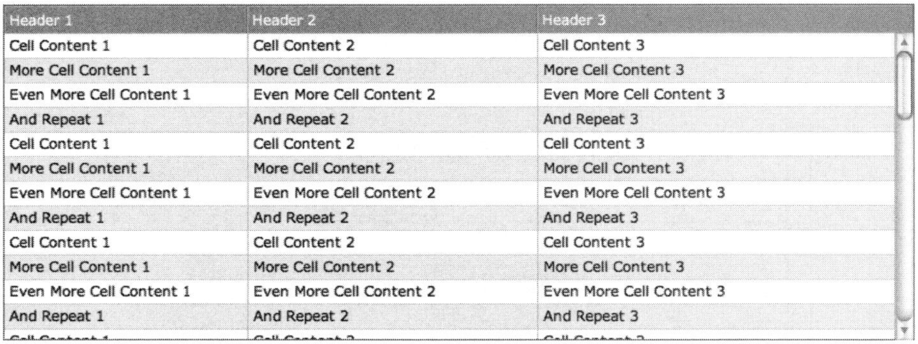

Header 1	Header 2	Header 3
Cell Content 1	Cell Content 2	Cell Content 3
More Cell Content 1	More Cell Content 2	More Cell Content 3
Even More Cell Content 1	Even More Cell Content 2	Even More Cell Content 3
And Repeat 1	And Repeat 2	And Repeat 3
Cell Content 1	Cell Content 2	Cell Content 3
More Cell Content 1	More Cell Content 2	More Cell Content 3
Even More Cell Content 1	Even More Cell Content 2	Even More Cell Content 3
And Repeat 1	And Repeat 2	And Repeat 3
Cell Content 1	Cell Content 2	Cell Content 3
More Cell Content 1	More Cell Content 2	More Cell Content 3
Even More Cell Content 1	Even More Cell Content 2	Even More Cell Content 3
And Repeat 1	And Repeat 2	And Repeat 3

Figure 3-15. A table with a fixed header and a scrollable body

There are several methods to achieve this, and—as usual, thanks to Internet Explorer—they can often be a little clumsy to implement. Most of them involve providing some CSS to modern browsers and then using an extra container `<div>` and some extra CSS. Examples include "Pure CSS Scrollable Table with Fixed Header" (`www.imaputz.com/cssStuff/bigFourVersion.html`); an alternative "(Almost) Pure CSS Scrollable Table with Fixed Header: Bullet Resistant Version" (`www.imaputz.com/cssStuff/bulletVersion.html`) with extra browser support; and "CSS Scrollable Table" (`www.agavegroup.com/?p=31`), which features a fixed header and footer with a scrollable middle.

Scripting tables

Finally, we come to enhancing your tables with JavaScript. Because you're writing well-formed, well-structured (X)HTML, many useful scripts can be used by simply linking to them in the `<head>` of your document and usually also giving your table a specific `id` or `class` attribute. The scripts can then apply behavior by traversing the DOM tree, and if for some reason users don't have JavaScript enabled, then the entire table is still available to them in all its unscripted glory. This is one of the basic notions of modern-day scripting (often referred to as **DOM Scripting** to distinguish itself from old-style DHTML) that JavaScript-enhanced functionality be separated from the content layer (just as we separate the presentation with CSS), so that in the absence of scripting support, the content remains available—no more inline `onmouseclick` events for the modern web developer.

Some of the scripts I refer to in this section duplicate the effects from the "Styling tables" section. Generally speaking, the only reason you would need to provide both script and CSS is for compatibility with Internet Explorer 6 and below.[9] When targeting Internet Explorer only, it is worth considering using conditional comments to filter your scripts to only that browser. A quick aside, then, to explain how these work.

Conditional comments

Conditional comments appear as regular (X)HTML comments to all browsers except for Internet Explorer. This means that you can include content or markup inside a conditional comment, and only Internet Explorer will take any notice of it. As these forms of comments have been knowingly built into the browser, they're not going to suddenly stop working. They're not dependent on a browser bug or quirk, and Microsoft recommends using them in place of hacks.[10]

A typical (X)HTML comment looks like this:

```
<!-- this text is commented out -->
```

---

9. Unless you consider the effect to be more behavioral than presentational, in which case, just use the scripts for all browsers and forget the CSS equivalent.

10. See `http://blogs.msdn.com/ie/archive/2005/10/12/480242.aspx`

A conditional comment inserts an if statement into that comment, like this:

```
<!--[if IE]> this text is now visible only ➥
  to Internet Explorer <![endif]-->
```

You're not limited to inserting just textual content in there—you can place @import rules for importing Internet Explorer–specific style sheets or <script> tags for including Internet Explorer–specific JavaScript. You can even specify which version, or versions, of Internet Explorer you intend to target, for instance:

```
<!--[if IE 5.5]> this text is now visible only ➥
  to Internet Explorer 5.5 <![endif]-->
```

Or perhaps you might want to only target versions of Internet Explorer with a version number of *less than* 6?

```
<!--[if lt IE 6]> this text is now visible only ➥
  to Internet Explorer 5.5 and below <![endif]-->
```

You can also use lte, which means "less than or equal to," and also gt ("greater than") and gte ("greater than or equal to").

And that's conditional comments in a nutshell. If you have any script or CSS that's specific to Internet Explorer, it's good practice to use conditional comments to target Internet Explorer rather than relying on browser bugs and hacks, which could stop working when a new version comes along.

> *And yes, Internet Explorer version 7 does* fix a lot of those hacks, so consider *yourself warned! You can find a detailed list of the Internet Explorer 7 fixes at* http://blogs.msdn.com/ie/archive/2006/08/22/712830.aspx.

Hovering with scripts

Let's start with something simple: replicating the :hover effect on table rows and cells. I've seen a few ways of doing this, but the simplest, leanest method is Patrick Griffiths's "Suckerfish :hover" (www.htmldog.com/articles/suckerfish/hover). The script can be used to add :hover to any element by just changing the referenced element in the opening lines, and it's pretty seamless, requiring you to only include the script on your page and change your style sheet from

```
tr:hover {background-color: red;}
```

to

```
tr:hover, tr.sfhover {background-color: red;}
```

Simple.

What about those zebra stripes? You have a few ways to add them. The simplest script I've seen to achieve this is "Automatic coloured rows" (http://bitesizestandards.com/bites/automatic-coloured-rows) by Juan Ignacio Serra. Weighing in at only nine lines long, it's simple and does exactly what you need: it loops through a table and applies a class name to alternate rows.

A slightly more complex and robust method is "Splintered Striper" (http://24ways.org/advent/splintered-striper) by Patrick H. Lauke. This script is not actually limited to tables—it can accept any type of parent element (and, if specified, only those with a specific class name). It can also assign two or more class names to the child elements (for multicolored stripes, if that's what strikes your fancy), it preserves any existing classes already applied to the child elements (the first script overwrites them), and it takes all of these options as parameters when you call the script on your page, so the one script can be used for a variety of uses.

Alternatively, if you'd like to have both a hover effect on your table rows *and* a zebra stripe effect, you could use the script provided by Matthew Pennell in his blog entry "Stripe your tables the OO way" (www.thewatchmakerproject.com/journal/309/stripe-your-tables-the-oo-way). This script achieves both tasks: it loops through a table and applies an alt class name to every other <tr>, and then it adds onmouseover and onmouseout functions for the hover effect.

Table sorting

If you've ever visited websites that include database-driven tables (e.g., eBay), then you may have noticed many of them allow you to sort the data in various ways by clicking the table headers. The way these web applications usually control this effect is by submitting that mouse click to the server and reloading the data in the desired order. But the user already *has* the data downloaded, so time can be saved by providing a JavaScript-based sortable table.

> *When implementing functionality with JavaScript, it's usually worth providing a server-side version that can be used if JavaScript is not available on the client side.*

Stuart Langridge came up with a script that does just that: http://kryogenix.org/code/browser/sorttable. It's a drop-in solution—you include the script in your page, add a class and id to your table, and your plain-vanilla table will then feature clickable headers, sorting each column in ascending or descending order as per the user request. It can even sort different data types. See Figure 3-16 for an example.

Name ↓	Salary	Extension	Start date
Bloggs, Fred	$12000.00	1353	18/08/2003
Fitz, Marvin	$3300	5554	22/05/1995
Mbogo, Arnold	$32010.12	2755	09/08/1998
Shakespeare, Bill	$122000.00	3211	12/11/1961
Shakespeare, Hamnet	$9000	9005	01/01/2002
Turvey, Kevin	$191200.00	2342	02/05/1979

Figure 3-16. A sortable table

Alternatively, you could use the following solution provided by Neil Crosby: www.
workingwith.me.uk/articles/scripting/standardista_table_sorting. This solution
goes a little further than the previous script, with a wider range of support browsers and
also an awareness of <thead>, <tfoot>, and <tbody>, but it is also a drop-in solution,
requiring you to only include some JavaScript and give your table a specific class name.
See Figure 3-17 for an example.

	Name			
Date	Fore ↑	Surname	Price	IP Address
17/10/2004	Annabel	Tyler	$104.00	192.168.2.17
01/02/2006	Becca	Courtley	$23.95	192.167.2.1
17/11/2005	Carl	Conway	$17.00	192.168.02.13
17/11/2004	David	Freidman–Jones	$14.00	192.168.2.1
21/01/2006	Neil	Crosby	$1.96	192.168.1.1
			$160.91	

Figure 3-17. Another sortable table

Summary

This concludes our examination of (X)HTML tables. They're not nearly as obsolete as you may have imagined, and they are far more complex than the average WYSIWYG editor lets on. With just a little work, tables can be made more accessible to both users of visual browsers and users of assistive devices, and they can also be made more semantic and more amenable to being styled and scripted cleanly and effectively.

3

We now turn our attention to forms, which—let's be honest—very few people really enjoy either creating or completing (but try not to let that put you off reading this chapter). Form markup has been with us for many years, appearing at least as early as the HTML 2 specification and not changing in any remarkable way since then. In essence, they're very simple things—they allow the user to input some data at one end, and then send that data on to the other end via a form handler that deals with it. Think of forms as the HTML equivalent of an intermediary for your data, located between you and the website.

It is fairly easy to create forms—just insert a couple of <input> tags, add a bit of text, slap a submit button on the end, and then you get to go home early—but it is a lot harder to create forms that are usable, accessible, and attractive. And although there's a lot you can achieve with markup alone, to create the ultimate usable form, you'll invariably have to turn to JavaScript or server-side code (or both) to help you with validating inputted data and providing users with appropriate and meaningful feedback in a timely fashion.

These are not things that should be left to the last minute. Your form may be the most important part of your website, particularly if it's a form that allows people to enter their credit card details, so it should be a model of simplicity and ease of use. It should not upset people, anger them, or put them off—it seems odd to have to say that, but I've seen some terrible forms in my time that did just that.

As with the previous chapter, I begin this chapter by working through the available form markup, examining how best to use the different types of form controls and how to enhance usability and accessibility with simple structural markup, before looking at some good practices when it comes to the functionality of your forms. After that, I cover how to enhance your forms with styles and scripts.

Form markup

Form markup is actually not that complicated, but like anything in (X)HTML, it can be used well, leading to well-formed, usable forms, or it can be used poorly and inappropriately, leading to needlessly complex and inaccessible forms. Let's take it all in, one step at a time.

The form container

A form consists of two things: a <form> container and any number of form controls within that container (plus any other body markup: paragraphs, headers, phrase elements, etc.). The <form> element itself is quite simple, existing only as a container with a handful of attributes: action, method, enctype, accept, accept-charset, and name.

> *Even though <form> is a block-level element, bear in mind that if you're writing XHTML, individual form controls must be contained within a further block-level element—generally a <div> or a <p>—in order to validate. Form controls are all inline-level elements, so you can place them adjacent to each other within a single block container, should you so desire.*

The action attribute tells the user agent what it's supposed to do with the contents of the form when the form is submitted (usually with a submit button, another form control; but you can also submit some forms by just pressing the Enter key when a text input has focus). (X)HTML does not actually provide any native mechanism for dealing with form data. All it can do is pass on the information to a form handler (a web page or script), which can be written in PHP, Perl, ASP, and so on.

The method attribute informs the user agent how the form data should be passed to the form handler. The two possible values are get and post. When the get value is used, form data is sent to the form handler in the form of a query string. For instance, the basic form shown in Figure 4-1 has a method value of get and an action value of formhandler.php.

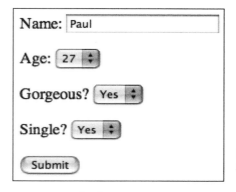

Figure 4-1.
A basic form

When you submit this form, the URL in your browser's address bar looks something like this:

```
formhandler.php?name=paul+age=27+gorgeous=yes+single=yes
```

When the post value is used, those values are not visible in the URL. The general rule of thumb is that if the form submission is active (i.e., modifying a server-side database in some way), your form should post.

> *Most browsers will warn you after the form has been submitted that if you return to the submission page, your information may be posted again to the server, possibly resulting in duplicated modifications to the database (such as payment details).*

If the form submission is passive, such as a search engine query, then use get. An advantage of having the queries visible in the URL is that you can bookmark a specific search query for repeated use.

> *When using the get value, only ASCII characters may be included in the query string. Forms sent with the post method have no such restriction.*

The enctype attribute is used to specify which MIME type should be used to encode the form data. If this attribute is left out of the markup, then the form will default to a MIME type of application/x-www-form-urlencoded, which should be suitable for most forms, unless the form is using a file input element (described further shortly), in which case this attribute should contain a value of multipart/form-data, allowing it to cope with processing binary code.

The accept attribute is also used when a file input element is in use. This attribute accepts a comma-separated list of MIME types pertaining to acceptable file types to upload to the server. For instance, if you include within your form the ability to upload JPG and GIF images to the server upon form submission, but you want to prevent users from uploading any other form of file, you would use an accept attribute like this:

```
<form accept="image/gif,image/jpeg,image/jpg">
```

Related to the accept attribute is the accept-charset attribute, which allows you to specify which character sets are permitted, such as ISO-8859-1 or UTF-8. Again, this attribute can be a comma-separated list of values if several character sets are acceptable.

Finally, the name attribute, used to identify the form to styles and scripts, is valid markup, but it was only included within the HTML 4 specification for backward compatibility. Instead of name, authors should use the id attribute for identifying their forms. However, *within* the form, all form controls that are passing data to the form handler *must* have a unique name attribute, otherwise it will not be possible to pass their values on to a form handler.

When a form is submitted, a process occurs to determine what data actually gets sent and what gets left behind. For data to be successfully sent, it must come from a control that has a control name paired with its current value, as shown in this example:

```
<input name="fullname" type="text" value="paul" />
```

The name/value pair here is fullname/paul. If the form was submitted using the get method, then the query string appended to the URL would be formhandler. php?fullname=paul.

Input

The <input> element is a self-closing inline element, like an image or a line break, so if you're writing XHTML, remember to include the closing forward-slash, and remember to enclose the element within a block element such as a paragraph:

```
<p><input /></p>
```

How the <input> element behaves and displays is dictated by the type attribute, which can take values of text, password, file, checkbox, radio, hidden, reset, submit, and button. If no type is specified, current web browsers assume it to be a text input.

> *As I cover the input types in the sections that follow, I provide screenshots for some of them, which show the controls as they appear in Camino, a Mac browser that uses the Gecko rendering engine (the same engine that Firefox, Mozilla, and recent versions of Netscape use). Because pretty much every browser on every operating system has a slightly different way of rendering form controls (and Camino uses the OS X widgets), don't be surprised if what you see here doesn't exactly match up to what appears in your own browser. That said, although they may appear differently depending upon the environment, the functionality of the types remains identical across all systems, and the visual differences should not be so radical that you wouldn't be able to recognize a submit button in Internet Explorer after only seeing it in Safari.*

The type attribute is used in all cases like so:

```
<input type="[value]" />
```

text

A text input is used, unsurprisingly, for typing text into. This is a single-line control and normally appears in the form of a rectangular box with an inset border, as shown in Figure 4-2.

The allowed length of the input string can be specified with the addition of a maxlength attribute, which takes a numerical value equating to the maximum number of allowed characters. There is no feedback mechanism provided in the event that the user tries to insert more than the allowed number of characters—the form control just ceases to accept extra characters and will truncate an overlong string if such a string is pasted into the control. If you wish to alert users that they've run out of room, you'll need to use JavaScript.

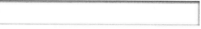

Figure 4-2.
A text input

You can also include a value attribute that presets the content of the text control:

```
<input type="text" value="Insert text here" />
```

Furthermore, a readonly attribute is available that prevents the text input content from being modified from its initial value. This is a Boolean attribute, so if you're writing HTML, you can simply use this:

```
<input type="text" value="You can't touch this" readonly />
```

whereas in XHTML you would write this:

```
<input type="text" value="You can't touch this" readonly="readonly" />
```

password

A password input is functionally almost identical to a text input; it shares the same possible attributes. The only difference is that character input is masked upon entry, usually by a series of dots or asterisks, as shown in Figure 4-3.

This type of input is not very secure—the form data will still be transmitted as plain text and will be visible in the URL if your form uses the get method. This masking is really only to hinder anybody peering over your shoulder from knowing the input (e.g., when you're in a public place and you're logging in to a site).

```
********
```

Figure 4-3.
A password input

file

A file input usually takes the form of a text input box followed by a Browse button, as shown in Figure 4-4. It appears as two controls, but it is actually only one.

Figure 4-4.
A file input

The file input control allows you to browse for a file on your local network. Once you have selected the file, the file path is then inserted automatically into the contents of the text input field, as shown in Figure 4-5.

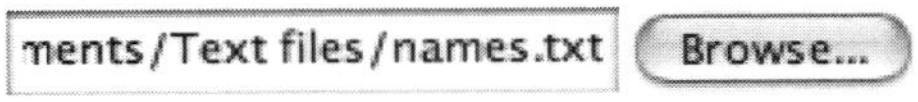

Figure 4-5.
A file input after a file has been selected

As with the text and password inputs, the value attribute can be used here to prefill the file path field. The accept attribute, described earlier, can also be used within this type of input to restrict the permitted types of files uploaded (but you will probably also need a server-side filter as well, just to be sure).

Safari is notable in that it is the only current browser that renders a file input in a different way from that described earlier. Whereas in other browsers, the file input control appears as two controls, Safari displays this control as shown in Figures 4-6 and 4-7.

Figure 4-6. A file input control in Safari, before the file has been selected

Figure 4-7. A file input control in Safari, after the file has been selected

It's not incorrect of Safari to display the control in this way, and it may have something to do with removing a security risk of a file input being used as a password input.[1] A downside of this approach, though, is that because the contents cannot be edited after a file has been selected (all you can do is change which file is being uploaded), it means users cannot back out of uploading a file once they submit the form, unless they reset or reload the entire form and start again.

checkbox

Figure 4-8.
Two check boxes, one checked and one not

A checkbox input takes the form of a square box, with a check mark or an "x" character appearing when the box is selected, as shown in Figure 4-8.

As with all the input types so far, you can preset the state of the check box, but rather than using the value attribute, you instead use the checked attribute. Like the readonly attribute, checked is a Boolean attribute, so if you're writing HTML you don't need to quote the value, but in XHTML you do.

radio

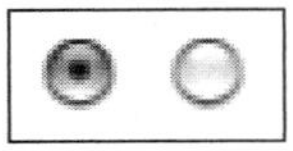

Figure 4-9.
Two radio buttons, one selected and one not

A radio button input takes the form of a circular inset, with a dot appearing inside the circular inset when the radio button is selected, as shown in Figure 4-9.

---

1. See https://bugzilla.mozilla.org/attachment.cgi?id=17860&action=view.

You use radio buttons to indicate that only *one* choice out of several—a **radio group**—can be selected. Figure 4-10 shows an example of a radio group.

Figure 4-10.
A group of radio buttons

To indicate to the user agent that a radio button is part of a group, you use the name attribute, giving each radio input element an identical name value. When the form is rendered, the user agent will not allow more than one radio input to be selected if that input shares a name value with another. Here's the markup for the preceding example:

```
<input type="radio" name="cheese" value="Cheddar" /> Cheddar
<input type="radio" name="cheese" value="Stilton" /> Stilton
<input type="radio" name="cheese" value="Brie" /> Brie
```

> *A real-world form would also include form labels, but we'll get to those in the section titled "Added structure."*

The state of a radio button can, like a check box, be preset with the checked attribute.

hidden

A hidden input element is used to include extra data within a form that is not visible to the user but is submitted along with the rest of the form data:

```
<input type="hidden" name="hiddenValue" value="42" />
```

reset

A reset button input resets all form controls within the same form to their initial values. Including a reset button used to be a common practice, but it's since become unfashionable due to the high risk of users accidentally resetting their form instead of submitting it. Without any undo function, reset buttons are of little use and should be used with caution, if at all.

> *Come on, we've all done it: reached the end of a form, tabbed to what we thought was the submit button, pressed Enter, and watched in despair as all our form data promptly vanished. If you're ever thinking of including a reset button on a form, just try to remember how many times in the past you have filled in a form, reached the end, and thought, "Actually, I think I'll just delete all of that and not bother." Exactly.*
>
> *For the same reason, I also strongly recommend avoiding Cancel buttons that return users to the previous page—the browser's Back button achieves the same thing and is harder to click accidentally. (An exception to this is when using a Previous button causes an application/form data to be saved, in which case it's actually preferable to using the browser's Back button.)*

submit

Figure 4-11.
A submit button

Submit Query

A submit button is used to submit all the form data to the file indicated in the form's action attribute. Figure 4-11 shows an example.

It is also possible to use an image as a submit button, using an input with a type of image and an additional src attribute that points to where the image file resides on the server, just like an <img>. Also like an <img>, remember to include an alt attribute for accessibility reasons.

Using an image for a submit button will also send x and y coordinates (the x and y coordinates of the part of the image you clicked) along as values; this is for when image submits are being used in conjunction with a server-side image map, as discussed in the previous chapter. And if your image has a name attribute, that will also get sent along with those coordinates. For instance, if your form has a method attribute of get, an image submit button like this:

```
<input type="image" name="imagesubmit" />
```

will pass values like this:

```
formhandler.php?imagesubmit.X=10&imagesubmit.Y=20
```

These extraneous values don't do any harm when they're submitted along with the rest of the form data, so don't worry about them. If you really want to prevent them from showing up in the URL, then you can change the method attribute of the form from get to post, which will hide all values from the user, as discussed earlier.

button

The input type of button creates a push button in the same style as a reset or submit button, but the difference here is that it has no default action. It can be clicked, but it won't do anything or have any affect on your form unless you specify this with a script or an event handler, discussed later in the section "Scripting forms."

Other input types

There are two more input types that I want to mention, but I'll stress now that they are *not* part of any current HTML specification, so their use will cause your document to fail validation. These types are search and range. The former is currently supported only by Safari (and has not, to my knowledge, been submitted by Apple to any standards working group for inclusion in any formal specification); the latter is supported by both Safari and Opera, and appears in the current Web Forms 2.0 draft specification at http://whatwg.org/specs/web-forms/current-work/#range (see Chapter 7 for more information on Web Forms 2.0).

What do these input types do? Well, search takes a text input control and turns it into a search control more like those used throughout the OS X environment, as shown in Figure 4-12.

Figure 4-12. A search control in the OS X Mail application

Apple also created several attributes to use within this proprietary input type: incremental, placeholder, autosave, results, and a new event handler called onsearch. The incremental attribute controls whether the search occurs straight away (using a handler defined in the onsearch or onkeypress attribute), the placeholder attribute is used to insert some grayed-out default text (but it's probably better to use value in this case so that nonsupportive browsers still get it), the autosave attribute allows you to set its value to a name of your choice, allowing visitors to return to your site in the future and re-search with the same search queries, and the results attribute controls how many past searches are displayed in the drop-down menu (and is a required attribute if you want that drop-down to appear at all). Thus, the following code results in the field and drop-down shown in Figure 4-13:

```
<input type="search" autosave="search.joeblade.com" results="5" />
```

Figure 4-13.
A search input field

A range input creates a slider control that defaults to returning a value of 0–100 (the allowed range can be controlled with the min and max attributes). The following code will appear as shown in Figure 4-14 in Safari and Opera:

```
Enter a value between 0 and 11: <input type="range" min="0" max="11" />
```

Figure 4-14. A range input field in Safari

The preceding code will appear as shown in Figure 4-15 in all other browsers.

Figure 4-15. A range input field in nonsupporting browsers

Am I really suggesting using invalid, proprietary markup in your document? Well . . . *possibly*. In the grand scheme of things, I think there have been far worse crimes against HTML, and unlike some previous proprietary markup, such as Microsoft's <marquee>, using these new types doesn't cause any known harm to nonsupportive browsers or prevent the form from being usable—they degrade gracefully to standard text input controls (as the default type value of an input is text, a browser that does not recognize the contents of the type attribute will revert to that default value). Yes, they're invalid, so their use may cause you mild feelings of guilt and anxiety if maintaining validity is important to you, and there is the possibility, however remote, that a minor browser exists somewhere (either now or in the future) that will break horribly when faced with invalid markup, but I think that it's a minimal amount of extra work that offers a minor benefit to a small audience and has few downsides, so I'm not going to lose too much sleep over it.

If validity is important to you—and it's no bad thing if it is—then you might consider using a DOM script to dynamically include those invalid attributes, so your markup remains valid but Safari still gets the enhanced search. Markus Stange has created such a script, which you can find at http://tests.themasta.com/safari.

Returning to the world of standards, the <input> element has several attributes that are shared across multiple types of input. These values include size, which takes a numerical value and converts it to either a pixel width in the case of submit or button types or a number of characters in the case of text and password inputs, and disabled, which prevents the form control from being used. An element with the disabled attribute set will not receive focus, it will be skipped during tabbing navigation, and its values will not be submitted.

> This is something to consider—if your form control is using a disabled attribute, does it even need to be visible in your form? Speaking as a user, it can be quite frustrating to be able to see a control but not be able to use it (and not know why I can't).

Other forms of input

Although the <input> element offers a wide range of options, other methods of providing users with the ability to input data are available—namely, the <textarea> and <button> elements.

The <textarea> element is similar in some ways to the text input element, but it allows multiple lines of input rather than just one. It uses a pair of attributes, cols and rows, to control its size, and instead of using a value attribute to preset any textual content, it uses the content of the element itself. It's a container element, rather than a self-closing element.

The following code creates a <textarea> that is 20 columns wide and 5 rows high (a scroll-bar will appear if the input exceeds the visible area). The result is shown in Figure 4-16.

```
<textarea cols="20" rows="5">Type your content here</textarea>
```

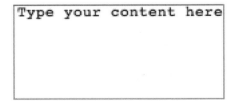

Figure 4-16.
A <textarea> 20 columns
wide and 5 rows high

The <button> element is much like an <input> with a type value of button, but they differ in that the <button> can contain content:

```
<button type="submit" value="submit">➥
<img src="arrow.gif" /> click me!</button>
```

The code preceding would normally render as shown in Figure 4-17.

Honestly, though, there's no good reason to use <button> in place of <input type="button" /> or <input type="image" />, particularly as Internet Explorer has issues discerning the correct value to pass to the server (it submits the content of the <button>, rather than the value contained within the value attribute). Although <button> allows you to create buttons

Figure 4-17.
A <button> containing an image and some text

that contain a combination of other elements (paragraphs, tables, etc.) instead of either text or an image, I can't imagine any situations where that would be required.

Finally, there also exists a deprecated <isindex> element. Web authors should use <input type="text" /> instead, as it does the same thing as <isindex> and is still current.

Menus

The <select> element is a container element, allowing any number of <option> and <optgroup> tags. It normally displays as a drop-down list, as shown in Figure 4-18.

Figure 4-18.
A <select> menu

This element has only three specific attributes: name, size, and multiple. The name attribute is used here to identify the control, and in the case of <select> it is *not* optional—every <select> must have a name. The size and multiple attributes are related. If the multiple attribute is set (multiple="multiple" if you're writing XHTML; otherwise, just multiple will do), then the <select> menu will normally display as a scrollable list box to permit multiple selections by the user, and the size attribute, which accepts a numerical value, determines how many rows of options are displayed. Figure 4-19 shows an example of a list menu.

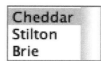

Figure 4-19.
A list menu, created with a <select> with an attribute of multiple

Each row within a <select> is contained within an <option> tag, like so:

```
<select name="cheesemenu">
  <option>Cheddar</option>
  <option>Stilton</option>
  <option>Brie</option>
</select>
```

The <option> tag has three specific attributes: selected, value, and label. The selected attribute is used to indicate to the user agent that a particular <option> should be selected initially; without it, the browser may display either nothing at all (just a blank select box) or the first <option> it encounters.

```
<select name="cheesemenu">
  <option>Cheddar</option>
  <option selected="selected">Stilton</option>
  <option>Brie</option>
</select>
```

The preceding markup renders as shown in Figure 4-20.

 Figure 4-20. A `<select>` menu with the second option preselected

Multiple `<option>` tags can have the selected attribute set, but only if the `<select>` has the multiple attribute (see Figure 4-21).

Figure 4-21.
A list menu with
multiple selections

A `<select>` that lacks the multiple attribute cannot have more than one `<option>` initially selected (after all, how would it be displayed?).

The value attribute is used here to allow the submission of a value that differs from the content of the `<option>`, and if it is not present, then the content is instead used as the value:

```
<select name="cheesemenu">
  <option value="ch01">Cheddar</option>
  <option value="ch02">Stilton</option>
  <option value="ch03">Brie</option>
</select>
```

Finally, we come to the label attribute. This attribute is designed to accept a short value, to use in lieu of displaying the content of an `<option>`. The menu in Figure 4-22, for instance, contains one `<option>` that is much longer than the others.

All of the cheeses in all of the worlds

Figure 4-22. A `<select>` menu with one option much longer than the others

This can be a problem if the menu is in a narrow location such as a fixed-width column. The label attribute can be used to provide an alternative display label, while still retaining the original content for the value passed to the server. The code for this looks like the following:

```
<select name="cheesemenu">
  <option>Cheddar</option>
  <option>Stilton</option>
  <option>Brie</option>
  <option label="All">All of the cheeses in all of the worlds</option>
</select>
```

Sadly, Internet Explorer does not support this attribute, so it cannot be relied upon, but there's no harm in providing it for supporting browsers, as it does not adversely affect the functionality of the form for nonsupporting browsers.

To help provide structure to your menus, you can use the `<optgroup>` element to group similar `<option>` elements. So, instead of the following markup:

```
<select name="cheesemenu">
  <option>- - - English cheeses - - -</option>
  <option value="cheddar">Cheddar</option>
  <option value="stilton">Stilton</option>
  <option> - - - French cheeses - - -</option>
  <option value="brie">Brie</option>
</select>
```

you would use this:

```
<select name="cheesemenu">
  <optgroup label="English cheeses">
    <option value="cheddar">Cheddar</option>
    <option value="stilton">Stilton</option>
  </optgroup>
  <optgroup label="French cheeses">
    <option value="brie">Brie</option>
  </optgroup>
</select>
```

The preceding markup would render as shown in Figure 4-23.

Figure 4-23.
A `<select>` menu organized with multiple `<optgroup>` elements

The label attribute used here *is* supported across browsers. A benefit of using `<optgroup>` tags to divide your `<option>` elements is that the `<optgroup>` label cannot be selected, nor can its value be submitted as data, whereas in the former example the web author would either have to live with erroneous submissions or provide a client- or server-side validator to ensure such dividers had not been submitted. Also, using `<optgroup>` is a clear example of using the right tag for the right job, and that's why we're all here.

You cannot validly nest <optgroup> tags, but the HTML 4 specification does suggest that browser vendors prepare for the possibility of that feature turning up one day in a future specification. At the time of this writing, it does not appear that any browser vendor has done so.

User agents are not actually limited to displaying <optgroup> menus, as in Figure 4-23. The HTML 4 specification suggests displaying the menu as an unfurling, cascading menu, and this is exactly how Internet Explorer for the Mac does it, as shown in Figure 4-24.

Figure 4-24. <optgroup> elements as rendered by Internet Explorer for the Mac

As far as I know, Internet Explorer for the Mac is the only browser that displays <optgroup> menus in such a way, and as development of this browser has long since been abandoned, it's reasonably safe to consider this display method as obsolete.

Added structure

The <fieldset> element allows web authors to divide form controls into thematically linked sections, making it easier for users to work through the form while also enhancing accessibility for assistive devices. Most browsers will display a <fieldset> with a simple border. For instance, the following markup displays the results shown in Figure 4-25:

```
<fieldset>
  <select name="cheesemenu">
    <option>Cheddar</option>
    <option>Stilton</option>
    <option>Brie</option>
  </select>
  <input type="submit" value="submit" />
</fieldset>
```

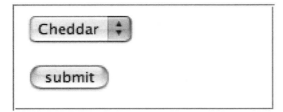

Figure 4-25. A <fieldset>

To identify each `<fieldset>`, you must use the `<legend>` attribute:

```
<fieldset>
  <legend>Cheeses of the world</legend>
  <select name="cheesemenu">
    <option>Cheddar</option>
    <option>Stilton</option>
    <option>Brie</option>
  </select>
  <input type="submit" value="submit" />
</fieldset>
```

The form will now look something like Figure 4-26.

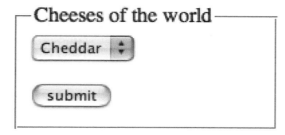

Figure 4-26.
A `<fieldset>` with a `<legend>`

The last form element to mention, `<label>`, also increases both usability and accessibility. This element is used to form an association between a textual label and a form control. In visual browsers, a user can then bring focus to the form control by clicking the associated label text as well as within the control itself.

> *The preceding statement is true in browsers except Safari. At the time of this writing, Safari offers no support for clickable labels, but you can try adding a dash of JavaScript to bridge the gap for now. See* `www.chriscassell.net/log/2004/12/19/add_label_click.html` *for more details.*

There are two ways of including clickable labels in the markup. The first is by enclosing the form control within `<label>`:

```
<label>Stilton <input type="checkbox" ➥
name="ch" value="stilton" /></label>
```

In the preceding example, the word "Stilton" causes the subsequent `<input>` to gain focus. This is nice and simple, but there are two downsides: Internet Explorer won't understand what you're trying to do, and it requires the label and control to exist together in the source markup. An alternative solution is to use the `for` attribute:

```
<label for="stilton">Stilton</label> ➥
<input type="checkbox" id="stilton" name="ch" value="stilton" />
```

101

Using the for attribute can be laborious. Each form control requires a unique id attribute to pair up with the label's for value, which involves a fair amount of hand-coding if your form is long. However, using labels in this way does mean Internet Explorer will understand how a label relates to a control. Another benefit of using the for attribute is that you do not have to keep the form control within the confines of the <label>, which is useful if your labels and controls cannot exist near each other—for instance, if you're using a table to lay out a form, with labels in one column and controls in another (which, ideally, you shouldn't be doing).

Finally, aside from some form-specific event handlers that I discuss in the section "Scripting forms," all form controls can use the tabindex and accesskey attributes described in Chapter 2. To reiterate, I believe these attributes to be of dubious value and feel they should be used *with* caution, and *without* the assumption that their inclusion automatically and dramatically increases the accessibility or usability of your website. You can usually negate any need for a tabindex attribute by placing your form elements in a logical order within your source markup, and the accesskey attribute suffers from a lack of consistency across sites and also from a lack of discoverability within the browsing environment. Personally, I never use either of them, and I do not recommend anybody else use them either.

Form usability

As mentioned earlier, it is easy to create a form, but it is much harder to create a really *good* form. Although in-depth knowledge of all the available form markup will help, it's not enough. Because a form is more of an application than a web page, you need to consider usability *seriously*. If your form is the point at which the general public starts giving you money, you need to test your form rigorously, observe people using it and record their reactions (even if your audience is just a few colleagues from the other side of the office), and make sure it works as well as it possibly can.

Exhaustive coverage of the subject of form usability is well beyond the scope of this book, but the guidelines outlined in the following sections should be enough to help you avoid some common form usability problems. Beyond the information you'll find in this chapter, I recommend reading *Don't Make Me Think: A Common Sense Approach to Web Usability* by Steve Krug (New Riders Press, 2000) and *Defensive Design for the Web: How to Improve Error Messages, Help, Forms, and Other Crisis Points* by 37signals (New Riders Press, 2004), both of which cover the topic in greater depth.

You may have noticed, by the way, that I'm talking about form usability before form styling—this is because it is more important that your form *works well* than *looks good*. Styling can come after you've made sure the form doesn't make people cry.

Use the right tag for the right job

So, you know about every input type there is, but which one is appropriate to use in a given situation? Some of these are obvious—a file input has only one purpose, and no other type of input can be used in its place—but what about, for instance, check boxes versus radio buttons?

A good rule of thumb is that if you have a list of two or more options, and the user *must* select one and *only* one of them, use radio buttons. Selecting one radio button should then deselect any other radio button that is part of the same named group. But if the list contains many options to select from, consider using a `<select>` menu instead. You'll retain the inability to select more than one option, and you'll save some space (at the expense of "discoverability").

Check boxes, on the other hand, are used when there are several choices to make, and users can leave them all blank or select as many as they like. Checking one check box does not deselect any others within the group. The menu equivalent of a series of check boxes is a `<select>` menu with the `multiple` attribute present, but check boxes are generally easier to use as they do not require the user to understand what keyboard/mouse combination to use (Ctrl-click? Command-click? What about keyboard-only users?), so you may wish to avoid multiple-select lists where possible.

You should also use a check box when there is a single option that users can switch on or off, such as agreeing for their data to be passed along to third-party companies. You would not use a radio button here because a radio button can only be deselected by selecting another.

Remember also to use labels, field sets, and legends to aid in both usability and accessibility.

Keep it short and simple

Collect only the information you need, and no more than that. Do you really need to know if I'm a Mr. or a Ms.? Do you really need my fax number? My occupation? My annual salary in dollars? Question the presence of every field you have in your form, and if it's a compulsory field, question again whether it needs to be. Your marketers may relish the opportunity to collect reams of personal data about your site visitors, but the longer your form is and the more irrelevant users start perceiving it to be, the higher the risk that they'll abandon it.

Don't make me think, don't make me work, and don't try to trick me

Make your form as easy to complete as possible. If at any point a user has to pause for a few seconds to try and work out what's gone wrong or what you mean, then that's a few more seconds when he might just think "Oh, forget it" and go off to make a sandwich. So, for instance, if your form contains compulsory fields, then let users know, as clearly as possible, which fields they are by making the labels bold, coloring the field background yellow, or adding the word Required somewhere in the label.[2] Whatever you do, make it clear from the beginning the fields that *must* be filled in, and don't wait until the form has been submitted and reloaded to tell users. Furthermore, please consider avoiding autotab functions, where the cursor automatically hops to the next form field after users complete one. Anybody who has ever attempted to go back to a field and correct a mistake in an autotabbing form will understand where I'm coming from on this; it's incredibly frustrating.

---

2. If you're short of space, use an asterisk (*), but contain it within an `<abbr>` tag, with a `title` attribute of "this form field is required."

If you need data in a certain format, don't rely on users entering it in that format—this is what your form handler is supposed to deal with. For instance, if a user needs to enter a credit card number, let her fill it in as 1234 5678 9012 3456 if she wants to (that's how it's formatted on her credit card), or 1234567890123456, or 1234-5678-9012-3456—whatever works for the user. The user doesn't want to be slapped back because nobody wrote code that converted her data into the appropriate format. Remember, computers are supposed to save *the user* time, not the other way around. Provide a guide to a preferred format if you like, but allow for the possibility of alternate entries.

If the user *has* made an error that can't be solved by server-side code, then let him know with a clear, meaningful, and appropriate error message—the sooner the better. Use JavaScript for instant feedback, and provide server-generated validation and error messages as a backup. The more complex your form, the more things that can go wrong, so test, test, test, and make sure there are no meaningless error messages such as "some sort of error" or "form submission failed." Provide the user with an explanation of the problem, the steps (if any) he can take to resolve the problem, some visual cues as to where the problem lies, and some contact information if all else fails.

If you do find you have to reload the page, make sure that all fields (with the exception of any password fields[3]) are now prefilled with the information the user just entered, including any opt-in/opt-out check boxes. Many times forms will ask users if they want to opt out of future mailings, only to then recheck the box when the page reloads. That's just *sneaky*.

Remember that the Internet is global

If your form is not specific to any one country, try not to fill it with references to "states" and "zip codes," and certainly don't make those fields compulsory if you do include them. Also relating to the previous point, don't try and restrict the format of the user's data, such as phone numbers. Maybe the user is from a country that has phone numbers with an extra two digits plus a secondary area code—who knows?

Styling forms

As mentioned earlier, nearly every browser on every operating system displays form controls in a slightly different way, ranging from the lickable aqua widgets of Safari to the chunky beveled boxes of Firefox. When it comes to styling forms and their controls, the first question you need to ask yourself is "*Should* I do this?"

> *For an exhaustive view on how operating systems display form controls, have a look at Roger Johansson's article "Styling form controls" at* `www.456bereastreet.com/archive/200409/styling_form_controls`.

---

3. Why? Because for a password field to be prefilled, the value attribute must be used, meaning that the password must appear, in plain, readable text, within the source markup. Someone could then view that password just by sifting through your browser cache.

It's one thing to adjust margins, padding, and alignments to lay out a form in a clear fashion, but it's quite another to start adjusting the way that buttons and check boxes appear. They may differ a little from browser to browser, but they're still fundamentally recognizable to the user, and too much tweaking can lead to a lot of confusion with little gain.

> At the time of this writing, neither Safari nor Camino allows for the styling of form fields, but this policy looks likely to change in the near future.

Remember that forms are a two-way process: you're not simply asking people to *read* them, but also to *interact* with them, and I believe that in almost every case, it's better to leave the browser to just get on with rendering the controls in roughly the same way it always does. It's better for users, as their expectations aren't being broken, and they can set about completing the form using a familiar set of controls. At this stage, you don't want users to have to *learn* how to fill in your form; rather, the form should be made as simple as possible to minimize the chances of users abandoning it halfway through. Experimenting with new visual styles when users are simply trying to buy a book or complete a magazine subscription order is a risky business.

On the other hand, this way of thinking leans a little toward the same sort of reasoning that caused famous usability experts in the 1990s to insist that links should *always* be blue, visited links should *always* be purple, and active links should *always* be red—and you'd better make sure they're underlined as well! So make of these suggestions what you will. I'm simply expressing my opinion, and to be honest, I can't back it up with any hard field research, so (tempting though it is) I won't insist that you *never* style form controls; I just want you to think hard about it before you go wild. (And given how stubborn some browsers can be when it comes to styling form controls, you may also save yourself quite a few headaches.)

Enough grumbling and soapboxing—on with the show.

Layout

Laying out a form is the one area of modern web design where using tables for presentation may seem like the only option. In fact, many people will argue that forms *are* tabular data, given that there is a relationship between text labels and form controls. Personally, I think that's a fairly tenuous argument, and I've found that in most cases forms only need a little CSS loving to lay them out. If you find yourself in a situation where your form is so complex that laying it out with CSS would just be too laborious, then it may be worth considering whether your form actually needs a bit of a rethinking, if possible.

The first thing we're going to look at is an alignment issue: how to turn the form in Figure 4-27 into the form in Figure 4-28.

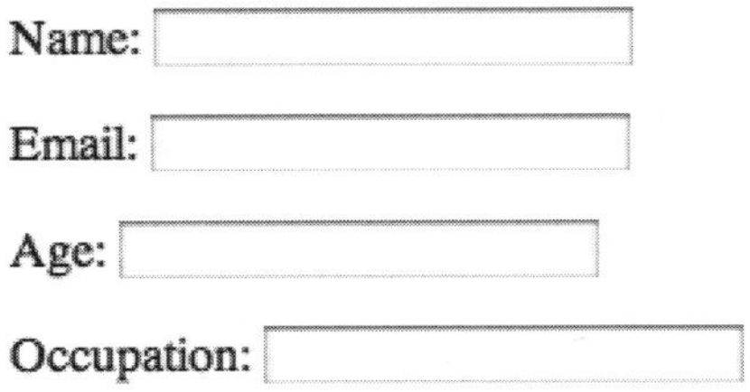

Name: [   ]   Name: [   ]

Email: [   ]   Email: [   ]

Age: [   ]   Age: [   ]

Occupation: [   ]   Occupation: [   ]

Figure 4-27. An unstyled form 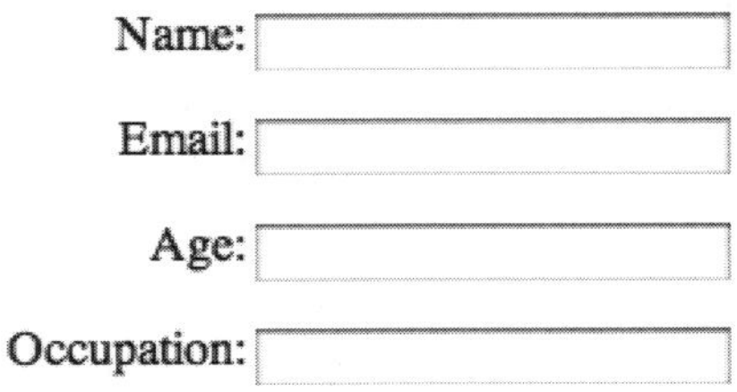   **Figure 4-28.** A form with labels and inputs neatly aligned

Figure 4-28 demonstrates perhaps one of the more common ways of presenting a form, and the reason behind it is clear. By simply aligning the labels alongside the inputs, the form becomes instantly neater and more professional-looking. You may previously have achieved this effect by placing all of your markup in a two-column table—text labels on the left, inputs on the right, and the left column cells all given align attribute values of right—but this effect is actually pretty easy to achieve with a bit of CSS.

First, we have to ensure our markup is top-notch and free of extraneous elements (we'll need no line breaks here). Here's a sample:

```
<label for="fullname">Your name: </label>
<input type="text" id="fullname" />
```

This is straightforward enough, and lean and accessible, but it will look a bit unappealing in the browser. To start, let's align the text within the label:

```
label {text-align: right;}
```

This won't have much of a noticeable effect, so let's make sure those labels are all the same width, which involves not only setting a width, but also turning the label into a block element:

```
label {text-align: right; width: 100px; display: block;}
```

These changes result in the form shown in Figure 4-29.

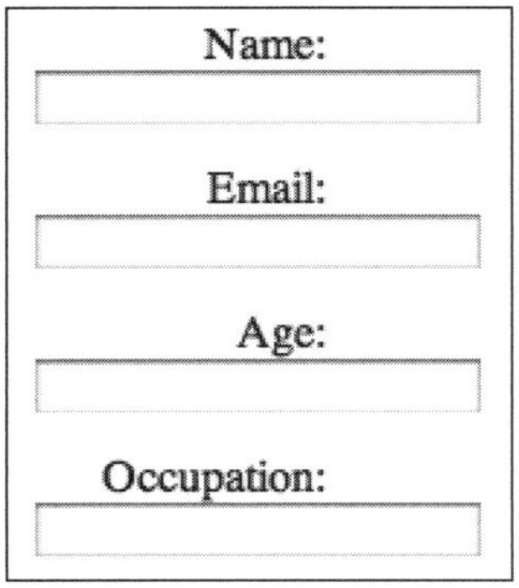

Name: [   ]

Email: [   ]

Age: [   ]

Occupation: [   ]

Figure 4-29.
A form with block-level
<label> elements

To get the labels and inputs back onto the same lines, we'll need to float the labels left, which causes the inputs to wrap up and sit alongside them. We'll also need those labels to clear the floats, to prevent subsequent labels from also wrapping up:

```
label {text-align: right: width: 100px; ➥
display: block; float: left; clear: left;}
```

Add we're done. Figure 4-30 shows the final version.

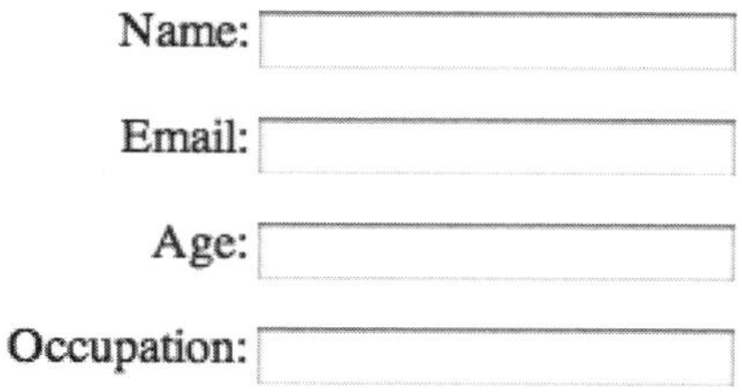

Name: _____

Email: _____

Age: _____

Occupation: _____

Figure 4-30. The finished product

Your form doesn't necessarily need to be laid out vertically. If you've used a couple of `<fieldset>` tags to group your controls into related areas, it's a simple matter of floating them as required. We can turn the simple vertical form shown in Figure 4-31 into the horizontal one shown in Figure 4-32 with this CSS:

```
fieldset {float: left; width: 50%;}
```

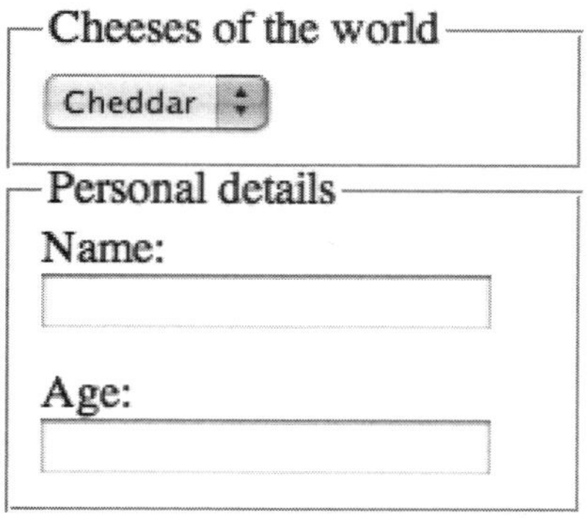

┌─Cheeses of the world─────────────
│ ┌────────────────┐
│ │ Cheddar ⬍ │
│ └────────────────┘
┌─Personal details──────────────
│ Name:
│ ┌─────────────────────┐
│ └─────────────────────┘
│
│ Age:
│ ┌─────────────────────┐
│ └─────────────────────┘

Figure 4-31. A form with two `<fieldset>`s

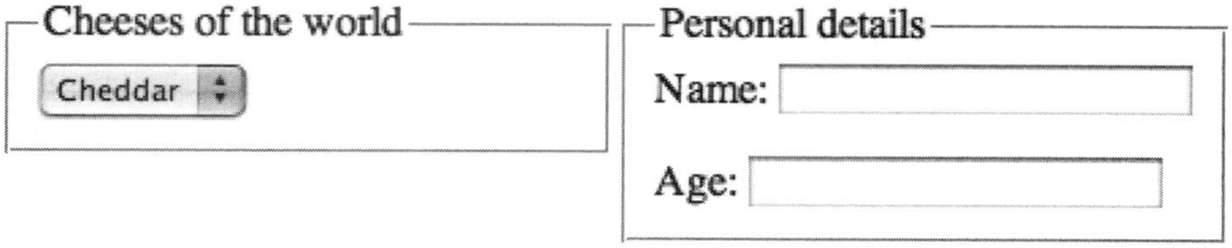

┌─Cheeses of the world────────┐ ┌─Personal details──────────
│ ┌────────────────┐ │ │ Name: ┌──────────────┐
│ │ Cheddar ⬍ │ │ │ └──────────────┘
│ └────────────────┘ │ │ Age: ┌──────────────┐
└─────────────────────────────┘ │ └──────────────┘

Figure 4-32. A form laid out horizontally

Even if your form isn't using `<fieldset>` elements, that doesn't mean you can't lay out the form nicely without recourse to tables as containers. It's perfectly possible to include `<div>`s within a form, and you can create the form shown in Figure 4-33 with just two floated container `<div>`s:

```
form div {float: left; width: 50%;}
```

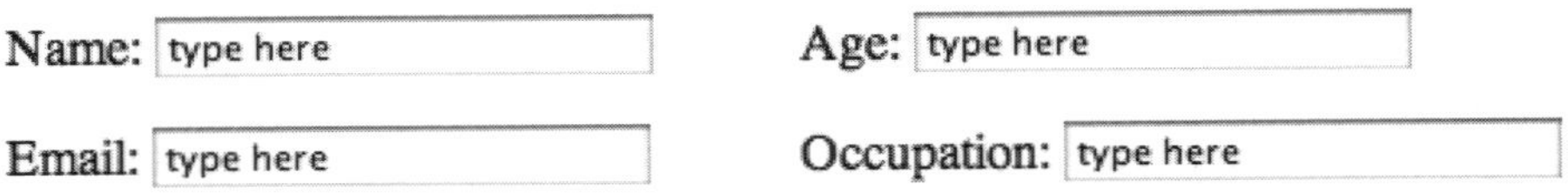

Name: type here   Age: type here

Email: type here   Occupation: type here

Figure 4-33. Two containing `<div>`s, both floated left

Form controls styling

Styling form controls consistently and reliably across browsers is problematic, which is part of the reason I suggest you apply only minimal styling. I do this myself with `<textarea>` and `<input>` elements. Not being a fan of the beveled border many browsers show by default, I tend to apply a slim-line CSS border instead (see Figure 4-34):

```
input {border: 1px solid #ccc;}
```

Figure 4-34. A text input with a single-pixel border

This single-pixel border removes the 3D effect, but the text input is still recognizably a text input. However, applying this border to all inputs, regardless of their type, is not always desirable. For example, Figure 4-35 shows what happens when a single-pixel border is applied to a radio button.

 Figure 4-35. A radio button with a single-pixel border

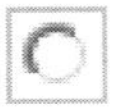

While the text input now appears crisp and professional, the radio button has an unsightly and unnecessary border. To prevent this, you need to be able to effectively say in your markup, "Only style inputs that have a type of text."

Selecting individual types of inputs can be a little trickier than it ought to be—because it's a single element that changes behavior depending on its type, you can't target *only* text inputs or *only* check boxes in the same way you can target a `<textarea>` or a `<fieldset>`. You have two ways of going about this. The first is with CSS2 attribute selectors. The following example targets only those inputs that have a type attribute of checkbox:

```
input[type="text"] {border: 1px solid #ccc;}
```

But Internet Explorer 6 and below (and other older browsers) do not support attribute selectors, so this solution is only viable for modern browsers. To make things backward-compatible, all of your inputs need to be given a class name, and then you can either style all inputs and override those classed as radio buttons and/or check boxes, or just target all inputs classed as text inputs:

```
input.text {border: 1px solid #ccc;}
```

Alternatively, as each of your inputs should have a unique id so as to pair up with a <label> (with its for attribute), you could save yourself a little work and target those instead:

```
#fullname, #address, #phonenumber, ➥
#age, #emailaddress {border: 1px solid #ccc;}
```

So, you can have messy markup and clean CSS, or clean markup and messy CSS. Pick the solution that you find the least unsightly and run with it.

> The tech reviewer of this book, Ian Lloyd, has come up with a JavaScript solution for removing CSS borders that involves applying the border to all inputs, but then removing the border for check boxes and radio buttons after the page has loaded. You can find his script at http://lloydi.com/blog/2006/08/30/remove-css-borders-radio-checkboxes.

CSS as an aid to usability

Now that you've started tweaking the controls, you can also use the CSS to enhance the usability of the form. To begin with, let's make use of the CSS2 :focus pseudo-class to help make it clearer to the user where they are in a form, by changing the background color and the border style to stand out from the crowd:

```
input:focus {background-color: yellow;}
```

> Internet Explorer version 6 and below do not support :focus on any other element but <a>, so nothing will happen in these cases.

Figure 4-36 shows the results of the preceding markup.

Figure 4-36. A text input that currently has the focus

Remember, though, that if you're setting a background color on your input, you should explicitly set a foreground color as well. Even if it all looks OK in your browser, you don't know what default font settings other people have, so if you're in doubt, hard-code that color in:

```
input:focus {background-color: yellow; color: black;}
```

109

Hard-coding the color is actually good advice to consider for all elements, not just form controls. When Netscape 3 and 4 were still in mainstream use, it was often easy to spot websites that had been tested in Internet Explorer only, because where Internet Explorer defaulted to a white background, Netscape defaulted to gray—so unless the web designer had explicitly set the body background to white, pages in Netscape would often look terrible.

The <legend> element is useful, as it aids in both usability and accessibility for all your users. Styling it, however, can be a real pain because it's impossible to override many of its characteristics. For instance, you can't set a width on a <legend>, nor can you set a height or a margin value. You can't float the element anywhere; you can't use position: absolute to try and break it out of the document flow; and if the contents of your <legend> are too long, it will stretch your <fieldset> and break out of your layout, so you need to manually insert <br /> tags where and if appropriate. It is one of the more *stubborn* elements.

Happily, though, you can (to some extent) change border values and background colors, and you can increase or decrease padding. Also, a wide range of CSS font properties are open to you, so you're not entirely left out in the cold (see Figure 4-37).

Figure 4-37. A heavily styled <legend>, as seen at www.cssplay.co.uk/menu/form.html

Something I think worth considering is providing users with some visual feedback to indicate that a <label> is actually clickable—something many people won't realize except through accidental discovery or by being otherwise told. You can do this using the cursor CSS property, as follows:

```
label {cursor: pointer;}
```

The mouse cursor will change in most browsers when hovered over a <label>, as shown in Figure 4-38.

Figure 4-38. A label being hovered over

It's a very quick, simple addition, but you should use it with caution. As noted earlier, Safari currently offers no support for clickable labels, which means users of this browser could be confused when their cursor changes to indicate that a label can be clicked—and that doing so achieves nothing. It's also arguable that, as most operating systems also don't offer visual feedback for their own clickable labels in dialog boxes, options panels, and the like, we shouldn't attempt to provide it in our websites either. I disagree with that idea—if providing visual feedback teaches people that labels can be clicked, then I don't see it as a bad thing. The lack of Safari support is a problem, but hopefully with enough nagging from web designers, Apple will provide this functionality in due course.

Scripting forms

I'll make this clear from the start: your form *must* work without JavaScript. I've repeated this statement throughout this book, but it's even more important in the case of forms, because if you rely on client-side scripting for your form to successfully submit, then you may be preventing people from using it, and those people may have websites, and they may write disparaging things about you if you upset them. The golden rule as I see it is this: if your form is using JavaScript to provide any sort of functionality, provide a server-side version or HTML version where relevant, to ensure the form works without scripts enabled.

So with that dire warning out of the way, let's look at how you can *enhance* your forms with JavaScript.

Validation

Client-side validation of form fields is a valuable aid to usability, as it provides users with instant feedback, alerting them to any potential (or actual) problems with their submission. Sometimes this feedback is provided at the end of the form, when users click the submit button, but it's even better if that validation can occur on a field-by-field basis so problems can be addressed right away.

Validation doesn't need to be limited to checking for well-formed e-mail addresses or other values entered by the user. It's currently becoming popular to use Ajax[4] to unobtrusively query server-side databases, allowing, for instance, near-instantaneous confirmation as to whether a desired username is available and alternatives if not, or a list of available concert tickets or airline seats on a given date. Because this book is primarily about (X)HTML, I'm not going to try and teach you Ajax—there's enough material there for a whole other book—but if this is an area you wish to learn more of, you could try starting with the tutorial "Ajax and XMLHttpRequest" (www.xul.fr/en-xml-ajax.html) and the article "Ajax: Getting Started" (http://developer.mozilla.org/en/docs/AJAX:Getting_Started).

The first bit of form validation you'll likely want to do is ensure that all required form fields have been completed, which is usually as simple as checking to see if the value of a form field is null, as detailed in the article "3 Steps to Writing JavaScript" (http://chunkysoup.net/basic/js3step/js_3step.3.html). It's also worth checking that any e-mail addresses entered are, in fact, actual e-mail addresses. There are a couple of ways of doing this, one of which is to include an extra field and ask users to enter their details twice, and then check that the contents of both fields match (this technique is useful for password fields as well). This can help prevent some errors, but it doesn't stop users from actually making the same mistake in both fields (particularly if they simply copy and paste from the first input).

A better way is to use **regular expressions** (strings that match certain patterns of other strings according to a given syntax) to check that the value is actually an e-mail address, and

---

4. Ajax stands for **Asynchronous JavaScript and XML**, a technique for making web pages feel more responsive by exchanging small amounts of data with the server behind the scenes, negating a need for a full page reload.

alert the user if it appears to be incorrect. Creating the regular expression can be a complicated business (see www.regular-expressions.info/email.html for more information), but once you have your expression, the script can usually be quite simple (see www.codetoad.com/javascript/is_valid_email.asp and www.quirksmode.org/js/mailcheck.html for examples).

> For more information on regular expressions, start with http://en.wikipedia.org/wiki/Regular_expression and take it from there.

How about validation of other common form values, such as telephone numbers and zip codes? Doing so would be possible using the same methods just described, but validation for these items should not be quite as severe—telephone numbers and zip codes can often vary wildly from state to state and country to country, so it's best to leave these things loose. You could also validate credit card details in a rudimentary way by checking to ensure that the card number is 16 digits, checking to make sure the expiration dates are valid dates, and so on. What you won't be able to do at this stage is check whether the credit card is actually a valid card; that level of validation needs to take place on the server, in communication with the banks. But at least you can attempt to ensure the details you receive are of a valid format prior to submission to these systems.

Forms as navigation

Forms are not always just used for collecting data. You've probably seen something like the menu shown in Figure 4-39.

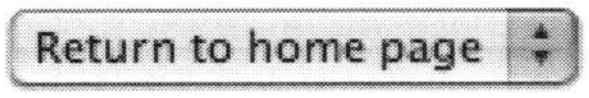

Return to home page

Figure 4-39.
A <select> menu used as a navigation menu

This is commonly referred to as a **jump menu**, and it consists of a <select> menu with a range of <option> elements, each containing a URL as their value. You can't make these menus functional with (X)HTML alone. All a form can do—all it was *designed* to do—is collect values from the form and pass them on as name/value pairs to the handler specified in the form's action attribute, so it isn't enough to provide URLs as values and hope that the browser will know what you mean. You still need to explain yourself with a script and a server-side handler.

Using <select> as a means of navigation has advantages: it saves a significant amount of space, it's unobtrusive, and clients tend to like it. It also has several disadvantages: search engines will not be able to crawl your site unless you also provide a text-based list of hyperlinks somewhere on the page, users won't be able to distinguish between unvisited and visited links, and there are problems with inaccessibility when it's not used well. Being a form, it still ought to provide both client-side and server-side functionality.

The most common JavaScript solution I've seen uses an onchange attribute that detects when an <option> has been selected and then changes the current document location to match the URL in the value. It's straightforward but inaccessible to keyboard users, as the menu registers a change as soon as users scroll down to the first <option>.

> *Cameron Adams came up with a solution that uses a bit more script but functions for keyboard users as well:* www.themaninblue.com/writing/perspective/2004/10/19. *This solution is better, but it still requires the user to have scripts enabled.*

Also needed are a submit button and a server-side form handler. If desired, you could hide the submit button from users who can use the JavaScript solution with a quick and dirty `<noscript>`:

```
<noscript><input type="submit" value="Go" /></noscript>
```

You would then need to provide a handler that took the value from the `<select>` menu and changed the browser location, making your jump menu accessible to more people.

Manipulation of disabled controls

As mentioned earlier, form controls all come with a `disabled` attribute. When set, the form control cannot be used, its value will not be submitted to the server, and the control itself will usually be grayed out or otherwise de-emphasized visually. On its own, this attribute doesn't have much use—if you're going to disable form controls on a static (X)HTML page, then you might as well just leave the control out altogether—but when combined with script, it can be more useful.

For instance, to help prevent duplicate form submissions (particularly useful during an online ordering process), many forms now programmatically disable the submit button after it has been clicked. At its simplest, this result can be achieved with a couple of event handlers:

```
<input type="submit" onclick="this.disabled=true;" ➥
onkeypress="this.disabled=true;" value="submit" />
```

> *Using both* onclick *and* onkeypress *event handlers means the script will fire for both mouse and keyboard users, and so is more accessible.*

Further uses of dynamic disabling could include disabling and enabling form controls based on user choices. For instance, if your form contains multiple paths depending on the choices the user makes, irrelevant fields can be dynamically disabled to guide those users along.

Form event handlers

As mentioned previously, several form-specific event handlers are available. onsubmit and onreset are both applicable to the `<form>` element and will fire events when the form is submitted or reset, respectively. onselect may be used only with the `<input>` and `<textarea>` elements and refers to when the user selects some text within the text field.

onchange may be used only with the <input>, <select>, and <textarea> elements and refers to when a control is no longer in focus *and* has changed since gaining focus. Finally, onfocus and onblur refer to when a control has focus or loses focus, respectively, and can be used on the <input>, <select>, <label>, <textarea>, and <button> elements.[5] My previous advice on the subject of event handlers still stands: where possible, use an external JavaScript that manipulates elements by traversing the DOM tree. Let's see how we can do that.

The onfocus event handler is pretty useful when it comes to adding a little usability to your form. Let's say that you have some placeholder text in all of your text inputs, as shown in Figure 4-40.

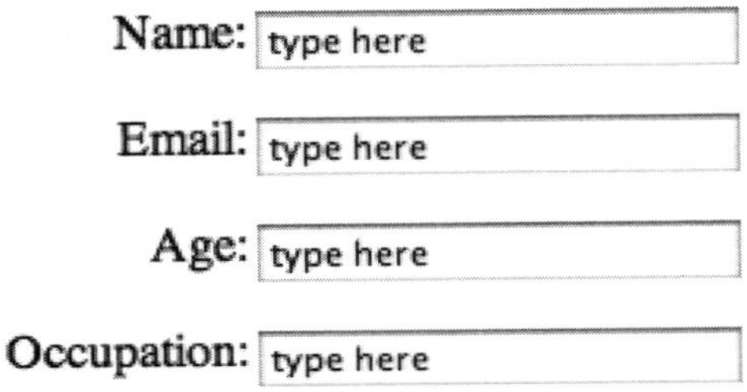

Figure 4-40.
Several text inputs with placeholder text

Somebody filling in your form would have to delete each instance of placeholder text before they could insert their own—not much fun. A quick and dirty way of alleviating that problem is with onfocus:

```
<input type="text" value="Your name here" onfocus="select();" />
```

Now, when the user tabs into that field, the text within it is automatically selected, as shown in Figure 4-41.

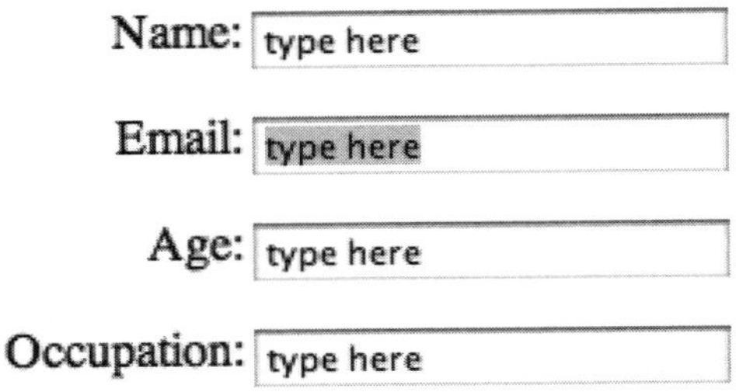

Figure 4-41.
Automatically selected text

Why does this matter? Well, the user can now start typing, and whatever the user types will instantly replace the selected text, so there's no need for the user to manually delete the

---

5. These last two event handlers can also be used on the <a> and <area> elements.

placeholder.[6] All well and good, but you would need to add that onfocus attribute to every <input> on your page, so this technique may be better for the user but not so much for you.

Instead, let's use an external JavaScript script:

```
function focusFields () {
  if (!document.getElementsByTagName) return false;
  var formfields = document.getElementsByTagName("input");
  for (var i=0; i < formfields.length; i++) {
    formfields[i].onfocus = function() {
      this.select();
    }
  }
}
window.onload = focusFields;
```

This script applies the select(); behavior to every <input> on your page. The principle is basically the same for all of these event handlers: you create an array containing all tags of a given name, and then loop through those tags applying a function, so you can apply numerous behaviors without having to modify your source markup.

Summary

This concludes our examination of form markup, usability, styling, and scripting. I hope you can see that, while it can be very easy to create a form, creating one that is as usable and accessible to as wide a range of people as possible, yet remains attractive, can be quite challenging. There will often be moments when you need to choose between usability and design, and I hope you'll always choose the former. A form may be bland or ugly, but if people can use it effectively, that's really what matters.

---

6. I've seen some people automatically clear placeholder text instead of selecting it. Please don't do this; it's incredibly frustrating when I find I have to go back to an input field and find it helpfully deleting my previous entry when it gains focus.

5 PURPOSE-BUILT SEMANTICS: MICROFORMATS AND OTHER STORIES

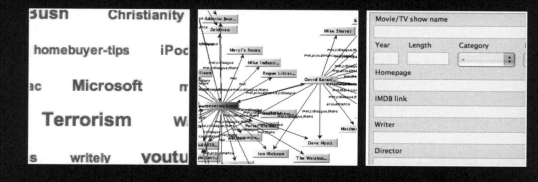

The preceding chapters have covered nearly every tag and attribute there is, with a few exceptions that you can find in Appendix B. Now that you're aware of all this markup available to you, you should be able to find a relevant tag for every element on your page and every fragment of text, right? Well . . . probably not. Try as you might to build your pages as free from generic <div> and <span> tags as possible, eventually you're going to have to face up to the fact that (X)HTML does not provide *everything* you need to describe your content, nor was it ever intended to; this is why generic <div> and <span> elements exist in the first place.

The purpose of this chapter is to examine how you can create your own semantics using the languages and tools already available to you (something you already do every time you give something a class name or id, or a rev or rel value), which is why it's as important to use semantic class names—names that describe the purpose or function, rather than the appearance—as it is to use semantic elements. We'll look at the use of metadata, microformats (what they are and why you should care, followed by a look in detail at some of the more common microformats already in use on the Web today, which will form the bulk of this chapter), the Dublin Core Metadata Initiative (DCMI), Structured Blogging (SB), and concepts such as the Semantic Web and Web 2.0.

We'll start with metadata and the <meta> element.

Metadata

Metadata is essentially data about data. When you buy a song from the iTunes music store, the song file itself (the AAC file) is the data; the track information that appears on your audio player—the title, the artist, the album the track is from, the duration of the track, and so on—is metadata, in this case stored at the beginning of the audio file in a format known as ID3. When you're writing an essay in Microsoft Word, you can retrieve information such as page count, word count (plus or minus footnotes), character count, paragraph count, line count, and so on; the essay is the data, and the information *about* the essay is the metadata.

In HTML, metadata about an HTML document has historically been included via the <meta> element, placed in the head of the document. This element has been around since HTML 2.0 and is fairly open-ended; it was designed to allow authors to include various types of metadata on their pages by specifying a property (via a name attribute, which can be any value you like) and a value (via a content attribute). For instance:

```
<meta name="Author" content="Paul Haine" />
```

The property here is Author and the value is Paul Haine.

You can also include a lang attribute, which defines the language of the value of the content attribute, allowing any screen-reading device with the ability to read <meta> content to alter its pronunciation appropriately:

```
<meta name="Author" lang="fr" content="Jacques Cousteau" />
```

It isn't always clear what the property value means, but there exists a scheme attribute that can be used to provide further information. Take this example from the HTML 4.01 specification:

```
<meta scheme="ISBN" name="identifier" content="0-8230-2355-9" />
```

This can help a user agent understand that the identifier is an ISBN and not a random string of numbers. However, this is only of use if the user agent understands what an ISBN is, so values are defined in an external **profile**, which is referred to as an attribute value in the <head> tag:

```
<head profile="http://example.com/profile/core">
```

The HTML specification does not have anything to say about what ought and ought not to be in a profile, so authors are free to create their own properties and associated values. Profiles can exist as an HTML document; microformats, which we'll examine later, use standard XHTML: a definition list with a class name of profile (http://gmpg.org/xmdp/samplehtmlprofile.html). The Dublin Core Metadata Initiative, something else we'll touch upon later, is an organization that promotes the adoption of interoperable metadata standards for bibliographic descriptions (http://dublincore.org/2003/03/24/dces) and uses RDF for their profiles rather than XHTML—but the underlying principle is the same: a dictionary of terms, each term having its own description.

> RDF stands for **Resource Description Framework**, a metadata model based upon making statements about resources in the form of a **triple**, a subject-predicate-object expression. From Wikipedia's entry on the subject: "One way to represent the fact 'The sky has the color blue' in RDF would be as a triple whose subject is 'the sky,' whose predicate is 'has the color,' and whose object is 'blue.' Predicates are traits or aspects about a resource and express a relationship between the subject and the object."

Finally, there exists an http-equiv attribute to be used in place of name; HTTP servers can then use this attribute to gather information for HTTP response message headers. You'll most likely have seen this already in the head of your web pages if you use Dreamweaver:

```
<meta http-equiv="Content-Type" ➥
content="text/html; charset=iso-8859-1" />
```

This informs the user agent that the document should be treated as text/HTML and uses a character set of ISO-8859-1. There are many other potential values,[1] but one common value you may have seen deserves a special mention as it should *not* be considered good practice:

```
<meta http-equiv="refresh" content="5;url=http://newwebsite.com/" />
```

---

1. Too many to list here. See http://htmlmastery.com/s/response-headers/ for an exhaustive list of HTTP response headers. Bear in mind that not all will be appropriate to use in the context of a <meta> element.

This is a way of informing the user agent that it should attempt to load http://newwebsite. com/ after a delay of five seconds (leaving out the URL means the page will just reload itself every five seconds instead). In the grand scheme of redirecting users to content that has moved, this is a quick, dirty, and ultimately unsatisfying method and is widely discouraged: it does not provide any feedback to the browser or search engine that the resource is in a different location, it breaks the user's back button, it is inaccessible because it allows the user no control over the rate of refresh, and it is not a guaranteed method anyway, since users may have disabled auto-refreshing.

A better, recommended way of redirecting is to use **HTTP redirects**, where redirecting is carried out on the server-side rather than the client-side. The server can then inform the user agent that the resource has been permanently redirected or temporarily redirected by sending an HTTP status code of 301 or 307, respectively.

Setting up HTTP redirects is only moderately more time-consuming but much more beneficial—how to set them up will vary depending on what server setup you have, but there are some useful links to instructions available at the W3C Quality Assurance website (www.w3.org/QA/Tips/reback) for the most common platforms (Apache and Microsoft IIS).

So, that's the <meta> element—just one standard way of including metadata in your web pages. There are other ways that you're almost certainly already using: the <title> on every page is metadata; the <address> element, used to provide contact information for the document, is also metadata; any time you use a title attribute, a cite attribute, or a datetime attribute, you're again creating metadata.

Unfortunately, metadata on the Web has a bit of a shady past. When name attribute value is either keywords or description, then the content attribute value can provide, respectively, a comma- or space-separated list of appropriate keywords relating to the document content and a concise summary of the document content. For instance, if you had written an essay on the history of Nintendo, you could use <meta> elements like this:

```
<meta name="keywords" content="nintendo, nes, snes, famicom, n64, ➥
gamecube, game boy, ds, zelda" />
<meta name="description" content="A brief history ➥
of Nintendo consoles from the inception of the Nintendo ➥
company to the present day." />
```

This would provide search engines with information about the essay before they'd even looked at the essay, in theory helping to create search results with greater accuracy. A sufficiently sophisticated engine could even learn that the Gamecube and Game Boy were created by Nintendo even if the word "Nintendo" never appeared in the article.

In practice, however, people realized that by stuffing their <meta> elements with inappropriate and misleading keywords and descriptions, they could trick search engines in an attempt to have their site rise in the rankings, even for unrelated searches. Eventually, search engines stopped referring to <meta> keywords altogether, as they could not be relied upon. Some engines may still display the description value on their results page, but generally only if the description contains the desired search term.

Spamming search engines with deliberately incorrect metadata is one of seven problems highlighted in an article by Cory Doctorow, "Metacrap: Putting the torch to seven straw-men of the meta-utopia" (www.well.com/~doctorow/metacrap.htm)—namely, that people lie. His analysis of the problems facing metadata can make for depressing reading; not only do people lie, but people can also be lazy and stupid, which introduces further inaccuracies or gaps. The gathering of metadata requires people to be both the observer and documenter of their own behavior, allowing personal bias and regional variations in terminology to creep in. And there is also the problem of differing *opinions* on what constitutes accurate metadata; the notion that there is a "correct" way of categorizing and describing all data is fallacious.

So it's all beginning to look a bit bleak, but Doctorow doesn't suggest abandoning metadata altogether: "Metadata can be quite useful, if taken with a sufficiently large pinch of salt. The meta-utopia will never come into being, but metadata is often a good means of making rough assumptions about the information that floats through the Internet." Google, for instance, does exactly that—it uses the information about how many people are linking to you to determine the importance of your site in relation to the rest of the World Wide Web; the number of people linking to you is metadata about your site. So despite the fact that, yes, people can lie, be lazy, be stupid, and argue, great things can still come from exploiting metadata.

We will now turn to the current golden boy of online metadata—microformats.

Microformats

Microformats are either wildly exciting or deeply bewildering, depending on how much you've read about them. I have to confess, when people first started talking about microformats a year or so ago, I didn't *entirely* understand what the big deal was; looking at the hCard microformat, it struck me as being an awful lot of extra markup—lots of `<span>` and `<div>` tags—for not much extra gain. But, like so many others, I finally began to understand how much potential they have and how useful they really are. Hopefully, if you're still looking at them with a skeptical glare, you'll have changed your mind by the end of this section.

So, first of all, what *is* a microformat? It's a good question, so let's start with the definition provided on microformats.org, which describes microformats as "a set of simple, open data formats built upon existing and widely adopted standards." The microformats-discuss mailing list (microformats.org/discuss/) provided this alternative definition: "Microformats are simple conventions for embedding semantics in HTML to enable decentralized development."

So what did *that* mean? Essentially this: marking up certain chunks of content in a standardized way that allows external applications, aggregators, and search engines to

- Recognize the content for what it is when crawling your website.
- Manipulate that content by providing access to it, collating it, or converting it into other, related formats for use in external applications and web services.

Let's look at some examples before we get too bogged down in high-level descriptions. For instance, you've already heard me make mention of the hCard microformat. I'll discuss it in more depth further on, but for the moment, just understand that it is a way of marking up your existing online contact details with standardized class names that allows for easy conversion to the vCard format (a portable electronic business card) or for search engines specifically searching for contact details to pick them out.

Another example is the XFN microformat. Standing for XHTML Friends Network, XFN is a way of using the rel attribute on hyperlinks to describe a relationship between yourself and the person you're linking to, allowing for the creation of automatically generated social networks based on that information.

So that's what a microformat is, basically—a means of taking advantage of existing standards to solve perceived problems. In the case of hCard, the problem was that there was no standard way to format and retrieve contact details from a web page, and in the case of XFN, the problem was that there was no standard way to express, semantically, personal relationships between a linker and one being linked to. They can look a little ungainly at first—in fact, the most common complaint I've heard about them is that due to their sometimes high use of generic elements, they appear to be the antithesis of the lean, meaningful markup we're all striving for these days. I can understand this complaint, as it's precisely the same thought I had when I first encountered hCards.

However, this doesn't necessarily need to be the case. Part of the guiding principles of microformat creation is that you should use the most appropriate semantic (X)HTML element where possible. If no such element exists, you use the most appropriate structural element instead, which could be a <div> or a <span> but could also be an <address>, a <li>, or even a <td>, depending upon the circumstances. While it is true that some microformat implementations will favor <span>, I don't think this is as bad as it initially feels. While it's good to avoid overusing generic elements, in this instance the tag is being used with meaning; it has been *given* semantic meaning, meaning that exists implicitly by context. Furthermore, using microformats can negate the need for extra presentational markup such as <br />, so when it comes down to it, your page is only gaining a few bytes around the hips.

Should you get excited about microformats? I definitely think they have great potential, and the more people who use them, the better things will be: the available range of data will be richer and larger, and the tools to make use of it all will be better integrated and more widely available. Some quite large sites other than Technorati (Upcoming.org, for instance, and various Yahoo! sites) are already making extensive use of them. We may even soon be seeing involvement from Microsoft, after Bill Gates was quoted in March 2006 as saying, "We need microformats and to get people to agree on them. It is going to bootstrap exchanging data on the Web . . . we need them for things like contact cards, events, directions . . ." (www.youtube.com/watch?v=Z9X-vHJ_Z-I). Could it be we'll see microformat data integrated seamlessly into Windows and Internet Explorer one day?[2]

Let's now look at some microformats with already-completed specifications: hCard, hCalendar, XOXO, XFN, VoteLinks, and three "rel-" microformats—rel-license, rel-nofollow, and rel-tag. I'm also going to show you hReview, despite it still being in draft form at this time, because it is already in use in some high-profile locations (Yahoo! Tech are using it, for instance) and so is unlikely to massively change between now and its formalization. Some of

---

2. And when that day comes, will they be referred to as Microsoft Microformats Executive Business Edition? Time will tell.

the formats still in draft form at this time will undoubtedly have been formalized by the time this book has been published, so do check microformats.org first of all for any new microformat news.

First of all, hCard.

hCard

The hCard microformat is a format designed to represent people and their companies, organizations, and locations using more or less the same properties and values of the vCard standard (www.imc.org/pdi/vcard-21.txt), but in (X)HTML. You may have used vCards in the past yourself; a vCard is an electronic business card, usually with a file extension of .vcf, that can contain—in the form of strings of plain text—not only name and address details, but also phone numbers, URLs, logos, and photographs (encoded in base64 or referenced by URI), and so on. They're not limited to specific operating systems or applications—most e-mail clients will support vCards—and they're completely portable. You can e-mail them, offer them for download on a website, or transfer them via Bluetooth, and generally you just need to open one on your computer, phone, or other device, and your preferred e-mail or address book application will allow you to save the contents of the vCard into your system address book. All well and good.

An hCard is a way of marking up your contact details in (X)HTML using class names that match as best as possible those names used in the vCard standard, allowing you to easily convert hCards to vCards. For instance, here is a sample vCard:

```
BEGIN:VCARD
VERSION:3.0
N:Haine, Paul
FN:Paul Haine
URL:http://unfortunatelypaul.com/
ORG:International Man of Mystery
END:VCARD
```

An equivalent of this as an hCard would be

```
<div class="vcard">
  <a class="url fn" href="http://unfortunatelypaul.com/">Paul Haine</a>
  <div class="org">International Man of Mystery</div>
</div>
```

Broken down into pieces, we have the following:

- A block-level container tag with a class of vcard to indicate to parsers that its contents should be treated appropriately

- An anchor tag with a class of url and fn—the URL is provided in the href attribute, and the fn, or the full name, in the content of the tag

- An additional container tag with a class of org, which stands for organization (This doesn't need to be a <div>—a <p> or a <span> would do the job just as well. The class name is the important part.)

In the end, as we're not using any visually distinctive tags, our hCard would render in a browser, very simply, as shown in Figure 5-1.

<u>Paul Haine</u>
International Man of Mystery

Figure 5-1. A basic hCard

Because any parser looking for hCard-specific markup will ignore anything it doesn't understand, we're not limited to displaying hCards in a traditionally formatted block of the sort you might find on the front of an envelope or in a corner of a formal letter. We can happily incorporate the hCard markup into natural language, like this:

```
<p class="vcard"><a class="url fn" ➥
href="http://unfortunatelypaul.com/">Paul Haine</a> is currently
working for <cite class="org">International Man of Mystery</cite>,
an organization dedicated to, ooh, all sorts of secret
and exciting things.</p>
```

This is exactly the same hCard as before, but now it renders as shown in Figure 5-2.

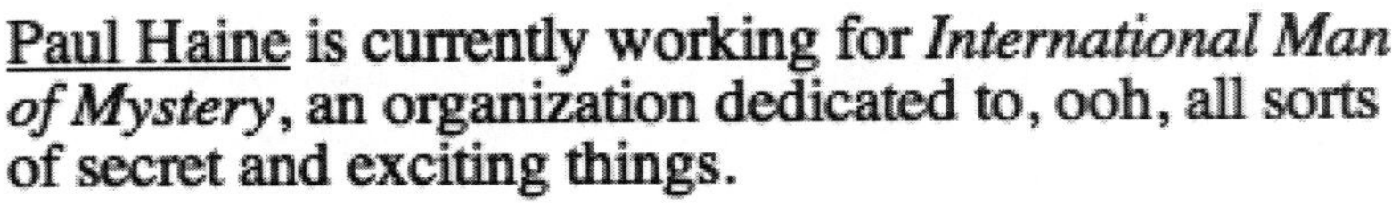

<u>Paul Haine</u> is currently working for *International Man of Mystery*, an organization dedicated to, ooh, all sorts of secret and exciting things.

Figure 5-2. An hCard incorporated into a natural sentence

Alternatively, we could have a table of people, each with their own hCard, by integrating the hCard class names directly into the table markup:

```
<table>
  <tr>
    <th scope="col">Name and URL</th>
    <th scope="col">Organization</th>
  </tr>
  <tr class="vcard">
    <td><a class="url fn" href="http://unfortunatelypaul.com">➥
Paul Haine</a></td>
    <td class="org">International man of mystery</td>
  </tr>
  <tr class="vcard">
    <td><a class="url fn" href="http://jukebo.cx">➥
Vikki Roberts</a></td>
    <td class="org">Jukebox</td>
  </tr>
</table>
```

which renders as shown in Figure 5-3.

Name and URL	Organization
Paul Haine	International man of mystery
Vikki Roberts	Jukebox

Figure 5-3. A table of hCards

So you can see that even though *examples* of hCards can tend toward high use of <div> and <span> tags, you're not at all limited as to how you integrate the hCard classes into your own markup.

So far we've been using a very simple example, one with only a full name, a URL, and an organization. As you might expect, there's a wide range of other properties available:

- fn, n (family-name, given-name, additional-name, honorific-prefix, honorific-suffix), nickname, sort-string
- url, email (type, value), tel (type, value)
- adr (post-office-box, extended-address, street-address, locality, region, postal-code, country-name, type, value), label
- geo (latitude, longitude), tz
- photo, logo, sound, bday
- title, role, org (organization-name, organization-unit)
- category, note
- class, key, mailer, uid, rev

Some of these properties have subproperties, which are the ones in parentheses in the preceding list. These are used by nesting them within other properties. Let's take this address as an example:

```
Verity Fane-Bailey
23 Acacia Avenue
London, United Kingdom
```

There are three distinct aspects to this address: a street name, a state, and a country; the hCard properties that match up to these are, respectively, street-address, region, and country-name, which are all subproperties of the adr property. To express this in our markup, we simply nest our properties:

```
<div class="vcard">
  <div class="fn">Verity Fane-Bailey</div>
  <div class="adr">
    <div class="street-address"> 23 Acacia Avenue</div>
    <span class="region">London</span>, ➥
<span class="country-name">United Kingdom</span>
  </div>
</div>
```

The adr property seen here is also implemented as a standalone microformat, known simply as adr. Along with the geo property, these are simply ways of providing geographical information without creating a full hCard. They currently exist only as draft specifications but are unlikely to change in any great way, as they are derived from the formalized hCard specification.

There also exists the notion of **types**, which allows you to be even more specific about an address element—for instance, providing a home, work, and fax number, which are all types of the tel property. You indicate types by nesting a type and a value within a property. Let's say you wanted to express this information as an hCard:

```
Christine Lockwood can be contacted via telephone
(cell: +44 1234 5656, work: +44 1234 7878)
or by fax (fax: +44 1234 7979).
```

This can be marked up as follows:

```
<p class="vcard"><span class="fn">Christine Lockwood</span>➡
 can be contacted via telephone (<span class="tel">➡
<span class="type">cell</span>: <span class="value">➡
+44 1234 5656</span></span>, <span class="tel">➡
<span class="type">work</span>: <span class="value">➡
+44 1234 7878</span></span>) or by fax (➡
<span class="tel"><span class="type">fax</span>: ➡
<span class="value">+44 1234 7979</span></span>).</p>
```

Now that's starting to look a bit clumsy, but it's actually fairly simple: a paragraph with a class of vcard, followed by a <span> element providing the full name, followed by three sets of <span> elements with a property of tel, each one containing a type and a value.

You could make the markup more readable with line breaks and tab or space indents, but extra whitespace in your markup can often translate into extra whitespace in the rendered document, so be wary—you may wish to break things up during development but collapse it all again when complete to remove extra visual spacing:

```
<p class="vcard">
  <span class="fn">Christine Lockwood</span> can ➡
be contacted via telephone (
    <span class="tel">
      <span class="type">cell</span>:
      <span class="value">+44 1234 5656</span>
    </span>,
    <span class="tel">
      <span class="type">work</span>:
      <span class="value">+44 1234 7878</span>
    </span>
  ) or by fax (
    <span class="tel">
      <span class="type">fax</span>:
      <span class="value">+44 1234 7979</span>
    </span>).
</p>
```

It is also possible to use a type of pref to indicate that a particular type should be the preferred means of contact. Using the preceding example, if the cell phone was preferred over the work phone, this could be indicated in the content like this:

```
Christine Lockwood can be contacted via telephone
(cell (preferred): +44 1234 5656, work: +44 1234 7878)
or by fax (fax: +44 1234 7979).
```

In the markup, we just need to include (<span class="type">pref</span>erred) between the cell type and the cell value—we use pref rather than the full word because pref is the keyword inherited from the vCard standard—so the markup now looks like this:

```
<p class="vcard"><span class="fn">Christine Lockwood</span>➥
can be contacted via telephone (<span class="tel">➥
<span class="type">cell</span>) (<span class="type">➥
pref</span>erred): <span class="value">+44 1234 5656</span>➥
</span>, <span class="tel"><span class="type">work</span>: ➥
<span class="value">+44 1234 7878</span></span>) ➥
or by fax (<span class="tel"><span class="type">fax</span>:➥
<span class="value">+44 1234 7979</span></span>).</p>
```

If you're concerned that all these extra classes and <span> tags are overwhelming and cluttered, take solace in the fact that they are at least meaningful and useful as well.

> To be honest, judging from the quality of some of the markup out there, if a few too many spans in your hCard is what makes your markup look unprofessional, then I congratulate you.

It's also possible to include rich media, such as a photo, a logo, or a sound, in an hCard. Continuing from the preceding example, let's add an image, so the rendered whole now looks like Figure 5-4 in a browser.

Christine Lockwood can be contacted via telephone (cell (preferred): +44 1234 5656, work: +44 1234 7878) or by fax (fax: +44 1234 7979).

Figure 5-4. An hCard with the addition of a decorative photo

There are two ways we can include that image in our resulting vCard: by referencing the URI of the image or by encoding it in base64. Let's try the first method, which is simply a matter of including an <img> within the hCard and giving it a class of photo:

```
<p class="vcard"><img src="http://htmlmastery.com/logo.gif"➥
alt="" class="photo" /><span class="fn">Christine...
```

Now, when the hCard is converted into a VCF file, it will gain a line like this:

```
PHOTO;VALUE=uri:http://htmlmastery.com/logo.gif
```

All well and good, but there's a problem with this method: it requires a connection to the Internet to retrieve the image; if there's no Internet connection available, or the remote server is down, or the owner of the website has absent-mindedly moved or renamed the image, then this isn't going to work. So, we turn instead to the slightly more technical solution of encoding the image in base64. This is a way of converting binary data (such as an image file) into plain text, allowing that data to be easily transferred over, for instance, e-mail. Once we've converted the image, we'll end up with something like this in our markup:

```
<p class="vcard"><img src="data:image/gif;base64, ➥
iVBORwOKGgoAAAANSUhEUg...
```

The src attribute no longer refers to an image on the server, but instead now states a MIME type of image/gif, the type of encoding (base64), followed by a lengthy string of ASCII characters. I'm not going to include the entire string here—it runs to nearly 5,000 characters, which you must ensure are written out by hand.

Kidding! There are plenty of conversion tools available online (www.motobit.com/util/base64-decoder-encoder.asp is one I've used in the past), or you can program one yourself in your coding language of choice. But before you get too excited, be aware that we've run into another problem—Internet Explorer can't display images when they're encoded in base64. It's possible to get around this using a PHP solution by Dean Edwards (http://dean.edwards.name/weblog/2005/06/base64-ie/) that sends the ASCII data back to the server, converts it back into an image, and then returns that image. An alternative solution is to include both forms of image in your markup, but only give the base64 data the class of photo, and use CSS to hide the inline image from all non-IE browsers.

A further solution, and the simplest of all, is to simply not worry about it and just don't display the image to Internet Explorer—the importance of the image being visible to all users depends on your circumstances.

So that, more or less, is what an hCard is and how you create one—there even exists an online hCard creator (http://microformats.org/code/hcard/creator) that can take some of the pain out of your hand-coding. When it comes to exploiting them, there's already an abundance of converters, aggregators, and search engines tailored to dealing with microformat data. Many of these deal with different varieties of microformat rather than specifically with hCards, and I'll list some of those toward the end of this section.

Technorati provides an hCard-to-vCard conversion tool (http://technorati.com/contacts/) that allows you to pass a URL to their server, and it will crawl the page found at that URL and return a VCF file containing one vCard for each hCard it finds. You don't need to even visit the Technorati site for this to work. By including a link like this on your own page:

```
<a href="http://feeds.technorati.com/contacts/yourdomain.com/">➥
Download vCard</a>
```

you can return a VCF file to your end user without that user ever appearing to leave your site. A JavaScript favelet is also available to allow you to retrieve vCards from any website you visit that has implemented the hCard standard.

*A **favelet**, also known as a **bookmarklet**, is a small snippet of JavaScript that provides one-click functionality for any number of services. It is stored as a URL within your browser bookmarks or within a link on a page.*

If you don't want to rely upon third-party services (which can become unavailable without warning), there's nothing to stop you from writing your own conversion tool in whichever server-side language you like, with reference to "hCard Parsing" by Tantek Çelik (http://microformats.org/wiki/hcard-parsing), or by downloading the code available from http://hg.microformats.org/.

Also of note is the way Andy Hume has implemented hCards for each person who comments on his blog posts (http://thedredge.org/2005/06/using-hcards-in-your-blog/), which also includes XFN data (see the section "XFN" later in this chapter) and a unique image for each commenter by using gravatars, or globally recognized avatars.[3] At the time of writing, those images are only displayed on the website version of the hCard; by simply adding class="photo", they could also be included within the hCard proper.

For even more information on hCards, do read the official hCard Wiki article (http://microformats.org/wiki/hcard), which lists many more implementations and contains even more in-depth instructions.

Now, let's turn our attention to the hCalendar microformat.

hCalendar

The hCalendar microformat is a lot like the hCard format, except it's used to describe events rather than contact details and is based on the iCalendar standard (http://tools. ietf.org/html/rfc2445) used by Apple's iCal, Google Calendar, Lotus Notes, and many more. The problem it set out to solve is that, despite bloggers discussing events both past, present, and future, there existed no standard way to retrieve event information from those discussions and add it to a personal calendaring application or service. By implementing the hCalendar standard on their websites, people can allow spiders, search engines, and other aggregators to retrieve that information and convert it into the iCalendar format (for downloadable iCalendar files, the file extension is usually .ics).

Now that you're familiar with hCard, working with hCalendar shouldn't pose much of a problem, as the principles are basically the same. Indeed, some of the iCalendar properties such as attendee, contact, and organizer are not even implemented in hCalendar, as you can use a nested hCard instead. The location can also be included within the hCard (but also exists in hCalendar), or you can use the adr or geo formats as mentioned in the "hCards" section earlier.

---

3. These represent a means of having the same image appear next to your name on any blog that's implemented the system. See www.gravatar.com for more info.

A typical event discussed online consists of the following elements: a summary or title, a location, a URL, a start date and time, an end date or time, and a description. For instance, this event:

**Future Noir: A retrospective look at *Blade Runner*
and its effects on the cyberpunk movement**
The 1992 release of the "Director's Cut" only confirmed what
the international film cognoscenti have known all along:
Ridley Scott's *Blade Runner,* based on Philip K. Dick's brilliant
and troubling SF novel *Do Androids Dream of Electric Sheep,*
still rules as the most visually dense, thematically challenging,
and influential SF film ever made.
Date: August 11th, 2006. Registration begins at 09:30,
discussion ends at 4:30 same day.
Venue: Orwell House Independent Theater

Expressed in plain vanilla (X)HTML, this can be straightforward enough:

```
<h1><a href="http://orwellhouse.com/futurenoir/">
Future Noir: A retrospective look at <cite>Blade Runner</cite>
 and its effects on the cyberpunk movement</a></h1>
<p>The 1992 release of the "Director's Cut" only confirmed
what the international film cognoscenti have known all along:
Ridley Scott's <cite>Blade Runner</cite>, based on
Philip K. Dick's brilliant and troubling SF novel
<cite>Do Androids Dream of Electric Sheep</cite>,
still rules as the most visually dense, thematically challenging,
and influential SF film ever made.</p>
<p>Date: August 11th, 2006. Registration begins at 09:30,
discussion ends at 4:30 same day.</p>
<p>Venue: Orwell House Independent Theater</p>
```

To turn this into an hCalendar, we first of all need to enclose it in a vevent container:

```
<div class="vevent">
  ...
</div>
```

Why vevent and not vcalendar? The vcalendar class is optional as its presence is implied by the presence of the vevent. If you're just displaying one event, it's superfluous; but if you're displaying multiple calendars on the same page, it should be used to group the vevents accordingly, like this:

```
<h2>A set of events</h2>
<div class="vcalendar">
  <div class="vevent">
    ...
  </div>
</div>
```

```
<h2>A set of events for a subject unrelated to the previous one</h2>
<div class="vcalendar">
  <div class="vevent">
    ...
  </div>
</div>
```

So, now we've informed the hCalendar-aware that here exists an event that's marked up in a way that can be exploited. We need to now fill in the details; let's begin with the title of the event, *Future Noir: A retrospective look at* Blade Runner *and its effects on the cyberpunk movement*. In our markup, the title is also acting as a link to another page (presumably a page giving more details about the event), so that makes it both a url and a summary, so our <a> now becomes the following:

```
<a href="http://orwellhouse.com/futurenoir/" ➡
class="url summary">Future Noir: A retrospective look at ➡
<cite>Blade Runner</cite> and its effects on the ➡
cyberpunk movement</a>
```

The title of the event is then followed by a description, which we indicate very simply by adding a class name of description to the containing <p>:

```
<p class="description">The 1992 release of the "Director's Cut"
 only confirmed what the international film cognoscenti have
known all along: Ridley Scott's <cite>Blade Runner</cite>,
based on Philip K. Dick's brilliant and troubling SF novel
<cite>Do Androids Dream of Electric Sheep</cite>,
still rules as the most visually dense, thematically challenging,
and influential SF film ever made.</p>
```

This is followed by the date of the event and the start and end times. This isn't as straightforward as just adding a class name. Dates in the iCalendar format need to be in the ISO-8601 format: so for our event, the date would be 20060811, which is the year, then the month, then the day—perfectly understandable for machines, but not very readable to us humans. A solution is to use an <abbr> element to present the date in a human-readable format, and then include the ISO-8601 version in the <abbr> title attribute.

Because we don't just want to display the date but also the start time and end time, we'll mark up the two times present in our event. The two class names we need for that are dtstart and dtend, so our markup will look now like this:

```
<p>Date: August 11th, 2006. Registration begins at
<abbr class="dtstart" title="20060811T0930">09:30</abbr>,
discussion ends at <abbr class="dtend"
title="20060812T1630">4:30</abbr> same day.</p>
```

So, any parser will now be able to retrieve both the start and end dates and times (the time is indicated by the T character), but people will be able to easily read the information as well. This is one of the principles of microformats: people first, machines second—first of all, you make sure the information can be used by ordinary people, and then you add the metadata for the machines.

Finally, we indicate that the event will take place in the Orwell House Independent Theater by adding a class name of location to our markup:

```
<p>Venue: <span class="location">Orwell House ➥
Independent Theater</span></p>
```

And that's it—that's our event now marked up in the hCalendar format. By running that through the Technorati hCalendar-to-iCalendar converter (http://feeds.technorati.com/events/), we end up with an ICS file looking somewhat like this:

```
BEGIN:VCALENDAR
PRODID:-//suda.co.uk//X2V 0.7.2 (BETA)//EN
VERSION:2.0
METHOD:PUBLISH
BEGIN:VEVENT
LOCATION;CHARSET=UTF-8:Orwell House Independent Theater
SUMMARY;CHARSET=UTF-8:Future Noir: A retrospective ➥
look at Blade Runner and its effects on the cyberpunk movement
DTSTART:20060811T000930
DTEND:20060812T001630
URL:http://orwellhouse.com/futurenoir/
END:VEVENT
END:VCALENDAR
```

Like vCards, iCalendars (somewhat confusingly referred to as vCalendars within the file itself) are just plain text files, so copying the preceding into a text file and saving it with an .ics extension should allow you to import the event into your calendar application of choice.

There's more you can do, of course. If your event is private, you can indicate this with a class name of class. What? Yes, a class name of class—like this:

```
<p>This meeting is <span class="class">private</span></p>
```

Events can also be public (assumed unless otherwise stated) or confidential, marked up in the same way with the desired value appearing as the content of a tag.

If your timetable includes different categories—our example event could belong to categories of film and cyberpunk—then this can also be expressed by using a class name of category, and, just like earlier, the category name is taken from the content:

```
<ul>
  <li class="category">Film</li>
  <li class="category">Cyberpunk</li>
</ul>
```

In our hCalendar file, this appears as follows:

```
CATEGORIES:Film,Cyberpunk
```

It's even possible, given hCalendar-aware technology, to subscribe to an hCalendar-enhanced feed from a website. Imagine you've just signed up for a conference that has not yet finalized its schedule, but when it does publish updates, it does so not just on the web, but also in an RSS feed as well, and it structures those updates with hCalendar markup. Some software such as the Endo newsreader software (`http://kula.jp/software/endo/`) can subscribe to that feed and pick out each vevent, adding it automatically to your calendar. Have a look at Drew McLellan's screencast to find out how that's done (`http://allinthehead.com/retro/288/hcalendar-in-endo`).

Finally, it's also worth knowing that you're not limited to describing events: you may also include to-do notes and journal entries, you may wish to set reminders and alarms, and with shared calendars you may wish to mark time out as being free or busy. The good news is that pretty much anything you can do in iCalendar you can reproduce in hCalendar, and you can find many more examples at the official hCalendar Wiki (`http://microformats.org/wiki/hcalendar-examples`).

"rel-" microformats

Remember the `rel` attribute from earlier? That attribute is often used in microformats, and the usage is generally very simple. The rel-license format, for instance, looks like this:

```
<a rel="license" href="http://creativecommons.org➡
/licenses/by-nc-sa/2.5/">➡
Creative Commons License</a>
```

By including a `rel` attribute with a value of `license` in the anchor tag, you can indicate that the destination of the hyperlink is a license for the content contained on the current page. The example I'm using is from my own design blog *Unfortunately Paul*, where the content has been made available under a "Creative Commons Attribution-NonCommercial-ShareAlike 2.5 License," which means that people are free to copy, distribute, and display my published entries and to make derivative works so long as I'm credited, it's for non-profit purposes, and any derivations are released under the same license. Creative Commons is an organization that provides a variety of "some rights reserved" copyright licenses, allowing content authors to release their content into the wild but retain some level of copyright.

The rel-license microformat is already in wide use, particularly thanks to the Creative Commons license generator (`http://creativecommons.org/license/`) that includes it in every generated license. Both Yahoo! (`http://search.yahoo.com/cc`) and Google (`www.google.com/support/bin/answer.py?answer=29508`) provide the means to search for content—which can be textual, audio, video, and so on—that has been released under such licenses, and they do that by searching for the presence of a rel-license microformat.

The rel-nofollow format is even more straightforward:

```
<a rel="nofollow" href="http://horriblenastyman.com">➡
This dingo ate my baby</a>
```

The value of nofollow in the rel attribute indicates to user agents that perform link analysis upon web pages (such as Google) that the destination web page should not be ranked or spidered or crawled in any way; it is a way of providing a clickable link to a person or organization without providing any implicit endorsement of it.

This microformat was actually originally created by Google as a means of preventing comment spam (http://googleblog.blogspot.com/2005/01/preventing-comment-spam.html), where spammers would repeatedly post spam ("visit my cialis soft-tabs holiday rentals in Spain v|agra site" and that sort of thing) in the comment sections of blogs, originally a severe problem for users of the Movable Type blogging software but later also affecting WordPress and Textpattern users as the popularity of those systems grew. The theory was that if blog software included nofollow values in every comment link, spammers would cease to use comment spam as a viable means of gaining page rank. Most popular blog systems now add nofollow values on commenter links by default.

Did it work? Not noticeably—just as e-mail spammers don't appear to selectively pick out the nonresponsive e-mail addresses from the masses they send to, comment spammers aren't leaving those with nofollow implementations out either. But it's not all bad—it no doubt *has* had a positive impact on the proliferation of spam in search results as Google, Yahoo!, and MSN are no longer crawling as many spam links. The only remaining issue is that if people are indiscriminately adding a nofollow value to all comment links, search engines are also no longer crawling *legitimate* comment links either, so it's a bit of a heavy-handed solution that actually breaks Google's own use of link metadata to gauge popularity. Fortunately, some blogging systems now only add nofollow values to comments by authors who have not yet posted a comment—assuming that anyone who has posted previously is therefore safe.

Finally, the rel-tag microformat. We've already touched upon the rel-tag microformat earlier, but let me go over it again. By adding rel="tag" to a hyperlink, you are indicating that the resource referred to in the href can be considered as a category for a particular subject—the content of the <a> becomes the tag. For instance, let's imagine that you had written an article about Nintendo, published on http://joeblade.com. Somewhere within the body of that article, you would include a link that looked like this:

```
<a href="http://joeblade.com/category/nintendo/" rel="tag">Nintendo</a>
```

Spelled out, that means "the resource available at http://joeblade.com/category/nintendo/ is a category (or subject, or tag) page for the subject detailed on *this* page." Anybody clicking that link would end up at a category page that collated all articles on http://joeblade.com that related to the subject of Nintendo, and then they could happily while away the hours reading up on what is clearly the greatest videogame company in the world.

But why bother including rel="tag" at all? Well, by including that link within the body of your article (or before the article, or beneath it—just somewhere where both browsers and aggregators can see it), you indicate to the entire world that your article is of the tag nintendo, allowing content searchers and aggregators such as Technorati to create their own category pages, ones that now include links to your article (e.g., http://technorati.com/tag/nintendo).

The notion of tagging content in this way is big business, not just because of Technorati—which uses them heavily—but also because of Flickr, the hugely popular online photo sharing application, which allows its users to descriptively tag their photos and browse collections of those tags, and YouTube, which allows its users to do the same with uploaded video clips.

The tagging of content has also led to a proliferation of tag-based navigation, sometimes seen as tag clouds, as Figure 5-5 illustrates.

Advertising   blogger   **Bush**   Christianity   **Education**
Environment   Hezbollah   homebuyer-tips   iPod   Iraq   Islam
Israel   Lebanon   Mac   **Microsoft**   most-recent   mp3   **NSA**
Politica   Review   **Sex**   **Terrorism**   War   web-20   **web2.0**
2.0   Windows   wordpress   writely   **youtube**

Figure 5-5. A weighted tag cloud—popular tags appear larger than the less-popular ones.

The idea behind tag-based navigation is that it is more natural and organic than the traditional rigid lists of categories—it is instead more freeform, adapting as you add to it over time. The rel-tag format is in wide use, with most current blog software offering tagging capability either natively or through plug-ins.

VoteLinks

The VoteLinks microformat provides another solution to the same problem that rel-nofollow aims to solve: namely that linking to a source implies endorsement when sometimes you'd rather be condemning. VoteLinks this time makes use of the rev attribute with three allowed values, vote-for, vote-abstain, and vote-against, allowing you to indicate endorsement, neutrality, and condemnation. The rev attribute is used here instead of rel because of the direction of the relationship. Have a look at this example, using rel:

```
<a href="http://example.com/" rel="vote-for">Example</a>
```

Remember how rel works? It describes how the resource indicated by the href location relates to the current document; this means that the preceding example, in plain English, says, "The person or organization located at http://example.com endorses this document," which isn't the meaning that is trying to be conveyed. The rev attribute, on the other hand, implies the opposite:

```
<a href="http://example.com" rev="vote-for">Example</a>
```

This example says, "The originator of this document endorses the person or organization located at http://example.com," which makes much more sense. You can also use this in combination with rel-nofollow, to allow for user agents that react to either one or the other but not both:

```
<a href="http://example.com" rev="vote-against" rel="no-follow">➥
Example</a>
```

At the time of writing, there are no major implementations of this format, though some Firefox extensions may soon provide visual access to the information. Criticism of VoteLinks has centered around the perceived "black-and-white" nature of the voting. For example, if I link to an article by someone who has disagreed with me, but I want people to read it, should I vote for, vote against, or abstain? Personally, I don't think it's that big of a problem—in this instance, I would abstain—as VoteLInks is still quite theoretical, and possibly only of use on occasion when someone wants to poll a very wide audience without using an actual polling system.[4]

XOXO

XOXO stands for eXtensible Open XHTML Outlines and is pronounced "ecks oh ecks oh," "zho-zho," or "sho-sho," depending on whom you ask. It's a very simple format (simpler than the pronunciation, it seems) used for describing an outline of a document or a blogroll-like subscription list. It's very easy to use—this example is from the XOXO Wiki (http://microformats.org/wiki/xoxo):

```
<ol class='xoxo'>
  <li>Subject 1
    <ol>
        <li>subpoint a</li>
        <li>subpoint b</li>
    </ol>
  </li>
  <li>Subject 2
    <ol compact="compact">
        <li>subpoint c</li>
        <li>subpoint d</li>
    </ol>
  </li>
  <li>Subject 3
    <ol>
        <li>subpoint e</li>
    </ol>
  </li>
</ol>
```

As you can see, all that distinguishes a XOXO-formatted outline from a garden-variety ordered (or unordered) list is the presence of a class name of xoxo at the very top, so there's nothing here very remarkable—but wait. Those of you who have been paying attention will notice the presence of the deprecated compact attribute. As discussed earlier, this attribute was designed to indicate to user agents that a list should be rendered

---

4. Technorati used VoteLinks during the 2004 US presidential elections, and http://folksr.de/ experimented with it during the 2006 World Cup.

"in a compact way." In the case of XOXO, the format specification suggests using a CSS2 attribute selector to hide any menu with this attribute, like this:

```
ol[compact="compact"] { display none;}
```

With this, the example preceding would render as shown in Figure 5-6.

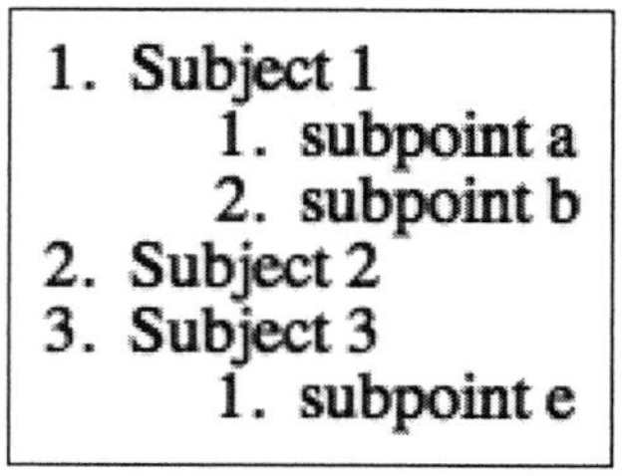

The compact attribute has been deprecated; the brains behind XOXO are aware of it and have claimed to be "repurposing" an obsolete presentational attribute for semantic use. Fair enough, I do the same with the <small> element, but be aware that using the compact attribute will cause your document to fail validation, which may or may not be important to you.

1. Subject 1
    1. subpoint a
    2. subpoint b
2. Subject 2
3. Subject 3
    1. subpoint e

Figure 5-6.
A XOXO-formatted list, with "compact" nested lists set not to display

Remember also that if you use display: none in the way suggested, you'll need to then use JavaScript to allow users to view the compact menu should they wish to. The menu will also be fully visible to any user agent not displaying the CSS or not understanding the CSS, unless said user agent knows what to do with a compact menu (most do not, which is why the attribute is obsolete in the first place).

It is possible to enhance your outline by using some common properties such as text, description, url, title, type, and rel, though these have not been standardized and are merely suggested within the XOXO specification. You can include these properties explicitly within the markup, like this:

```
<ol class='xoxo'>
  <li>
    <dl>
      <dt>text</dt>
        <dd>item 1</dd>
      <dt>description</dt>
        <dd> This item represents the main point ➥
we're trying to make.</dd>
      <dt>url</dt>
        <dd>http://example.com/more.xoxo</dd>
      <dt>title</dt>
        <dd>title of item 1</dd>
      <dt>type</dt>
        <dd>text/xml</dd>
      <dt>rel</dt>
        <dd>help</dd>
    </dl>
  </li>
```

This can be a little unwieldy though, and it's possible to include much of this information with standard (X)HTML attributes, like this:

5

```
<ol class='xoxo'>
  <li><a href="http://example.com/more.xoxo" ➥
title="title of item 1" type="text/xml" rel="help">item 1</a>
    <dl>
       <dt>description</dt>
         <dd>This item represents the main point we're ➥
trying to make.</dd>
    </dl>
  </li>
```

The XOXO format is being used on the Web already (podcast website Odeo displays user subscription lists as XOXO-formatted outlines), though at the time of writing it's not nearly as prevalent as hCard or hCalendar. It can be argued that, as the root class name of xoxo can be implied rather than included explicitly, XOXO is actually used an enormous amount already, but that may be being overly generous.

XFN

XFN, or the XHTML Friends Network, uses the rel attribute, this time to describe, as a list of space-separated values, the relationship between you and the person you're linking to rather than the relationship between documents. With the increasing popularity of online social networks, XFN allows for the creation of a network based upon personal relationships rather than simply "who's linking to whom." It is again, like rel-nofollow and VoteLinks, an attempt to convey additional information about the relationship between A and B (and between B and A, if the two parties are linking to one another with identical or differing values) while remaining within the boundaries of standard markup.

There is a small range of values available (purposefully small—the intention was to create a small range and then expand if it proved necessary, rather than create a large range of values that never got used), grouped into seven categories: friendship, physical, professional, geographical, family, romantic, and identity. The values allowed for each category are as follows:

- **Friendship**: contact, acquaintance, friend
- **Physical**: met
- **Professional**: co-worker, colleague
- **Geographical**: co-resident, neighbor
- **Family**: child, parent, sibling, spouse, kin
- **Romantic**: muse, crush, date, sweetheart
- **Identity**: me (used to link to yourself at a different URL)

They're all fairly self-explanatory, and some of them are symmetric; if you described a relationship with someone you met at a conference with rel="met", the reverse relationship would naturally be the same. Some are inverse; the inverse of rel="child" is rel="parent".

There are many advantages in describing your relationships in this way. Ultimately, this is not so very different from any other social network service such as Friendster.com, but its key difference is that it does not rely on any external service. People are already linking to one another, and XFN doesn't require much in the way of specialist knowledge beyond that which it took to create the link in the first place (unlike, for instance, the Friend of a Friend, or FOAF, service, which requires information stored in RDF-XML—I'll mention this service again in the "The Semantic Web" section later in this chapter). So it's very quick and easy to include this metadata—most blog software already comes with the ability, either natively or via plug-ins, to include XFN information in your lists of links.

It is a very natural way of creating a social network with very little effort, and the more people use it, the richer and more useful the network becomes. And as it's not relying on a single service, but is instead distributed across millions of blogs and other websites, it has no single point of failure either; if one person drops off the Internet, there are many others to keep things going (and provide relationship information even about someone whose web presence is no longer available—whether that's a good or bad aspect, I'll leave up to you).

XFN is already in wide use today, and there are a number of tools that allow you to spider websites to see how people relate to one another such as XFN Graph (http://xfngraph. sourceforge.net/), shown in Figure 5-7, and XFNRoller (http://xfnroll.new-bamboo. co.uk/).

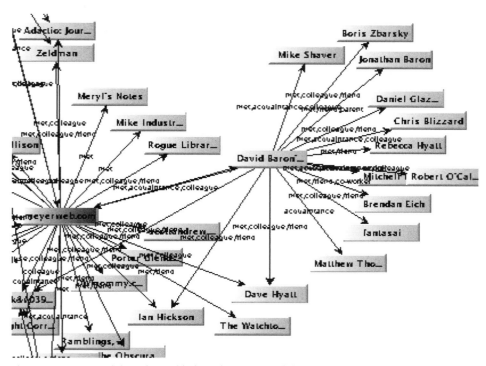

Figure 5-7. XFN Graph in action, spidering Eric Meyer's website

Rubhub (`www.rubhub.com/`) is a simple XFN lookup engine for determining the relationships between people. You enter a URL, and it returns a list containing details of outgoing, reciprocal, and incoming relationships, as Figure 5-8 demonstrates.

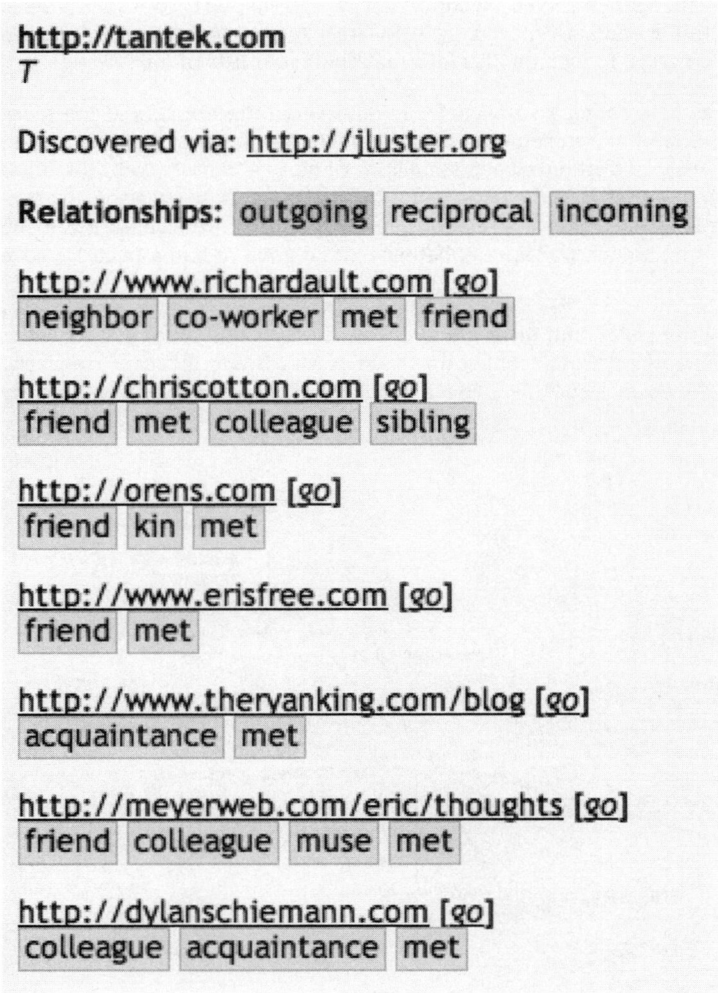

Figure 5-8. A page of Rubhub results, with details of all outgoing, reciprocal, and incoming relationships related to a single website

There's also a wide variety of favelets and browser extensions that reveal XFN metadata as you browse; have a look at the XFN implementations page (`http://microformats.org/wiki/xfn-implementations`) for details.

hReview

Finally we have the hReview microformat, a format that describes reviews of products, businesses, events, places, and so on. I'm covering it here and now, despite it still being in draft form, because it is already in use in various places and makes use of existing microformats as well. The chances are that it won't change in any great way (and if it does, then it is likely to be backwardly compatible with itself as you'll see further in this section) but do check the hReview Wiki (http://microformats.org/wiki/hreview) before implementing it yourself.

The intention of the format is to greater facilitate the sharing, distribution, syndication, and aggregation of reviews. Just as hCard encourages the standardization of contact details and hCalendar encourages the standardization of event listings, hReview encourages the standardization of reviews for much the same purpose; for instance, if you wanted to read reviews of a new brand of LCD television, an aggregator could theoretically deliver to you any number of hReview-formatted reviews in one go, saving you from having to hunt around different review websites and trying to compare disparate review methodologies.

There are only two required components of an hReview: a root class name of hreview and some item info, which must at least provide a full name of the item under review (fn). So at its absolute minimal, an hReview can look like this:

```
<div class="hreview">
  <p class="item"><span class="fn">The Royal Tenenbaums
  </span></p>
  <p>Hilarious, touching and totally original comedy about a
  dysfunctional family's sudden, unexpected reunion.</p>
  <p>The Royal Tenenbaums tells the story of Royal Tenenbaum
  (Gene Hackman) and his wife Etheline (Angelica Huston)
  who had three child prodigies...</p>
</div>
```

Most reviews will come with a little more metadata though (and probably a few more paragraphs of actual review, but that isn't why we're here)—the name of the reviewer, the product type, the date of the review, a rating, and so on. The current hReview specification (0.3 at the time of writing) provides the following properties, all of which are optional except for item as already mentioned: version, summary, type, item, reviewer, dtreviewed, rating, description, tags, permalink, and license.

Let's start by adding a version, which relates to the version of the hReview specification rather than the version of the review itself. By adding in a version number, you're stating that your review is written specifically to that version of the hReview specification. Omitting it means you're stating that your review is backwardly compatible with past versions, which is the preferred case. If you do find you need it or want it, then you add the version like this:

```
<span class="version">0.3</span>
```

This number would be fairly meaningless to anyone not familiar with the hReview spec, though, so you can incorporate that span into a natural sentence, like this:

5

```
<p>This review uses version <span class="version">0.3</span>➥
of the hReview specification.</p>
```

Because the version of the review format is not crucial information, I would suggest visually deemphasizing references to it, perhaps with a smaller font or a low-contrast color.

Next, we'll include a summary, which should be a short overview of the review and can act as a title. In our example, this is as simple as adding a class name of summary to one of the opening paragraphs:

```
<p class="summary">Hilarious, touching and totally original
comedy about a dysfunctional family's sudden, unexpected reunion.</p>
```

Now let's look closer at the item property. We've already included an item and an fn to indicate the name of what's being reviewed, but we can also provide a URL for the item under review and a photo URL. This is also where previous microformats come in—if the item being reviewed is a person or a business, then the item information must be provided in the form of an hCard; if the item is an event, then the item information must be provided in the form of an hCalendar vevent. Because the item we're reviewing is a movie, we'll just provide a URL to the movie's entry on the Internet Movie Database (http://imdb.com):

```
<p class="item"><a href="http://imdb.com/title/tt0265666/" ➥
class="url fn">The Royal Tenenbaums</a></p>
```

Furthermore, we can use the type property to indicate what it is that's being reviewed, with allowed values of product, business, event, person, place, website, and url.[5] Our review is a movie, which is a product:

```
<span class="item"><span class="type">product</span></span>
```

It's probably wise to hide this with CSS, as describing something as a "product" is going to be of little use to your readers. Some types can be inferred; for instance, if the item information is in an hCard, the type will be either a business or a person; similarly, if the item information is in an hCalender vevent, the type is naturally going to be an event.

Who's reviewing this film, anyway?

```
<p>Reviewed by <span class="reviewer vcard">➥
<span class="fn">Paul Haine</span></span></p>
```

As you can see, the hCard crops up here as well. If the reviewer is specified, the reviewer details must be provided as an hCard. The reviewer can be deduced by a competent parser. If no reviewer is found within the hReview, the parser should look at the rest of the page for an <address> element, and if it still cannot provide an author, it should look in any available Atom or RSS feeds for the <author> element. This could be a little unpredictable, so it's best to include reviewer information if possible or explicitly use the name "anonymous" as the reviewer name.

---

5. It's noted within the specification that this list may grow in the future.

How about the date of the review? We use the dtreviewed property here, which must be in the ISO-8601 format. As discussed previously, we can provide that in the form of a title attribute on an <abbr> element to create a human-readable and a machine-readable date at the same time:

```
<abbr class="dtreviewed" title="20060813T1849">August 13, 2006</abbr>
```

The review itself is marked out by the description property. As a typical review could run for several paragraphs and contain lists and other block-level elements, a <div> is the most appropriate element to use here:

```
<div class="description">
  <p>The Royal Tenenbaums tells the story of Royal Tenenbaum
  (Gene Hackman) and his wife Etheline (Angelica Huston)
  who had three child prodigies...</p>
</div>
```

We then have the rating property. A typical hReview will provide a rating from 1 to 5, with 1 being the worst rating and 5 the best. The hReview creator (http://microformats.org/code/hreview/creator) formats ratings with an <abbr> element, a title attribute, and the use of a star entity (★):

```
<abbr title="4" class="rating">➥
&#x2605;&#x2605;&#x2605;&#x2605;&#x2606;</abbr>
```

which displays stars as shown in Figure 5-9.

The title attribute is used here in the same way as with the dtreviewed property: to give aggregators and search engines the actual rating, while the stars are used to give a visual indicator to human readers. But what if you don't want to rate things on a scale of 1 to 5? What if you prefer to give marks out of 10, 15, 20, or more? This is also accounted for with the ability to provide a best or worst value. Imagine that we wanted to rate *The Royal Tenenbaums* as 25 out of 30. In hReview, we would do this:

Figure 5-9.
A four-star rating. The title attribute is used on the <abbr> element to provide an actual numerical value.

```
<p class="rating">Rating: <span class="value">25</span>➥
out of <span class="best">30</span></p>
```

In this way, you're free to use whichever rating system you like (within reason), and hReview aggregators can still determine what your rating of the item is.

Finally, you've seen the tags, permalink, and license properties elsewhere. The tags property is simply the rel-tags microformat described previously in this chapter, the permalink property is actually just rel-bookmark that was discussed back in Chapter 2, and the license property is simply the rel-license format also described previously in this chapter, so there's no need to cover them again here.

As I've said, hReviews are already turning up all over the place. Yahoo! is a particular fan of them, with Yahoo! Local (http://local.yahoo.com/), Yahoo! Tech (http://tech.yahoo.com/), and Yahoo! UK Movie Reviews (http://uk.movies.yahoo.com/movie-reviews/) all now formatting user reviews with hReview properties and giving the format a certain amount of corporate credibility. Other implementations include Cork'd (http://corkd.com/), a wine review site created by Dan Cederholm and Dan Benjamin; OpenGuides (http://openguides.org/), a community-maintained guidebook project; Vitamin (www.thinkvitamin.com/), a web designer resource site; and many others that you can find on the hReview home page along with a range of ways to create reviews, from WordPress plug-ins to Amazon-specific creators.

And so, that's microformats. As you've now seen, there are numerous ways already to implement and take advantage of them, from the hCard, hCalendar, and hReview creators to the Technorati microformats search engine that indexes them, to the Dreamweaver microformats extension (www.webstandards.org/action/dwtf/microformats/) that provides a quick-and-easy way to insert microformats into your content without hand-coding.

In the end, the strength and usefulness of microformats lives or dies with the number of people using them. It's a chicken-and-the-egg scenario: if there are no mainstream tools to take advantage of microformat metadata, there's no point in including microformat metadata on our pages; but if there's no microformat metadata on our pages, nobody will develop the tools. Luckily though, it seems that tools and data are both being very healthily developed right now—there's a lot of enthusiasm about microformats within the web standards world, and many tools have already been created that take advantage of them. The notion of extending our documents in a rich, semantic way is a very web standards way of thinking, which could explain the appeal—we're all striving to write hardcore, well-structured, meaningful markup, and the ideas and guiding principles behind microformats fit very well those efforts.

It is, of course, quite conceivable that they will fail, perhaps being abused by spammers and charlatans like the <meta> element, or perhaps they will simply find a niche but never revolutionize the mainstream. It's very easy to get carried away when something like this is new, so I don't want to embarrass myself by loudly proclaiming now that microformats are the future and everyone should get in on the ground floor, only to look back a year or two later and find that it didn't happen.

But, they *might* be the future, and given how little extra effort it is to encode your <address> as an hCard or your blogroll as an XFN- and XOXO-formatted list, you could help them on their way with very little cost but substantially more gain. And then, if they do turn out to be wildly successful, you'll be able to say that you were in there on the ground floor as well.

> *If you are interested in immersing yourself more deeply in microformats, you'll be interested in the forthcoming book* Microformats *by John Allsop (friends of ED). It should be available in early to mid 2007.*

The Semantic Web

So far, we've just been looking at ways in which (X)HTML can be enhanced with our own home-grown semantics and structures. This is fine; it's easy to implement as you only need to know (X)HTML, there are practically no issues with browser support or compatibility as no new standards are being used, and provided these structures are all well-formed, then a variety of parsers, aggregators, and the like can exploit their presence.

But, using plain-vanilla (X)HTML can only get you so far. Ultimately, (X)HTML is just a markup language for marking up chunks of a document, and there's very little way to express how those chunks relate to one another, what they mean, or even what they are. Because web pages are designed generally for humans first and machines second, we can infer relationships and structure from what we see (or hear, if the content is being read aloud).

For instance, if we are looking at a list of products on an online store, we can work out which price and description relates to which item due to the proximity of the different elements and various other factors—humans are, by and large, pretty good at working these things out. Machines, on the other hand, are not. Because (X)HTML provides no way to say that *this* price and *this* description relate to *this* product—or even to say that *this* is a price and *this* is a description—beyond a very liberal, open classification and identification with the id and class attributes, machines are unable to make much sense of the listing.

If machines *were* able to make sense of such things, understanding how the data related to real-world objects, the advantages would be that it would be easier to share data between disparate applications, and machines would be able to research and gather information with less human intervention. This, then, is the objective of the Semantic Web: to make web pages understandable to machines, to ultimately benefit humans; for the web to not simply be about the interchange of documents, but also about the interchange of data. The Semantic Web project is currently under the direction of Tim Berners-Lee, the creator of the World Wide Web, so it has a certain amount of credibility. As Tim stated in 1999:

"I have a dream for the Web [in which computers] become capable of analyzing all the data on the Web—the content, links, and transactions between people and computers. A 'Semantic Web,' which should make this possible, has yet to emerge, but when it does, the day-to-day mechanisms of trade, bureaucracy and our daily lives will be handled by machines talking to machines. The 'intelligent agents' people have touted for ages will finally materialize."

So, it all sounds wonderful, so long as we don't allow our machines to go all *Terminator* on us, but how's it going to work? Well, the technical specifics of it all are a little beyond the scope of this book, but I'll try and give you a meaningful overview without lapsing into a "The Internet is a series of tubes"-style gaffe.[6]

There are several technologies that make up the Semantic Web. First of all, there's the eXtensible Markup Language, XML. XML allows people to create their own tags to describe their content (for instance, you could store a collection of recipes in XML format with

---

6. If you don't get the reference, you're not online *nearly* enough.

recipe-related tags such as <recipe>, <ingredients>, <quantity>, and so on) and then various scripts, services, and applications can manipulate those tags in a variety of interesting and useful ways. However, using XML doesn't automatically make this content useful to machines as there's no meaning being conveyed. To a human, it's easy to see that the <recipe> is the root container tag, but to a machine that's just a generic root container tag—it may as well be a <div> or a <body>.

The meaning is therefore expressed using the Resource Description Framework, or RDF. RDF works by storing information about what an item is. It does this with a subject/verb/object structure known as a triple, as I mentioned earlier. In other words, an item (for instance, a person, such as myself) has various properties (such as "is the author of"), and these properties have values (*HTML Mastery*). In this way, information about what the objects described by the XML structures actually mean can be expressed. Further to this, each subject, verb, and object is given a Universal Resource Identifier, or URI; this means that each term is tied to a unique definition that allows other people or machines to locate it.

> *For a more detailed overview of RDF, I suggest "What Is RDF?," originally written by Tim Bray in 1998 but updated by Dan Brickley in 2001 and Joshua Tauberer in 2006, at* www.xml.com/pub/a/2001/01/24/rdf.html.

So now we have a syntax (the XML), a dictionary (of sorts) to explain what that syntax means (the RDF), and a map detailing what each of those meanings refers to (the URIs). By describing our content and data in such a way, we're allowing both the data and the rules *about* that data to exist together—allowing any capable system to interpret and utilize it, even if the data and rules were developed in an entirely different system.

It doesn't end there though; this system has a possible flaw, in that multiple databases could conceivably use different URIs for the same thing. For instance, a database describing city features could refer to both *pavement* and *sidewalks*, the same thing but with potentially different URIs. Any system trying to utilize this data needs to somehow know that these should be considered as different terms for the same item.

A solution to this is the use of an **ontology**, a document that defines terms and the relationships between them—basically a taxonomy that uses inheritance principles, classes and subclasses, and a set of logical rules to derive and infer information from it. (For instance, there's an ontology for tags of the microformat variety available here: www.holygoat.co.uk/owl/redwood/0.1/tags/.) These ontologies can then be referred to by any service that needs to determine a meaning. These ontologies are created in another technology known as Web Ontology Language, or OWL for short.

> *Yes, that should probably be WOL instead of OWL, but why pass up an opportunity for a good acronym, eh? OWL is an extension of RDF and is derived from the DAML+OIL Web Ontology Language. Confused yet? It also comes in three varieties: OWL Lite, OWL DL, and OWL Full, and if you're interested in learning more, I suggest looking at the "W3C OWL Web Ontology Language Overview" at* www.w3.org/TR/owl-features/.

The final piece of the puzzle is the notion of **agents**. Agents will be the tools that reach out into the Semantic Web to answer your queries, piecing together data from a variety of sources before returning you an answer (or multiple possible answers). Think of them as intelligent search engines; for instance, if you needed to book an appointment with a doctor who specialized in the treatment of a particular condition, but your appointment shouldn't clash with any other appointment in your diary, you should be treated somewhere within a reasonable distance from your home at a clinic with a trusted rating, and you should be able to afford the treatment. On today's Web, to determine this would require you to

- Locate some appropriately nearby clinics.
- Locate information on the quality of the clinics.
- Locate information on the doctors at the clinics.
- Locate information about possible appointments available at the clinics.
- Cross-check those available appointments with existing appointments in your calendar.
- Check that you can afford the treatment by looking at your bank details.
- Do it all again if nothing appropriate comes up.

On the Semantic Web, because (ideally) data could be freely interchangeable between services—in this case, clinical data, information on the doctors, bank details, personal calendar details, location details—a suitably intelligent agent would be able to filter through all of that information on your behalf, possibly delegating areas of responsibility to other agents, and return to you a list of possibilities. From your perspective, this could take a matter of moments, whereas before it might have taken hours, and you would have had to locate and sift through the data yourself.

But is all of this just theory? Not entirely—though we're a long way off from the situation where agents can seamlessly scour the web for free data and understand it well enough to understand our own queries, there are some implementations already.

The Dublin Core Metadata Initiative

With the current enthusiasm regarding microformats, it's easy to overlook those who have been getting on with metadata quite nicely for a few years now, thank you very much. The Dublin Core Metadata Initiative, or DCMI, is one such initiative, which may not be as fashionable among standards-based designers—certainly not as fashionable as microformats currently are—but nevertheless has been around for roughly 10 years and has carved out a healthy niche in the public and academic sectors; universities, libraries, publishers, governments, and so on. It's a nice reminder to us who are firmly entrenched in the web standards world that there exists a whole lot of other work out there that's worth considering as well.

The DCMI provides, via the Dublin Core Metadata Element Set (DCMES), 15 metadata elements: title, creator, subject, description, publisher, contributor, data, type, format, identifier, source, language, relation, coverage, and rights, all of which are optional and can be repeated within the same document. Those 15 belong to the simple set; there's also a larger **qualified set** that includes audience, provenance, and rightsholder elements plus a number of **qualifiers** that allow you to further specify and refine your meta-data. The intention of Dublin Core is much like that of the original <meta> element: to provide extra information on what a resource *is* and what it contains. The overall aim is to aid in effective search and retrieval. The Dublin Core organization itself describes Dublin Core as being a "small language for making a particular class of statements about resources."

The guiding principles, listed here, of the DCMI have much in common with other meta-data initiatives:

- **The one-to-one principle**: This means that DC metadata refers to one version of a resource and one only; the creator of a digital image of a painting is not necessarily the same as the creator of the original painting.

- **The dumb-down principle**: This relates to the potential for refining the original 15 metadata elements with qualifications; the metadata should still be understandable *without* those qualifications—which are about refining the metadata rather than extending it.

- **Appropriate values**: Basically this just means that it might be a machine reading your metadata but it might also be a human, so use values that are appropriate and useful as an aid to discovery.

Most of the DCMES are pretty self-explanatory, and they can either be included with your content via a <meta> element or a <link> element if the content is (X)HTML, or separately from the content in the form of an RDF file (which is of more use if you're categorizing non-text documents, files, and objects). Let's look at including them within an XHTML document. Take the date property, for instance; within a document, it would be referenced like this:

```
<meta name="DC.date" content="2006-08-16" />
```

This property can be refined by including qualifiers of created, valid, available, issued, modified, dateAccepted, dateCopyrighted, and dateSubmitted. Qualifiers are used like this:

```
<meta name="DC.date.created" content="2006-08-16" />
```

If the DC element is a reference to an external resource, it's preferable to use the <link> element instead:

```
<link rel="DC.relation" href="http://www.example.org/" />
```

Qualifiers of the relation property include isVersionOf, isReplacedBy, replaces, requires, isPartOf, and several others. Usage of qualifiers within a <link> is the same as in <meta>:

```
<link rel="DC.relation.replaces" href="http://www.example.org/" />
```

What about RDF? A DC RDF file could look something like this (this example was taken from "Using Dublin Core," http://dublincore.org/documents/usageguide/#rdfxml):

```
<rdf:RDF
    xmlns:rdf="http://www.w3.org/1999/02/22-rdf-syntax-ns#"
    xmlns:dc="http://purl.org/dc/elements/1.1/">
    <rdf:Description rdf:about=➥
"http://media.example.com/audio/guide.ra">
        <dc:creator>Rose Bush</dc:creator>
        <dc:title>A Guide to Growing Roses</dc:title>
        <dc:description>Describes process for planting
and nurturing different kinds of rose bushes.</dc:description>
        <dc:date> 2001-01-20</dc:date>
    </rdf:Description>
</rdf:RDF>
```

This example is describing an audio recording of a guide to growing roses. The resource was created by someone named Rose Bush on January 20, 2001, and comes with a title and a description. This RDF file can then be stored in a database or on a server and used as a reference point for the audio file.

The DC also includes the notion of a **controlled vocabulary**, which is a set of predefined terms to avoid inconsistencies (like our earlier example of both *pavement* and *sidewalk*). If the vocabulary can be controlled, then metadata can be more accurate and machines more likely to understand it. Examples of such vocabularies include the US Library of Congress Subject Headings and the US National Library of Medicine Medical Subject Headings. A downside is that controlled vocabularies need someone to control them, an administrative body of some kind—someone to create, review, update, and distribute the information. Those creating the metadata must also be trained in using the vocabulary, so they know that there exists an approved term in the first place.

As you might expect of a system that's been around for more than a decade, there's an abundance of tools available for creating, using, and searching for DC metadata. When it comes to viewing DC metadata, there's naturally a Firefox extension to view DC metadata by Patrick Lauke (www.splintered.co.uk/experiments/73/). There's a variety of DC retrieval tools, such as a URL search and citation tool by StudentABC (www.studentabc.com/search), which allows you to retrieve DC metadata from a resource and format it as a citation, and also some DC creation tools, some automated and some not. A detailed list of resources can be found on the DC website (http://dublincore.org/tools/).

Structured Blogging

Structured Blogging (www.structuredblogging.org/), or SB, is a recent initiative that combines microformats with some of the principles of the Semantic Web. Plug-ins are offered for the Movable Type and WordPress blogging platforms that create tailored post windows specific to different types of content. For instance, if you wanted to write a review of *The Royal Tenenbaums* in a regular blog, you would normally insert all of your content into the same window as all of your other articles, reviews or not. While you could style posts in review categories differently with a little server-side script, a little client-side styling, and a bit of cunning, this is only going to change the appearance; underneath that, you're still lumping all of your data in the same way. There's no semantic difference between a review of a movie and, say, a rant about the queues in your local supermarket, or an explanation of a new coding technique.

With the Structured Blogging plug-ins, each type of article comes with a range of type-specific fields. Figure 5-10 is a screenshot from WordPress of the "review movie" type.

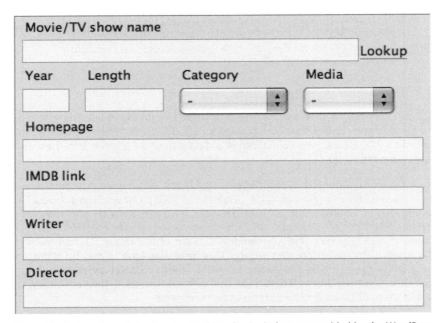

Figure 5-10. A section of the "post a movie review" window, as provided by the WordPress Structured Blogging plug-in

As you can see, there are a lot of extra fields there: links to IMDB, information about the director, the studio, the writer, the cast, the duration, the genre, and so on—enough to create a comprehensive overview of a movie. Alternatively, you could review an album, a book, a café, a club, a restaurant, a hotel, some software, or write up an event, talk about a video or a song, and much more besides; each type comes with its own range of specific fields, allowing the author of the content to focus on filling the information in instead of worrying about how to format with the traditional single–text area blog post editor. Further advantages include being able to access specific fields from the database instead of trying to pick bits out of an entire article.

I said that it used microformats, and it does. The reviews, for instance, are formatted with hReview markup; other formats currently supported are hCard, hCalendar, rel-license, rel-tag, XFN, and XOXO. This markup is present not only when the content is viewed in a web browser, but also within syndicated feeds, so the data and the metadata are intertwined.

What the SB plug-ins also do is output the same content as XML—also within the content, so it's present not just in browsers but in feed readers as well. This XML isn't visible unless the source is viewed, and looks somewhat like this:

```
<script type="application/x-subnode; charset=utf-8">
  <!-- the following is structured blog data for machine readers. -->
  <subnode alternate-for-id="sbentry_1" ➡
  xmlns:data-view="http://www.w3.org/2003/g/data-view#" data- ➡
  view:transformation=➡
  "http://structuredblogging.org/subnode-to-rdf-interpreter.xsl"➡
  xmlns="http://www.structuredblogging.org/xmlns#subnode">
  <xml-structured-blog-entry xmlns="http://www.structuredblogging.org➡
  /xmlns">
  <generator id="wpsb-1" type="x-wpsb-post" version="1"/>
  <review type="review/movie"><subject ➡
  name="The Royal Tenenbaums" year="2001" length="109" ➡
  category="comedy" media="dvd"
  imdburl="http://imdb.com/title/tt0265666/" ➡
  writer="Owen Wilson" director="Wes Anderson" producer="Wes➡
  Anderson" studio="Touchstone Pictures" distributor="Bennyvista"➡
  image="http://www.royaltenenbaums.com/images/royal_tenenbaums_➡
  dvd.jpg">
  <upc media="dvd"/></subject><rating max="5" min="0">4</rating>
  <description>The Royal Tenenbaums tells the story of Royal Tenenbaum
  (Gene Hackman) and his wife Etheline (Angelica Huston) who had three
  child prodigies...</description></review>
  </xml-structured-blog-entry>
  </subnode>
</script>
```

By including this XML within the boundaries of each post, machines are better able to exploit it and understand the meaning of the content of the post itself. Aggregators, applications, and search engines can all use this information without trying to parse the natural language of the review. The XML essentially is a way of saying to external services, "Here's what all this means, do what you like with it."

Criticisms of SB point out one of the flaws that Doctorow discussed in his article on metadata: people are lazy. In an article entitled "Structured Blogging Will Flop" (http://paul.kedrosky.com/archives/002215.html), Paul Kedrosky argues that this level of structuring is simply beyond the interests of most people, pointing out the common situation of Outlook inboxes being packed with thousands of e-mails despite the functionality to create folders and structure. A counter argument is that people are happy to fill out extra fields if there's a perceived benefit to them—hence why thousands of people make little complaint about filling in product details on eBay. Of course, the easier this is, the better, and both eBay and the SB plug-ins contain "lookup" functionality to prefill many common fields.

Other implementations

The Friend of a Friend, or FOAF (www.foaf-project.org) mentioned earlier can be considered as an implementation of the Semantic Web as it uses RDF and OWL to create descriptions of how person A is related to persons X, Y, and Z, and those people can also create their own FOAF file that refers to still more people. It's much like XFN, except it uses a different language (you don't need to know how to write RDF as there's a FOAF-creator available at http://htmlmastery.com/s/foaf/). There are also existing ways to browse FOAF data, such as the FOAF Explorer (http://xml.mfd-consult.dk/foaf/explorer/), Foafnaut (http://foafnaut.org/), and FoaFiler (www.foafiler.com/).

Other implementations include Piggy Bank (http://simile.mit.edu/piggy-bank/), a Firefox extension that turns the browser into a "Semantic Web browser" by extracting information from existing web pages and storing it locally in RDF (either by extracting from existing RDF files or by a process known as "screen scraping"). That data can then be browsed independently from the original website and in conjunction with data from other websites—for instance, combining restaurant location information, cinema times, and Google Maps data to allow you to plan your evening through one interface, rather than three different websites.

> It's true that there are plenty of "mash-ups" between Google Maps and other services, but these all still require somebody to code it up for you; the idea behind the Semantic Web is that all data would be interoperable, so you wouldn't need to create special cases—everything would just work with everything else.

There are criticisms of the Semantic Web, though—there are concerns, for instance, about a possible lack of privacy. As the system relies upon everything (not just web pages but people too) being uniquely identifiable, it could be much harder to remain anonymous; there's also an issue of censorship; if the machines can understand our data that much easier, then it therefore becomes easier to recognize and block certain types of content—a handy ability for both repressive governments *and* overzealous parents.

Another criticism is that there appears to be a need for a rigid taxonomy, which isn't where the web appears to be heading right now, preferring loose, organic collections of user-authored categories, sometimes referred to as a **folksonomy**. Could the Semantic Web make use of such collections?

Despite these concerns, it remains an area with a lot of potential to make life easier for us all, so it's certainly worth keeping an eye on where it goes in the future.

Web 2.0

To round off this chapter, let's talk about **Web 2.0**, something that I'm sure many of you have heard of already. The most common Web 2.0–related question I've heard is, "What is it?" and the answer can depend on whom you ask. Is it Ajax? Is it marketing? Is it Flickr? Is it Google Maps? Is it the Semantic Web, a concept, a methodology, a new way of thinking? The answer is all of the above (just not necessarily all at once).

Web 2.0 began life as a title of a suits-and-boots web conference by O'Reilly (www.oreillynet.com) in 2003, and was used simply as a means of explaining to the crowd of VCs and corporate minions that not only was the web not going away but that it seemed to be changing for the better. New websites and web-based applications were continuing to crop up, companies that had survived the dot.com bubble burst appeared to be thriving, and people were more and more becoming not just *spectators* of content but *producers* of it as well. As a marketing term, Web 2.0 is quite effective, indicating a new and improved "version" of the web, but a lot of the typical Web 2.0 behaviors stemmed from websites that predate the term by a good number of years.

These days, Web 2.0 means a lot more than just a management-friendly buzzword, having been appropriated by the web development community at large to refer to a new ideology about how websites and web applications ought to be developed, an ideology that has much in common with the ideas found in microformats and the Semantic Web—open, sharing networks where data is interoperable and people participate as much as they consume (if not more).

There are a few elements that people have come to associate with self-styled Web 2.0 sites and applications; on the design side we see reflections, drop shadows, and pastel colors, and on the code side, we see Ajax in action and references to Python and Ruby on Rails. So common have these elements become that you can even check to see whether your website is Web 2.0 by running it through a tongue-in-cheek Web 2.0 Validator (http://web2.0validator.com/). It's easy to make fun, but the visuals can be just as important as the functionality; delivering a rich, usable, and innovative interface to the user is a key Web 2.0 concept.

There are several other guiding principles as laid out in "What is Web 2.0" by Tim O'Reilly (www.oreillynet.com/pub/a/oreilly/tim/news/2005/09/30/what-is-web-20.html). One of these is "the web as platform," basically meaning that the Web itself is used as the basis of your applications rather than the local operating system, leading to a greater level of device independence and greater mobility; your data is no longer tied to a specific desktop PC.

Using the web as an application base is not a new idea—go back a few years to when Microsoft and Netscape were both trying to provide *the* browser via which you would access the Web, and you'll find very similar notions then. The difference between then and now is that it's less about the browser and more about the web services themselves. As it turned out, there wasn't as much value in being the default browser as hoped for; instead, the value came from the services online.

Then there's the notion of harnessing collective intelligence—Wikipedia, BitTorrent (a file-sharing network where you share chunks of the same file you're downloading, while you're downloading it), Flickr, Amazon, and del.icio.us (a web-based bookmark manager with social networking capability) all do this, with their usefulness determined by the number of people using the services. The fact that the data these services collate is also easy to include on your own pages and in your own services is very important; I've mentioned several times now the notion that data should be interoperable and easily accessible.

Web 2.0, and what it means, has provoked seemingly endless debate online, but I think once you get past the hype, the marketing and the pastel-flavored gradients, there exists some great ideas that ultimately benefit all of us. Anything that can make content easier to find and use, anything that can make the machines do more of the work instead of the other way around, anything that puts people at the heart of the Web, can only be a good thing.

Summary

As you can see, there's a lot more to online metadata than just stuffing <meta> elements with keywords and descriptions, and there's a lot you can do to enhance your content no matter what level of ability you're at, from ensuring you use semantic class and ID names, to microformatting your data, all the way up to using XML and associated technologies.

Once you've started including metadata in your pages, how little or how much you take advantage of it is up to you. Perhaps you just want to use semantic class names to make your markup more understandable and more reusable. Perhaps you just want to mark up your contact details as an hCard so you start turning up in microformat-specific searches. Perhaps you won't take advantage of it yourself, but allow others to take advantage of it instead. Whatever the situation, including accurate metadata may be an extra overhead on the author, but ultimately everyone benefits from it, and the more people get on board, the more useful it will be in the future.

6 RECOGNIZING SEMANTICS

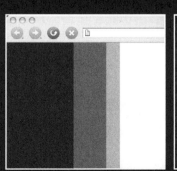

An important part of creating well-formed, well-structured, semantically-rich websites is recognizing the opportunities to use semantic and structural markup when they come along—and they come along more often than people realize. Many web authors, particularly those transitioning from table-based layouts to CSS-based layouts, can easily overlook the fact that the average layout can be teeming with semantic and structural opportunities: paragraphs, headings, lists, and more.

The purpose of this chapter is to help you learn to see a design structurally and semantically instead of simply visually, to learn to recognize opportunities to hook scripts and styles onto meaningful elements. We'll look at a range of common page elements—navigation lists, footers, decorative text fragments, and so on—and examine how best to convert them into solid, well-formed (X)HTML representations.

Throughout this chapter, I'll talk about the dreaded *divitis*, *span-mania*, and *classitis*. These are problems that most of us have suffered from to some degree or another. They occur when your markup becomes saturated with unnecessary structural markup—with divs, spans, and class attributes, the three worst offenders—usually as a result of thinking too much about how a particular page element *looks* and not enough about what it *means*, and also from not being aware of the alternative markup options.

Avoiding divitis

The habit of using divs in place of structural markup such as headings and paragraphs was not initially a problem of bad practice, but of bad browsers. The problem arose when Netscape 4 was taken into consideration. A web author could include, for instance, an <h1> on his or her page, and then override its default margins and padding with CSS—except Netscape wouldn't *override* those default values, but would instead *add* to them, making it that much harder to get your design pixel-perfect in both Netscape 4 and Internet Explorer 4/5. The <div> element, on the other hand, comes with no default margins or padding, so a <div> with 30px of padding looks the same in both major browsers. Divitis in this case was hard to avoid.

Nowadays, however, there is no longer any excuse for using a <div> when there's perfectly good structural and semantic markup available to us. Although there may be variations in margins and padding across browsers, these differences will normally be trivial and easy to override with CSS.

> *An extreme method of dealing with margins and padding is with the Global White Space Reset technique, described here:* http://leftjustified.net/journal/2004/10/19/global-ws-reset.

When it comes to marking up our content, dozens of different tags are available to us. When it comes to styling, each element can be styled to include its own background color; a background image (one that can repeat horizontally, vertically, or both); and a border on the left, right, top and bottom sides, each of which can be given a unique color and style. And you can also apply margins, padding, and a wide range of font styles. The modern-day web designer is not lacking choice.

But let's just be clear on something: using a <div> is not necessarily a *bad* thing, and I would be surprised if you could build a complex website without using a <div> at some point. <div> was created for a reason—in this case, to describe divisions within your content. If the elements on your page can be grouped thematically (some into a header, some into a sidebar, some into a footer), then do so. That's what <div> is there to do, and it will make your life easier in the long run.

> Also see the <section> element that's part of the XHTML 2.0 draft specification. Chapter 7 provides further details on this element.

Avoiding divitis is more of a methodology than a simple checklist of "Use X tag in place of <div>." The key is to stop thinking *visually*. If you are working from a design in Photoshop or Fireworks, then when it comes to building the site, I've found that it helps to begin by just forgetting about the style and typing in all your content—or placeholder text if you don't have all of your content at the time (http://lipsum.com is a good source of filler text)—straight into your document. By "content," I mean *everything*—not just body text but also any navigation, headers, footers, and so on. If something may end up as an image in the end (e.g., a corporate logo), then don't worry about it at this stage. Just include some text in its place; you can always replace it with an inline image later if required.

As you do this, think about the content you're typing, think about how you would describe it to someone else, and think about what tags are available that fit your description. Forget about how things are going to look for now—don't think of an <h1> as being "large, ugly, and bold" because that's just how it appears by default; everything can be restyled.

Assume while you're doing this that the <div> tag does not exist. Doing this will help you avoid divitis, because it will force you to think of alternatives. So, where you may once have marked up your company logo—often the first element on the page—like this:

```
<div id="header"><img src="logo.gif" alt="Company name" /></div>
```

you'll now need to find an alternative. So, what to use instead? The most likely candidate to me seems to be the first-level heading (the <h1>) making your company name (or blog title, etc.) the most important heading on the page:

```
<h1><img src="logo.gif" alt="Company name" /></h1>
```

As noted in Chapter 2, whether your website/company name gets to be wrapped in an <h1> or whether your page title or blog article headline gets that honor instead is pretty much up to you—there are no hard and fast rules about this. Similarly, the number of times you use an <h1> on a page is also not set in stone, though you'll find the general consensus is often that there should be only one. Also, wrapping *everything* in an <h1> is an old search engine optimization trick, so overuse could see you being penalized.

6

A quick aside: When displaying alt *text in place of an image, most modern browsers will respect the surrounding markup and display the text according to either the browser defaults (so large and bold in the case of the* <h1> *) or any defined styles for that element. For this reason, it's a very good idea to test your site with images disabled and make sure that the* alt *text is readable—it just being present in the markup may not always be enough, particularly if you're using dark background colors that will still be displayed even if images are not. It's also a good reason to avoid including the optional* width *and* height *attributes on the* <img>*, as the* alt *text may not entirely fit within the boundaries and thus become unreadable.*

Styling the body

An element that often gets overlooked when it comes to style and structure is the <body> itself. You'll often see something like this:

```
<body><div id="container">...
```

But people forget that the <body> can also be a container—it can be given a width and margins, it can be centered within the browser viewport, and so on. For instance, the simple, single-column layout in Figure 6-1 doesn't need a master container div.

Lorem ipsum

Lorem ipsum dolor sit amet, consectetuer adipiscing elit. Duis massa diam, consequat ut, porttitor ut, mollis sed, nisl. Quisque facilisis magna nec lacus. Nam libero massa, auctor ut, viverra non, luctus sit amet, sem. Mauris eget enim at ante varius scelerisque. Sed dapibus augue et lacus. Cras varius posuere dolor. Phasellus et purus et ante fringilla bibendum. Lorem ipsum dolor sit amet, consectetuer adipiscing elit. Suspendisse potenti. Vestibulum ante ipsum primis in faucibus orci luctus et ultrices posuere cubilia Curae; Ut condimentum, libero quis mollis pellentesque, ante velit congue ipsum, in aliquet enim lorem eget nisi. Etiam eu velit ac libero fringilla sagittis. Vestibulum quis velit eu nulla facilisis volutpat. Maecenas augue velit, dignissim sed, bibendum at, molestie ultrices, nulla. Nunc odio nisi, convallis non, rhoncus at, lobortis in, nibh. Curabitur diam lectus, consectetuer non, mattis eu, facilisis sed, libero. Mauris sit amet purus a odio ornare aliquet. Vestibulum at massa id augue sollicitudin mattis. Proin posuere magna vel lorem varius semper. In interdum.

Figure 6-1. A simple, single-column web page

> *I've heard it argued in the past that using a wrapper or container <div> is no worse, semantically speaking, than wrapping all of your content in a single-celled table, which would also give you that elusive 100% height container. I disagree with this. By including your content within a table—even a single-celled table—you're saying to the world at large that your website consists exclusively of tabular data, which is unlikely to be true.*

All we need to do is directly style the body with the same styles we would have applied to the container. In this case, we just need to center the body and give it a border and some margins. First, let's deal with the centering, which involves a short digression.

When we wanted some content centered in the past, we used to use the <center> tag, like this:

```
<center>Your content</center>
```

This is clearly presentational, and as noted earlier, the tag is deprecated in HTML 4.0[1] and absent from XHTML 1.0, so it shouldn't be used. I've noticed that the alternative, particularly in WYSIWYG-generated markup, is to do either this:

```
<div align="center>Your content</div>
```

or this:

```
<div style="text-align: center">Your content</div>
```

Both of these options will get the job done, it's true, but if you do it these ways, then you may as well be using <center>, as it has the same meaning and is just as presentational. The first example uses the deprecated align attribute, and the second example uses an inline style—both are including presentational information within the document markup.

Instead, use CSS. If you want to center the content within an element, then use the text-align property:

```
p {text-align: center;}
```

If you apply that to only one paragraph, you can see that the text is centered within the paragraph but the paragraph itself remains in the default alignment, as shown in Figure 6-2.

6

---

1. Deprecated with a vengeance—the tag appears only once, in only one sentence (see http:// htmlmastery.com/s/center). In actual fact, this tag was introduced by Netscape simply as a shorthand way of writing <div align="center"> and was only included in the HTML 3.2 specification because it was already in common usage.

Lorem ipsum dolor sit amet, consectetuer adipiscing elit. Duis massa diam, consequat ut, porttitor ut, mollis sed, nisl. Quisque facilisis magna nec lacus. Nam libero massa, auctor ut, viverra non, luctus sit amet, sem. Mauris eget enim at ante varius scelerisque. Sed dapibus augue et lacus. Cras varius posuere dolor. Phasellus et purus et ante fringilla bibendum. Lorem ipsum dolor sit amet, consectetuer adipiscing elit. Suspendisse potenti.

Vestibulum ante ipsum primis in faucibus orci luctus et ultrices posuere cubilia Curae; Ut condimentum, libero quis mollis pellentesque, ante velit congue ipsum, in aliquet enim lorem eget nisi. Etiam eu velit ac libero fringilla sagittis. Vestibulum quis velit eu nulla facilisis volutpat. Maecenas augue velit, dignissim sed, bibendum at, molestie ultrices, nulla. Nunc odio nisi, convallis non, rhoncus at, lobortis in, nibh. Curabitur diam lectus, consectetuer non, mattis eu, facilisis sed, libero. Mauris sit amet purus a odio ornare aliquet. Vestibulum at massa id augue sollicitudin mattis. Proin posuere magna vel lorem varius semper. In interdum.

Figure 6-2. The first paragraph has had `text-align: center;` applied to it, centering the text within the paragraph

The `text-align` property doesn't just affect text either—an image within a paragraph would also be affected.

If you want to center a block on the page, then use the `margin` property:

```
p {margin-left: auto; margin-right: auto;}
```

This informs the browser that the left and right margins of the element in question should expand automatically to fit within its container, which means that for this to work, the `<p>` either needs to be in a container with an explicit width or it needs to have an explicit width itself. If no width is specified, then the width value itself defaults to auto, and in such a case, those left and right margins then default to zero.[2] So, after adding some width, we end up with the result shown in Figure 6-3.

Lorem ipsum dolor sit amet, consectetuer adipiscing elit. Duis massa diam, consequat ut, porttitor ut, mollis sed, nisl. Quisque facilisis magna nec lacus. Nam libero massa, auctor ut, viverra non, luctus sit amet, sem. Mauris eget enim at ante varius scelerisque. Sed dapibus augue et lacus. Cras varius posuere dolor. Phasellus et purus et ante fringilla bibendum. Lorem ipsum dolor sit amet, consectetuer adipiscing elit. Suspendisse potenti.

Vestibulum ante ipsum primis in faucibus orci luctus et ultrices posuere cubilia Curae; Ut condimentum, libero quis mollis pellentesque, ante velit congue ipsum, in aliquet enim lorem eget nisi. Etiam eu velit ac libero fringilla sagittis. Vestibulum quis velit eu nulla facilisis volutpat. Maecenas augue velit, dignissim sed, bibendum at, molestie ultrices, nulla. Nunc odio nisi, convallis non, rhoncus at, lobortis in, nibh. Curabitur diam lectus, consectetuer non, mattis eu, facilisis sed, libero. Mauris sit amet purus a odio ornare aliquet. Vestibulum at massa id augue sollicitudin mattis. Proin posuere magna vel lorem varius semper. In interdum.

Figure 6-3. A centered paragraph

As you can see, the entire paragraph has been centered on the page, but the text within the paragraph remains aligned to the default left.

So that's how content gets centered these days, which means that to center our `<body>`, we just need to do this:

---

2. See `www.w3.org/TR/REC-CSS2/visudet.html#q6`.

```
body {
  margin-left: auto;
  margin-right: auto;
  width: 20em;
}
```

Our example also has a visible border and a background color. Again, this can be achieved by styling the body directly:

```
body {
  background-color: #ccc;
  border: 1px solid black;
  margin-left: auto;
  margin-right: auto;
  padding: 20px;
  width: 20em;
}
```

Now it looks as shown in Figure 6-4.

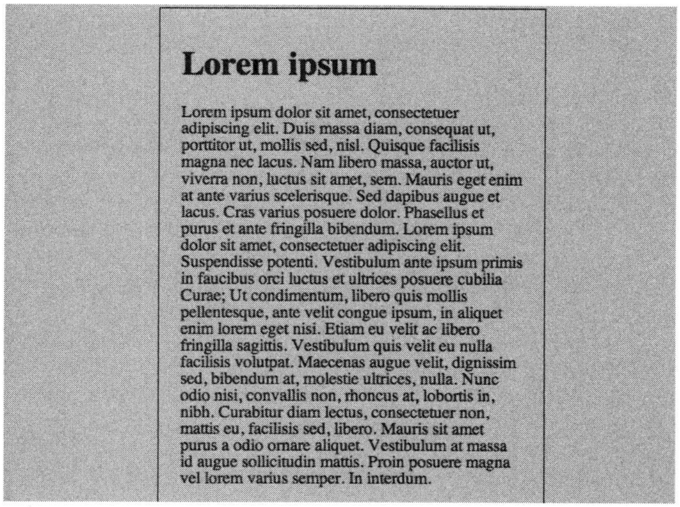

Figure 6-4. The body has been centered and bordered, but something's not right . . .

Ahh . . . what's happened here? The dimensions of the body are clear: the column of text is narrow, it has a border, and its been centered on the page, just as we wanted. But the background properties (in this case, background-color) are not respecting that, filling the entire viewport instead. This is because browsers treat the <body> element in a "special" way, different from that of a regular <div>, and it's this special treatment that allows you to, for instance, set a vertically repeating background image on your page that runs the full height of your browser, even if there's no content, like this (see Figure 6-5):

```
body { background: url(body_bg.gif) top left repeat-y;)
```

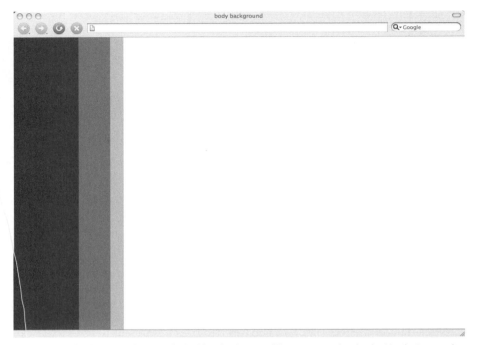

Figure 6-5. The body has been styled with a background image repeating in the Y axis. It stretches the full height of the browser viewport, even though there's no content on the page and even when the viewport is resized.

You may have tried this with a <div> before and found one of the most well-known limitations of using CSS over tables for layout: while a table could be created, given a width and height of 100%, and then scale to fill the viewport, <div> elements just don't work that way (see Figure 6-6):

```
div { background: url(body_bg.gif) top left repeat-y;)
```

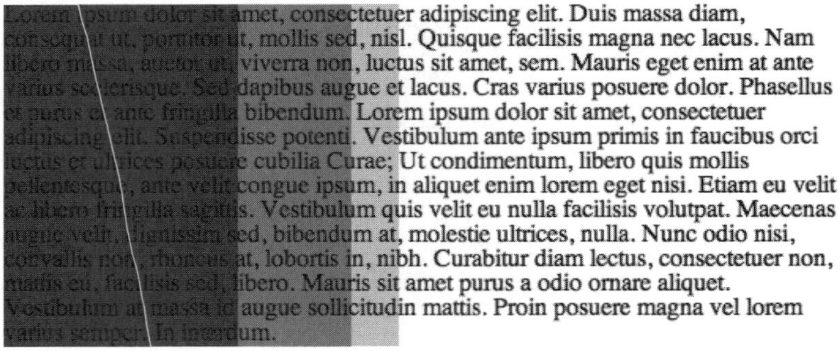

Lorem ipsum dolor sit amet, consectetuer adipiscing elit. Duis massa diam, consequat ut, porttitor ut, mollis sed, nisl. Quisque facilisis magna nec lacus. Nam libero massa, auctor ut, viverra non, luctus sit amet, sem. Mauris eget enim at ante varius scelerisque. Sed dapibus augue et lacus. Cras varius posuere dolor. Phasellus et purus a ante fringilla bibendum. Lorem ipsum dolor sit amet, consectetuer adipiscing elit. Suspendisse potenti. Vestibulum ante ipsum primis in faucibus orci luctus et ultrices posuere cubilia Curae; Ut condimentum, libero quis mollis pellentesque, ante velit congue ipsum, in aliquet enim lorem eget nisi. Etiam eu velit ac libero fringilla sagittis. Vestibulum quis velit eu nulla facilisis volutpat. Maecenas augue velit, dignissim sed, bibendum at, molestie ultrices, nulla. Nunc odio nisi, convallis non, rhoncus at, lobortis in, nibh. Curabitur diam lectus, consectetuer non, mattis eu, facilisis sed, libero. Mauris sit amet purus a odio ornare aliquet. Vestibulum at massa id augue sollicitudin mattis. Proin posuere magna vel lorem varius semper. In interdum.

Figure 6-6. The div is only as large as the sum total of its height plus any margin, padding, or height/min-height values applied to it.

In this case, the div will stretch vertically only if there is content in it, and if height, min-height, or padding has been applied to it.

For our example, where we're styling the <body> directly, we need our <body> to act like a <div>; otherwise, the background color will overspill. One solution is to style the <html> element, because applying background properties to <html> will cause browsers to treat *that* element in this special way, and the <body> will then treated just like any other <div>.

```
html { background-color: white; }
```

That does the trick, as shown in Figure 6-7.

Lorem ipsum

Lorem ipsum dolor sit amet, consectetuer adipiscing elit. Duis massa diam, consequat ut, porttitor ut, mollis sed, nisl. Quisque facilisis magna nec lacus. Nam libero massa, auctor ut, viverra non, luctus sit amet, sem. Mauris eget enim at ante varius scelerisque. Sed dapibus augue et lacus. Cras varius posuere dolor. Phasellus et purus et ante fringilla bibendum. Lorem ipsum dolor sit amet, consectetuer adipiscing elit. Suspendisse potenti. Vestibulum ante ipsum primis in faucibus orci luctus et ultrices posuere cubilia Curae; Ut condimentum, libero quis mollis pellentesque, ante velit congue ipsum, in aliquet enim lorem eget nisi. Etiam eu velit ac libero fringilla sagittis. Vestibulum quis velit eu nulla facilisis volutpat. Maecenas augue velit, dignissim sed, bibendum at, molestie ultrices, nulla. Nunc odio nisi, convallis non, rhoncus at, lobortis in, nibh. Curabitur diam lectus, consectetuer non, mattis eu, facilisis sed, libero. Mauris sit amet purus a odio ornare aliquet. Vestibulum at massa id augue sollicitudin mattis. Proin posuere magna vel lorem varius semper. In interdum.

Figure 6-7.
The <html> root element has been styled, which causes the <body> element to be treated as a regular <div>.

Rounded-corner menus

Now consider Figure 6-8.

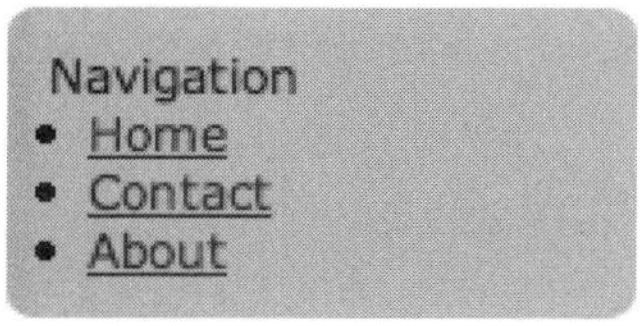

Navigation
- Home
- Contact
- About

Figure 6-8. A navigation list with a rounded top and bottom

The temptation here can often be to create markup such as this:

```
<div id="toproundedcorners"></div>
<div>Navigation</div>
  <ul>
    <li><a href="/">Home</a></li>
    <li><a href="/contact/">Contact</a></li>
    <li><a href="/about/">About</a></li>
  </ul>
<div id="bottomroundedcorners"></div>
```

To start with, let's look at how the markup can be improved, and forget about those rounded corners for now. This is just a list with a heading, so it should be marked up simply as follows:

```
<h4>Navigation</h4>
<ul>
    <li><a href="/">Home</a></li>
    <li><a href="/contact/">Contact</a></li>
    <li><a href="/about/">About</a></li>
  </ul>
```

> *I've chosen to use <h4> in this example just because it's a low-level heading, denoting less importance than the higher levels, but what you use will depend on your circumstances, what other headings are on the page, and how important you deem this list to be.*

Now, those corners—we don't need any <div> tags, nor do we need to use any inline images. Because the corners are purely decorative, we should keep them out of the markup and they should instead be included with CSS, as background images. Remember that every block element can be given its own background image, and that these can be positioned anywhere within that element. In our example, we have five available blocks to use—an <h4>, a <ul>, and each of the <li> elements—more than enough for our purposes. The uppermost rounded corner image can be included as a background to the <h4>, while the bottom image can be included as a background to the <ul>, positioned on the bottom. First, here's the <h4>:

```
h4 {
   background: url(toproundedcorner.gif) top left no-repeat;
}
```

Figure 6-9 shows the result.

Navigation

Figure 6-9. The text overlaps the image.

Not quite what we want—the rounded edge needs to sit above the text, but here it's directly behind it. We could give the <h4> a fixed height, but that wouldn't help, as the size of the element would increase downward and the text would remain in the same place. So instead, we need to add some padding:

```
h4 {
    background: url(toproundedcorner.gif) top left no-repeat;
    padding-top: 10px;
}
```

This creates a buffer zone for the image to sit in, and it has the advantage that if the text size is increased, the space reserved for the image will remain the same, as shown in Figure 6-10.

Figure 6-10. The image now sits above the text.

Figure 6-11 shows the image with the text size increased a bit.

Figure 6-11. Still fits . . .

Including the bottom image works along the same principles. First the image is included:

```
ul {
    background: url(bottomroundedcorner.gif) bottom left no-repeat;
}
```

Then a touch of padding is added to create a space for the image to rest in:

```
ul {
    background: url(bottomroundedcorner.gif) bottom left no-repeat;
    padding-bottom: 10px;
}
```

And that's our div-less headed menu with rounded corners.

News excerpts

Another common page element is a news headline or blog excerpt, similar to the one shown in Figure 6-12.

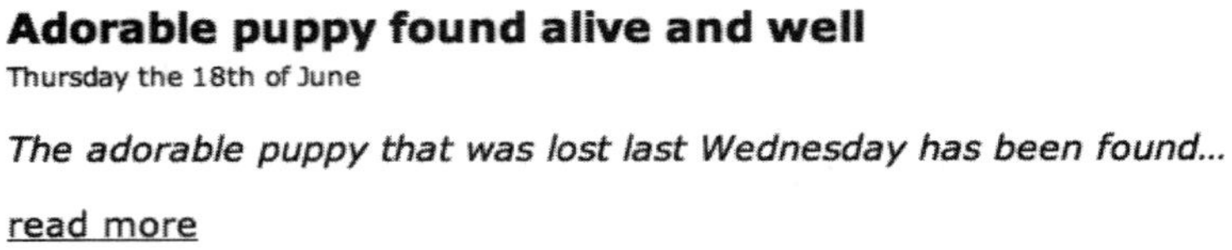

Adorable puppy found alive and well
Thursday the 18th of June

The adorable puppy that was lost last Wednesday has been found...

read more

Figure 6-12. A news headline with date, excerpt, and a read more link

This could very easily be a festival of <div>:

```
<div class="newsitem">
  <div class="headline">Adorable puppy found alive and well</div>
  <div class="date">Thursday the 18th of June</div>
  <div class="newsstory">The adorable puppy that was lost last ➡
Wednesday has been found...</div>
    <div class="readmorelink"><a href="/fullstory.html">➡
read more</a></div>
</div>
```

Let's again forget about appearances and think about the meaning of each item. First of all, we see a headline. As I'm sure you're aware by now, anything that can be described as a headline is likely to need to be marked up as an <hn> of some kind—let's go with an <h3> for now.

```
<h3>Adorable puppy found alive and well </h3>
```

Then there's the date. There's no <date> element, so what can we use here? I'd say it should be a paragraph, but you might also consider it to be a <span> with a meaningful class name of "date-time," "datetime," or something similar—endowing a nonsemantic element with your own semantics. Or you could use the <abbr> trick you learned from the section on microformats in the previous chapter. Just remember that as inline elements, those must be included in a block element. Does this mean you're resigned to using a <p>?

No. Look at that first <div> that contains the whole block: <div class="newsitem">. This is actually a <div> with a purpose—it's denoting where one news item begins and ends, so it's fine to leave this one in, and it also means you don't have to describe everything within another block-level element. Because of this, it would be perfectly valid to leave the date floating on its own if you wanted to, but that would make it trickier to style; you would have to style the surrounding <div>, allow that text fragment to inherit the styles, and then override them if you wanted the other elements to appear differently.

The presence of the wrapper <div> will also help us to distinguish between headings and paragraphs that are part of a news item and those headings and paragraphs that are not, which is useful if you wish to style or script your news elements in a different fashion from your non-news elements.

Then we have the news story itself, which in our example is a single paragraph, presumably an excerpt from the main story. So, as I've just said, it's a paragraph:

```
<p>The adorable puppy that was lost last Wednesday has been
found...</p>
```

Finally, we come to the read more link. This can be treated in the same way as the date—it could be a paragraph, or it could be a generic <span>, or it could even just be wrapped in an <a> and left as is. So ultimately, our almost-div-less news item will look more or less like this:

```
<div class="newsitem">
  <h3>Adorable puppy found alive and well </h3>
  <span class="datetime">Thursday the 18th of June </span>
  <p>The adorable puppy that was lost last Wednesday has ➡
been found...</p>
  <a href="/fullstory.html">read more</a>
</div>
```

It's lean, meaningful, and easier to target with CSS selectors:

```
.newsitem {}
.newsitem h3 {}
.newsitem .datetime {}
.newsitem p {}
.newsitem a {}
```

I think that the ultimate example of divitis has to be when people try to create tables with divs instead of table markup, after taking too literally the notion that "tables are bad." If it's tabular data—that's any content that logically fits in a row/column structure—use a table, because although it's possible to make a div-based layout look like a table, the relationships between the data and headers are completely lost, making it all but useless if CSS is removed. Refer to Chapter 3 for more information on tables.

> *Eric Meyer created a tableless calendar as a demonstration of how a div-based calendar created far more inefficient markup than one of the table-based variety, though he also noted that it was a good way to learn how the CSS* float *property operated. See* http://archivist.incutio.com/viewlist/css-discuss/35082 *for more information.*

Footers

Which of the following two examples is preferable:

```
<div id="footer"><p>© 2006 Paul Haine</p></div>
<p id="footer">© 2006 Paul Haine</p>
```

Is the first example a case of divitis or not? Possibly—this is one of those borderline cases that can cause small holy wars between designers. The answer is, I think, yes it is, and no it isn't, and even if it is then it's only a mild case anyway.

The first example appears to be using an extraneous <div>. Because the entire content is also encapsulated in a <p>, you don't really need the <div> as well. But isn't the <div> marking out a distinct section? Yes, it is, but if any adjacent sections above or below the footer (if, in fact, you'd have any sections below a footer) are contained in their own

<div>, then the existence of a distinct footer section can be implied. So, it's an unnecessary <div>.

However, it may be worth thinking ahead. If you ever need to include a *second* paragraph in your footer, then the second example will no longer work, and you'll need to include a containing <div>, so if that may be possible, then why not include it just in case?

Avoiding span-mania

A similar condition to divitis exists where <span> is overused or misused, and this is sometimes known as *span-mania*, *spanitis*, and other variations on the theme. It's generally not as prevalent as divitis, but it does happen, and for the same reasons. As with <div>, though, using <span> is not necessarily a bad thing—you're not automatically docked ten web-standards points per <span>—so long as it's used with intelligence and purpose.

Avoiding overuse is, again, simply a matter of stopping to think about the meaning of your content and identifying a possible alternative tag. For instance, remember this example from Chapter 1?

```
<p><span class="leadingWords">The first</span> ➥
two words of this paragraph can now be styled differently.</p>
```

Let's think about this some more. Does this really need to be a <span>? There's no CSS available that can target an arbitrary number of words in a paragraph, so there needs to be *something* there to hook our style onto. We need to think about what we're trying to achieve by styling those first two words differently from the rest of the text. Are we trying to emphasize those words? If that's the case, we should probably be using either <em> or <strong>:

```
<p><em class="leadingWords">The first</em> ➥
two words of this paragraph can now be styled differently.</p>
```

This can still be styled in any way you like, just as the <span> could be, for instance (see Figure 6-13):

```
em.leadingWords { font-style: normal; font-variant: small-caps; }
```

THE FIRST two words of this paragraph can now be styled differently.

Figure 6-13. The two leading words are now both visually and semantically emphasized.

It's a judgment call—decide what you're trying to achieve and then think about if there's a more meaningful tag available. In the preceding example, you might consider this to be a purely presentational effect, in which case it's better to remain with the <span>.

Another example I've seen in the wild is markup like this:

```
<span class="error">All required form fields
need to be completed</span>
```

Although the author-defined semantics present in the class name are fine, there's a better alternative to using a <span>:

```
<strong class="error">All required form fields
need to be completed</strong>
```

The author-defined semantics are now completed by the <strong> tag, which indicates that the content should be strongly emphasized. You don't actually *need* the class name, but providing it allows you to style error messages in a different way from any other strongly emphasized content (e.g., coloring the text red).

There's also the example mentioned in Chapter 2: when marking up text that's in an alternative language, it may be preferable to use the <i> element with a lang attribute instead of a <span> with a lang attribute and a class attribute for styling purposes.

A quick aside; if you are marking up text in a foreign language, then you may also find of use the <bdo> element (that's "bidirectional override") and the dir attribute, which control the direction of a text fragment and a block of text, respectively, and are best used when marking up Hebrew and other languages that are written from right to left instead of the Western left to right. Use <bdo> when the word or phrase is inline within a block of text written in a right-to-left language (and I'm afraid I don't know any Hebrew, so please excuse my English-language examples; they're nonsensical but they help get the point across):

```
<p>When rendered by a browser, <bdo dir="rtl">these words</bdo>➥
will appear as 'sdrow eseht'</p>
```

This markup renders as shown in Figure 6-14.

When rendered by a browser, sdrow eseht will appear as 'sdrow eseht'

Figure 6-14. The words "these words" have been reversed by the <bdo> element.

If an entire block is in a right-to-left language, use the dir attribute (with a value of rtl for right-to-left languages and ltr for left-to-right languages) on the container tag:

```
<p dir="rtl">When rendered by a browser, this will appear ➥
aligned to the right.</p>
<p>But this paragraph lacks a <code>dir</code> attribute. </p>
```

This markup renders as shown in Figure 6-15.

.When rendered by a browser, this will appear aligned to the right

But this paragraph lacks a `dir` attribute.

Figure 6-15. The entire first paragraph is now formatted to be read right-to-left instead of the default left-to-right.

In this example, the entire first paragraph is now aligned to the right, and the punctuation has also moved, but the text remains in the order it is written in the source markup, the assumption being that if an entire block of text is set with a dir attribute, then it has been written to be readable in that direction already. The second paragraph is untreated and is there for comparison only.

Finally, don't forget about all the different phrase elements discussed in Chapter 2: elements for citations, keyboard input, defining instances of terms, and so on. Remembering what inline elements are available to you can be a valuable aid in avoiding unnecessary spans.

You'll probably have seen the effect shown in Figure 6-16 before, if not on the Web then at least in print.

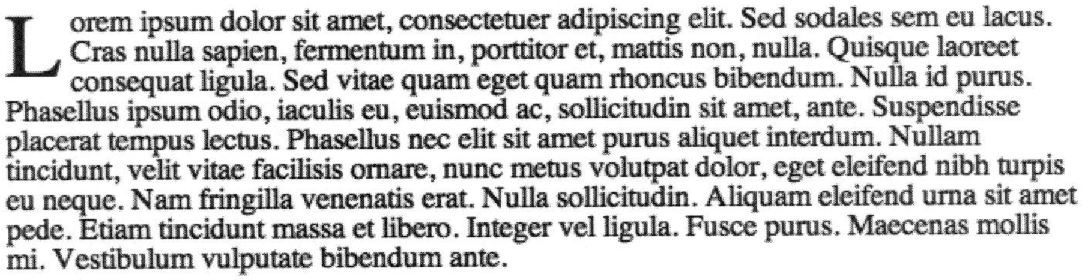

Lorem ipsum dolor sit amet, consectetuer adipiscing elit. Sed sodales sem eu lacus. Cras nulla sapien, fermentum in, porttitor et, mattis non, nulla. Quisque laoreet consequat ligula. Sed vitae quam eget quam rhoncus bibendum. Nulla id purus. Phasellus ipsum odio, iaculis eu, euismod ac, sollicitudin sit amet, ante. Suspendisse placerat tempus lectus. Phasellus nec elit sit amet purus aliquet interdum. Nullam tincidunt, velit vitae facilisis ornare, nunc metus volutpat dolor, eget eleifend nibh turpis eu neque. Nam fringilla venenatis erat. Nulla sollicitudin. Aliquam eleifend urna sit amet pede. Etiam tincidunt massa et libero. Integer vel ligula. Fusce purus. Maecenas mollis mi. Vestibulum vulputate bibendum ante.

Figure 6-16. A drop cap, where the initial letter of a sentence is visually enhanced

Figure 6-16 shows a *drop cap*, where the first letter of a paragraph has been styled to appear much larger than the rest of the text.

A detailed look at how you can calculate the appropriate size of your drop cap in relation to the size of your text can be found at `www.citrusmoon.net/dropcaps.html`.

It's a purely visual effect, so you might think that this is an acceptable place to use a <span>:

```
<p><span class="dropcap">T</span>his paragraph has a drop cap.</p>
```

Here's the CSS:

```
span.dropcap {
  float:left;
  display:block;
  font-size:300%;
  line-height:100%;
  padding-right: 0.1em;
}
```

This *is* a valid use of a <span>, but CSS2 provides us with a less invasive alternative. Remove the <span> from your markup and change your CSS to this:

```
p:first-letter {
```

:first-letter is a pseudo-element and targets the first letter of a paragraph (or any other element you apply it to. But watch out, as browsers can be a little quirky in how they react to this. For instance, if you use it on a list element, some browsers will include the bullet character along with the first letter).

Intentional spans

Sometimes, though, what appears to be span-mania is actually markup with a purpose—such as when you're describing multiple types of telephone numbers in the hCard micro-format discussed in the previous chapter. Two good rules of thumb to determine whether you should use a <span> are as follows:

- Are you using the markup purely as a hook to apply decorative styles to?
- Can the meaning of the content be described only with a class name?

If the answer to either of these questions is yes, then use a <span>. Otherwise, investigate other options—it's likely that there's a more appropriate alternative.

An example of using span markup for purely presentational reasons is using them to create rounded corners in flexible boxes. If your content is of a fixed width, then you can usually just include an image of the same width with both left and right corners included, but if your content is flexible (or elastic, or fluid), then it's trickier to achieve. A common solution is to include one <span> per corner and include each corner as a background image. You can usually recognize the technique by markup similar to this:

```
<div><p><span><span><span><span>Lorem ➥
ipsum...</span></span></span></span></p></div>
```

Mmm, lovely. Once those spans are in place, you apply a different background image to each one:

```
div {background: #a7a7a7;}
p {padding: 10px;}
div span { background: url(corner_tr.gif) top right ➥
no-repeat; display: block; }
div span span { background: url(corner_br.gif) bottom right ➥
no-repeat; }
div span span span { background: url(corner_bl.gif) bottom left➥
  no-repeat; }
div p span span span span { background: url(corner_tl.gif) top left ➥
no-repeat; }
```

Figure 6-17 shows the result.

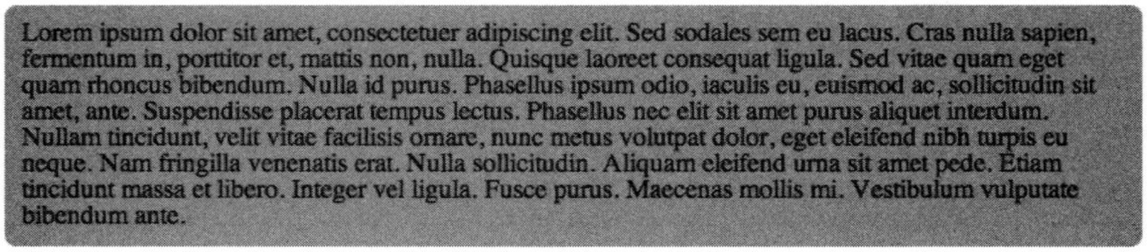

Lorem ipsum dolor sit amet, consectetuer adipiscing elit. Sed sodales sem eu lacus. Cras nulla sapien, fermentum in, porttitor et, mattis non, nulla. Quisque laoreet consequat ligula. Sed vitae quam eget quam rhoncus bibendum. Nulla id purus. Phasellus ipsum odio, iaculis eu, euismod ac, sollicitudin sit amet, ante. Suspendisse placerat tempus lectus. Phasellus nec elit sit amet purus aliquet interdum. Nullam tincidunt, velit vitae facilisis ornare, nunc metus volutpat dolor, eget eleifend nibh turpis eu neque. Nam fringilla venenatis erat. Nulla sollicitudin. Aliquam eleifend urna sit amet pede. Etiam tincidunt massa et libero. Integer vel ligula. Fusce purus. Maecenas mollis mi. Vestibulum vulputate bibendum ante.

Figure 6-17. A paragraph with rounded corners

If the paragraph is not of a fixed width or height, then the corners stay in the correct places even when the size and shape of the container changes, as shown in Figure 6-18.

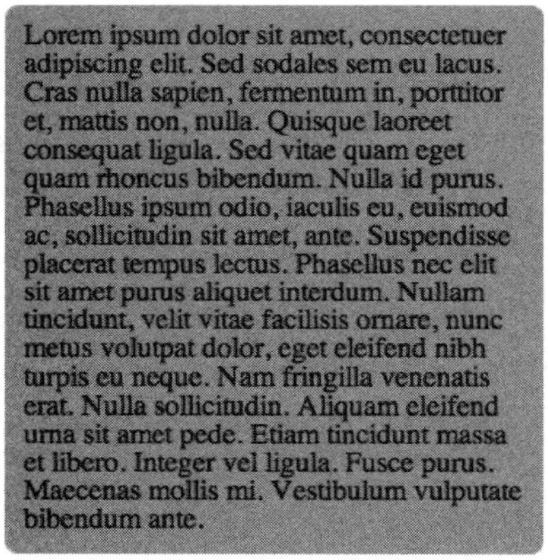

Lorem ipsum dolor sit amet, consectetuer adipiscing elit. Sed sodales sem eu lacus. Cras nulla sapien, fermentum in, porttitor et, mattis non, nulla. Quisque laoreet consequat ligula. Sed vitae quam eget quam rhoncus bibendum. Nulla id purus. Phasellus ipsum odio, iaculis eu, euismod ac, sollicitudin sit amet, ante. Suspendisse placerat tempus lectus. Phasellus nec elit sit amet purus aliquet interdum. Nullam tincidunt, velit vitae facilisis ornare, nunc metus volutpat dolor, eget eleifend nibh turpis eu neque. Nam fringilla venenatis erat. Nulla sollicitudin. Aliquam eleifend urna sit amet pede. Etiam tincidunt massa et libero. Integer vel ligula. Fusce purus. Maecenas mollis mi. Vestibulum vulputate bibendum ante.

Figure 6-18.
The corners are persistent,
no matter the size of the container.

If you want to have an image in each corner of your block and have the block be fluid in both the X and Y axes, then at the moment this is more or less the only way you can do it. Although the CSS3 draft specification allows you to include any number of background images on a single element, the browser support for this is minimal, with only Safari currently offering support (see http://htmlmastery.com/s/css3bg/ for a demonstration of this).

You can clean up your markup a bit by using JavaScript to dynamically insert the <span> tags. This means people without scripting enabled won't see your corners, but that's probably OK if the corners are just decorative.

Roger Johansson's article "Transparent custom corners and borders" (http://htmlmastery.com/s/customcorners) provides a comprehensive script solution for this issue.

Another good use of seemingly superfluous spans can be found in Andy Budd's remote rollovers technique, which allows you to hover over one element and cause an image change elsewhere on the page. Full details of this technique can be found in Andy's *CSS Mastery: Advanced Web Standards Solutions* (friends of ED, ISBN: 1-59059-614-5).

Avoiding classitis

Classitis is a similar condition to divitis, except it occurs when the web designer has overused the class attribute instead of the <div> tag. Classitis can be avoided through a better understanding of CSS selectors. A typical example of classitis is markup such as this:

```
<ul id="nav">
  <li class="navlist"><a class="navlink" href="p.html">Link</a></li>
  <li class="navlist"><a class="navlink" href="p2.html">Link 2</a></li>
  <li class="navlist"><a class="navlink" href="p3.html">Link 3</a></li>
  <li class="navlist"><a class="navlink" href="p4.html">Link 4</a></li>
</ul>
```

In the style sheet, both .navlist and .navlink are then independently styled, but the fact is that not a single one of those classes is necessary, as you can target both the list items and the anchors with **descendent selectors** (i.e., selectors that target the descendents of a particular element, or hierarchy of elements):

```
ul#nav li a { /* your CSS styles here */ }
```

This CSS looks for any <a> that is a descendent of an <li>, which is in turn a descendent of a <ul> element, with an id value of nav (so this is actually an example of an ID selector as well as a descendent selector). Targeting elements in such a way is beneficial for two reasons: it cleans up your markup, making it more readable, lighter, and easier to maintain, and it does the same for your CSS.

But, again, using class attributes is not intrinsically bad, and it can often be your only option when targeting an element, particularly because of Internet Explorer 6's lack of support for advanced CSS2 selectors. For instance, the example shown in Figure 6-19 is similar to the "leadingWords" example from earlier.

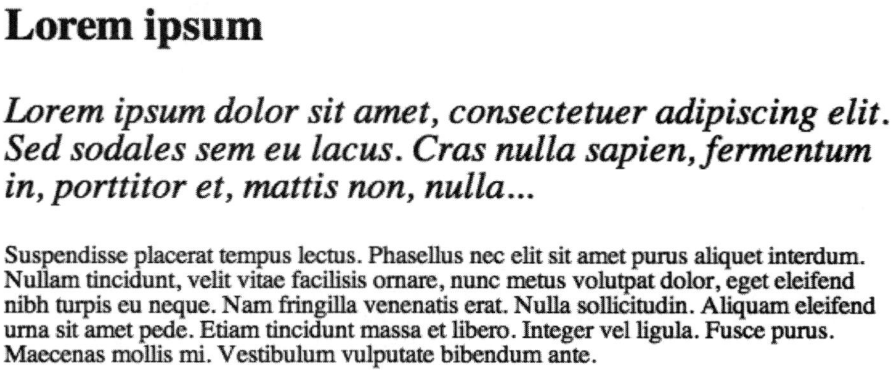

Lorem ipsum

Lorem ipsum dolor sit amet, consectetuer adipiscing elit. Sed sodales sem eu lacus. Cras nulla sapien, fermentum in, porttitor et, mattis non, nulla...

Suspendisse placerat tempus lectus. Phasellus nec elit sit amet purus aliquet interdum. Nullam tincidunt, velit vitae facilisis ornare, nunc metus volutpat dolor, eget eleifend nibh turpis eu neque. Nam fringilla venenatis erat. Nulla sollicitudin. Aliquam eleifend urna sit amet pede. Etiam tincidunt massa et libero. Integer vel ligula. Fusce purus. Maecenas mollis mi. Vestibulum vulputate bibendum ante.

Figure 6-19. The leading paragraph is visually emphasized.

The first paragraph is serving as an introduction to the rest of the article, and it's similar to a style you'll see in magazines and newspapers, with the introductory text much larger than the rest of the copy. We can style this paragraph in a number of ways. For example, we could use a CSS2 **adjacent sibling** selector:

6

```
h3+p { font-size: 150%; font-style: italic;}
```

This targets any <p> that directly follows an <h3> in the markup:

```
<h3>Title</h3>
<p>First paragraph</p> <-- this paragraph is being targeted
<p>Second paragraph>
```

But because Internet Explorer 6 and below don't support adjacent sibling selectors (Internet Explorer 7 does), if this effect is important, we must find another way. And really, the only other way is to add a class name to that paragraph:

```
<h3>Title</h3>
<p class="intro">First paragraph</p>
<p>Second paragraph>
```

Now, what about the semantics? Like the <span> example from earlier on, aren't we trying to emphasize that first paragraph? So, could we slip an <em> in there?

```
<h3>Title</h3>
<p class="intro"><em>First paragraph</em></p>
<p>Second paragraph>
```

The paragraph with the class of intro has now been emphasized. Here's the corresponding CSS:

```
.intro em { font-size: 150%; font-style: italic; }
```

This way, the intended emphasizing is present in both the CSS and the markup—but remember to only use an <em> if you actually intend semantic emphasis, not just visual emphasis (which could actually be the same thing).

I mentioned the :first-letter pseudo-element earlier on. There also exists a :first-line pseudo-element, which is used in the same way as :first-letter, but targets the first line of the element (and recalculates what the first line is on the fly, so when you resize your content, the applied effect only ever affects the first line):

```
p:first-line { font-weight: bold; }
```

Figure 6-20 shows the result.

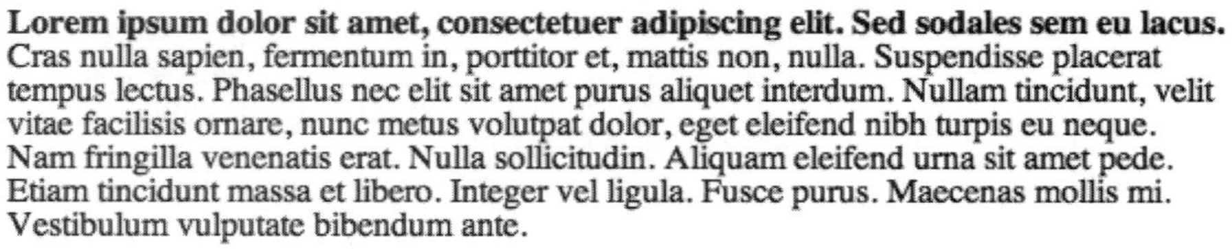

Lorem ipsum dolor sit amet, consectetuer adipiscing elit. Sed sodales sem eu lacus.
Cras nulla sapien, fermentum in, porttitor et, mattis non, nulla. Suspendisse placerat tempus lectus. Phasellus nec elit sit amet purus aliquet interdum. Nullam tincidunt, velit vitae facilisis ornare, nunc metus volutpat dolor, eget eleifend nibh turpis eu neque. Nam fringilla venenatis erat. Nulla sollicitudin. Aliquam eleifend urna sit amet pede. Etiam tincidunt massa et libero. Integer vel ligula. Fusce purus. Maecenas mollis mi. Vestibulum vulputate bibendum ante.

Figure 6-20. The :first-line pseudo-element is being used to embolden the first line of the paragraph.

Figure 6-21 shows this effect again, but in a narrower browser window.

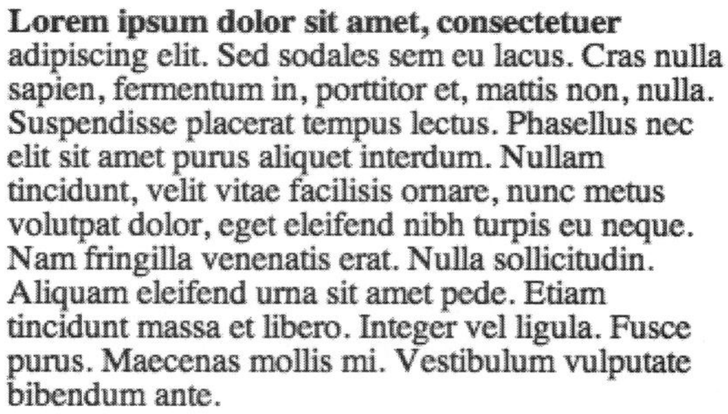

Lorem ipsum dolor sit amet, consectetuer adipiscing elit. Sed sodales sem eu lacus. Cras nulla sapien, fermentum in, porttitor et, mattis non, nulla. Suspendisse placerat tempus lectus. Phasellus nec elit sit amet purus aliquet interdum. Nullam tincidunt, velit vitae facilisis ornare, nunc metus volutpat dolor, eget eleifend nibh turpis eu neque. Nam fringilla venenatis erat. Nulla sollicitudin. Aliquam eleifend urna sit amet pede. Etiam tincidunt massa et libero. Integer vel ligula. Fusce purus. Maecenas mollis mi. Vestibulum vulputate bibendum ante.

Figure 6-21.
The paragraph has been resized and what constitutes "the first line" has been automatically recalculated.

Using the :first-letter and :first-line pseudo-elements doesn't involve you modifying your markup in any way, and although you do lose support in older browsers, they'll still be able to display your content. However, you may not want to apply these pseudo-elements to every paragraph, so you can still target a paragraph that has a specific class or ID value:

```
<p class="intro">First paragraph</p>
```

Here's the CSS:

```
p.intro:first-letter { /* your styles here */ }
```

Semantic navigation

Navigation on a website can come in many different shapes and sizes—horizontally, in the form of tabs, vertically as a nested list of expanding and collapsing categories, breadcrumb trails, drop-down menus, and so on. Regardless of how it's presented, though, it's almost always the case that navigation can be marked up as an ordered or unordered list. Let's look at a few examples of this, starting with breadcrumb trails.

A **breadcrumb trail** is a navigational aid where links are provided that lead you from the current page back up to the root of the website, through any preceding categories, as shown in Figure 6-22.

Home > Archives > Movies > Shaun of the Dead

Figure 6-22. A typical breadcrumb trail

Markup for a breadcrumb trail will often look something like this:

```
<p><a href="/">Home</a> &gt; <a href="/archives/">➡
Archives</a> &gt; <a href="/archives/movies/">Movies</a>➡
 &gt; Shaun of the Dead</p>
```

But hold on—isn't this, basically, just a list? So shouldn't we mark it up as one? Yes! Let's start with the markup:

```
<ol>
  <li><a href="/">Home</a></li>
  <li><a href="/archives/">Archives</a></li>
  <li><a href="/archives/movies/">Movies</a></li>
  <li>Shaun of the Dead</li>
</ol>
```

Notice that in both examples, the final option isn't hyperlinked. This is intentional, as links that link to the same page that they're on can cause mild confusion as people click them and find they haven't moved from the page they are on.

I'm using an ordered list because these links do have a clear order. If you reordered them, then they would no longer describe a hierarchical trail, and that's the acid test for deciding upon whether you should use an ordered or unordered list. If you can reorder the list items and the list still makes sense, then it's probably an unordered list; if the list no longer makes sense, then it should be marked up as an ordered list.

Also, I've removed the > entities from the markup. These entities create the greater-than symbol (>), but a better, often-overlooked entity available to use is → (or →, which is the numerical equivalent), which creates a right-pointing arrow (→) and is more meaningful in this context. Using the greater-than symbol in place of an actual arrow is semantically dubious.

Figure 6-23.
A breadcrumb trail in its unstyled list form

I've removed the entities because they're there only for decoration, and if we keep them directly within the markup, then screen readers will read them out—so our first example will most likely be read out as "Home greater archives greater movies greater Shaun of the Dead." Which . . . OK, that *sort of* makes sense if you twist your brain around it a little, but it's not ideal.[3] Instead, we'll include our decorations with CSS. At the moment, our breadcrumb trail will look like Figure 6-23.

Let's first deal with the list:

```
ol {
  list-style-type: none;
}
```

This markup removes the numbering from the list. In a production environment, you'd probably also include some specific margins, padding, and font styles, but this is fine for our purposes.

---

3. Have a listen to the various samples of how the JAWS screen reader reads out different characters in an article entitled "The Sound of the Accessible Title Tag Separator" at Standards Schmandards (http://htmlmastery.com/s/sounds). It might put you off of using the right double angle bracket (») ever again.

Next, we tweak the list items a little:

```
li {
  display: inline;
  padding-left: 0.5em;
}
```

This causes the list items to display horizontally, and the padding will just make things look a little nicer. So far, our breadcrumb trail looks like Figure 6-24.

Home   Archives   Movies   Shaun of the Dead

Figure 6-24. The breadcrumb trail is now more trail-like.

Now, there are two ways to include our arrows. The first way we'll look at uses the CSS background-image property, which will work in all current CSS-supporting browsers (Internet Explorer included), and the second uses the CSS2 content property, which is used in conjunction with the :after pseudo-element and not supported by any current version of Internet Explorer (version 7 included).

The first solution involves more effort on your part, as you'll have to create an arrow image in your graphics application of choice. Once you've done that, it's simply a matter of including it as a background image on your list items:

```
li {
  background: url(arrow.gif) right no-repeat;
  padding-right: 20px;
}
```

Which gives us the result shown in Figure 6-25.

Home → Archives → Movies → Shaun of the Dead→

Figure 6-25. A breadcrumb trail using background images for the decorative arrows—but what's that last arrow pointing at?

We'll have to override the background image on the closing <li>, so give it an id of last-item and add this to the CSS:

```
li#last-item {
  background: none;
}
```

And we're done. (See Figure 6-26.)

Home → Archives → Movies → Shaun of the Dead

Figure 6-26. The completed breadcrumb trail

The second method, using CSS-generated content, is easier and neater, but it lacks support from Internet Explorer, and screen readers *may* read out generated content. The markup is almost the same as in the previous solution, but instead of adding a background image in the CSS, we add this:

```
li:after {
  content: '→'
}
```

Then we just add a little padding to the right side of the <a>:

```
a {
  padding-right: 0.5em;
}
```

Now, in modern browsers, the result is as shown in Figure 6-27.

Home → Archives → Movies → Shaun of the Dead→

Figure 6-27. A breadcrumb trail using CSS generated content to insert the arrow figure

Finally, add an ID value of last-item to the final <li>, and add to your CSS:

```
li#last-item:after {
  content: '';
}
```

> *In case it's not clear: the* content *property is simply being passed an empty value. There's nothing between those single quotes.*

We're all done! Figure 6-28 shows the result.

Home → Archives → Movies → Shaun of the Dead

Figure 6-28. The finished trail

The same principles can be applied to horizontal menus, such as the one shown in Figure 6-29.

Home | About | Contact

Figure 6-29. A collection of links presented horizontally

The markup for this type of menu will often be in the form of a paragraph:

```
<p><a href="/">Home</a> | <a href="/about/">About</a> ➡
| <a href="/contact/">Contact</a> </p>
```

Again, though—this is a list. It's a small list of only three items, but a list nonetheless:

```
<ul>
  <li><a href="/">Home</a></li>
  <li><a href="/about/">About</a></li>
  <li><a href="/contact/">Contact</a></li>
</ul>
```

As before, we can lose the pipe character (|) separator (which a screen reader can read out as "vertical bar," so the full list would be read out as "Home vertical bar about vertical bar contact," which is not ideal), and this time we can just use the CSS border property to re-create it. First of all, we lose the list bullet:

```
ul {
  list-style-type: none;
}
```

Then we get all the list items up onto the same line, add a bit of padding and margin, and add a border to act as a visual separator:

```
li {
  border-right: 1px solid;
  display: inline;
  padding-right: 0.5em;
  margin-right: 0.5em;
}
```

And the finished result is shown in Figure 6-30. It's not identical to the paragraph version, but it could be styled further.

Home | About | Contact |

Figure 6-30. A horizontal list of links, marked up as a list but presented horizontally

If you don't want the closing link to have a border, just add an id to the last list item again and add border: 0; to your CSS.

The importance of validity

One of the reasons people can suffer from divitis and classitis is because they can write that sort of markup and still have the W3C validator give them a shiny "Valid XHTML!" badge at the end of it. It's important to understand that validation does not equal best practice—validating is commendable, in the same way that writing with perfect grammar is commendable, but being grammatically correct doesn't necessarily mean that the meaning of your text or speech is clear.

When you view your pages in a web browser, the browser doesn't actually know if you've written valid (X)HTML or not. You may have declared with your doctype that you're writing to the XHTML 1.0 specification, but the web browser isn't downloading a copy of the DTD and checking up on you. All that happens when a doctype is present is that the browser switches to standards mode,[4] and when the document is validated it informs the validator what DTD it needs to be checking against. This is why you can write to an XHTML standard but then chuck in an HTML 3.2 tag (written in uppercase) or attribute (with an unquoted value) and find that it still works without complaint—support for these older standards and markup methodologies is hard-coded into the browser.

Does this mean that we should question the importance of creating (and maintaining) a valid document? After all, if validating doesn't guarantee intelligent use of the markup, what good is it?

We should also consider those that have been successful with invalid markup, such as Macromedia (now Adobe) with their Flash product. The standard way to include Flash movies on your page is invalid, as it partly relies upon the <embed> tag and some other nonstandard markup. It's invalid, but it works, and it has worked so well that 80–90% of web browsers now have the ability to view Flash media. Invalid markup has not, it seems, harmed Flash's market penetration.

So, again, what good is it?

In my mind, there are two basic types of validation error:

- **Structural failures**, such as a missing </div> (or one too many </div>s), which can cause massive rendering problems on your page
- **Nonstructural failures**, such as an unencoded ampersand, a missing required attribute (such as an image alt attribute), or an unquoted attribute value, the presence of which are unlikely to cause any noticeable problems, because a browser understands how to read an unquoted attribute value or how to parse an unencoded ampersand, irrespective of what doctype you're writing to

> *If you're serving your XHTML with a MIME type of application/xhtml+xml, then some of these nonstructural failures will cause your pages to break, displaying an XML parse error instead of any content, in addition to all of the structural failures. However, this is still not about checking for validity—it's actually only breaking if the markup is not well-formed, so you can still include attributes and tags not part of the XHTML specification, as long as the attribute values are quoted and the tags are all nested and closed correctly.*

But you still need to be able to spot the difference between a structural failure and a nonstructural failure, and the best way to do that is to avoid both types altogether. If you've forgotten to close a <div>, but you're also missing a few dozen alt attributes and a few

---

4. Or almost-standards mode, as discussed in Chapter 3.

hundred unencoded ampersands in your URLs, the error message highlighting the problem with the <div> is likely to get lost amid all of the other errors. By aiming for strict validation, you make it far easier to spot structural problems, particularly as one failure earlier in the document can trigger several other failures further down the line.

Furthermore, by aiming for strict validation, you help to future-proof your website. At the moment (in late 2006/early 2007) we can look at the browser situation and say, "Yes, I can get away with a lot of invalid markup." But we don't always know what's coming—perhaps Internet Explorer 8 or Firefox 3 will be far less forgiving of our errors, or browsers will begin actually taking note of what DTD we're using instead of using it only as a rendering mode trigger. Perhaps serving content with a MIME type of application/xhtml+xml, with its draconian error-handling, will become much more common. Perhaps a brand-new browser—maybe a mobile phone browser, or a browser on an as yet unimagined device—will come along and choke on invalid markup. We don't really know.

But realistically, strict validation is not always easy. In a business environment with third-party ad servers spitting out advertisements marked up as tables with lots of font tags and crufty URLs, or clunky CMSs that generate twentieth-century markup but are too expensive and important to rebuild or replace, or even a blog environment with open comments (where you have limited control over what the commenter decides to write), it may not even be *possible*.

So it's something to aim for, and I think it very much *should* be aimed for—but if it can't be managed, and for good reason, try not to judge yourself or others too harshly because of it.

Summary

So now you've seen that there are more opportunities to create semantically and structurally sound websites than you might have thought. Despite the limited number of (X)HTML tags available, many page elements can be broken down into simple forms: lists, paragraphs, and so on. It's often just a case of stepping back from your content and thinking about what it really is.

7 LOOKING AHEAD: XHTML 2.0 AND WEB APPLICATIONS 1.0

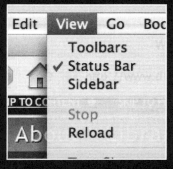

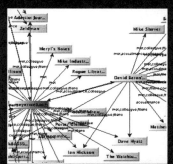

So, you've now seen covered every element from the HTML 4.01 and XHTML 1.0 specifications (with the exception of frame markup, which will be covered in Appendix B), from the obscure—<bdo> and <optgroup>—to the common—<p> and <h1>. You've looked at tables and found that they're just as useful today as they always have been, when used correctly, and you've looked at forms, and how giving them a bit of semantic structure can notably enhance their usability and accessibility. You've taken in microformats and the Semantic Web, and looked at a few common page elements and how to express them more semantically, avoiding divitis and classitis as you go.

To finish things off, I'm going to give you a brief look at future (X)HTML technologies, the successors to XHTML 1.1 and HTML 4.01. They are, at the time of writing, still in the draft stage, and it is likely to be a while yet before they can be used in a production environment—but then again, this is the Internet. The Internet moves pretty fast, and as a great man once (more or less) said, if you don't stop and look around once in a while, you could miss it.

At the time of writing, the successor to XHTML 1.1 is XHTML 2.0—as far as the W3C is concerned. Complicating the issue somewhat is Web Applications 1.0 and Web Forms 2.0, also collectively known as HTML 5. As both of these technologies are still being worked upon, what I'm about to write is entirely subject to change, so I won't go into too much depth for that reason. It's unlikely you'll be using either in any serious way for some time, but it's still nice to know what's happening so that when the time comes to take sides and have fiery, impassioned debates about XForms versus Web Forms or the <hr> element versus the <separator> element, you'll be ahead of the game.

First, in the blue corner, XHTML 2.0.

XHTML 2.0

Whereas the purpose of XHTML 1.0 was to reformulate HTML into XML, the purpose of XHTML 2.0 ("XHTML 2.0, W3C Working Draft," www.w3.org/TR/xhtml2/) is to progress from that point, addressing the problems of HTML as a markup language, making it easier to write with greater accessibility and device independence, improving internationalization, and supplying enhanced forms and more meaningful semantics. For example, the notion of six levels of headings (<h1> through <h6>) has been supplanted by a new <section> element (a container for dividing up content, much like a <div>) and any number of <h> elements,[1] where the document structure is inferred from the placement and hierarchy of these sections and headings. So, where you may be used to this with current (X)HTML:

```
<div>
    <h1>Page Title</h1>
    <h2>Page Slogan</h2>
</div>
```

---

1. The heading tags (<h1> through <h6>) will still be supported to help with the transition between XHTML 1 and 2.

```
<div>
    <h3>Article Title</h3>
    ...
    <h4>Subheading</h4>
</div>
```

in XHTML 2, you would do this:

```
<section>
    <h>Page Title</h>
    <h>Page Slogan</h>
</section>
<section>
    <h>Article Title</h>
    ...
    <h>Subheading</h>
</section>
```

Also of note is that the src attribute is no longer limited to images and scripts; in XHTML 2.0, it can be applied to any element, negating the need for alt attributes or CSS-based image replacement techniques. So, where you may once have done this:

```
<h1><img src="/foo.jpg" alt="Page Title" /></h1>
```

in XHTML 2.0, you could simply do this:

```
<h src="/foo.jpg">Page Title</h>
```

If, for whatever reason, the image is not available or the visitor to the site has disabled images, the text within the <h> tags will display instead.[2]

Other new tags and attributes in XHTML 2.0

XHTML 2.0 will also be bringing to the table a few new tags and attributes for us to play with, such as the <blockcode> tag (a combination of <pre> and <code>), a new list tag for navigation lists (the <nl> tag), and the <separator> and <l> elements (that's an "l" for "line"), replacing <hr> and <br>, respectively.

Accessibility is also made marginally simpler with the new nextfocus and prevfocus attributes (replacing the tabindex attribute and negating the need to maintain your own hard-coded numbering of tabindexes), and the role attribute to describe to screen readers the purpose of a particular element. Also new is the ability to better specify metadata with the property attribute, used like this:

```
<h property="title">Page Title</h>
```

---

2. This renders the <img> element obsolete, but as with the six original header tags, it will be included in the XHTML 2.0 specification for backward compatibility.

This means you would not have to write out the title of the document twice (once in the `<title>` tags and again within the document)—the browser could extrapolate from the document what the title should be.

XForms

There's a lot to be said about XForms, the technology that aims to replace the old (X)HTML forms and form controls that you will be familiar with—enough to write a book on, in fact. Designed from the ground up to overcome many of the problems associated with existing forms, XForms promises exciting things such as device independence, client-side validation of form fields (without scripting or reloading the page), a simpler construction process for the web author, and built-in integration with XML ("XForms 1.0 Frequently Asked Questions," www.w3.org/MarkUp/Forms/2003/xforms-faq.html).

A major difference between (X)HTML forms and XForms is that XForms specifies what form controls should *do* rather than how they should *look*. This shouldn't be an unknown concept—it's part of what this very book is about; thinking about how things should act and what they mean rather than their appearance. So, for instance, where an (X)HTML form might have a `<select>` element for a multiple-choice menu and an `<input>` element with a type value of radio for a single-choice option, an XForm would have the `<select>` element and the `<select1>` elements, with the appearance left to the display device or the author's stylesheet.

For example, where you may have written something like this:

```
Chicken or beef:
<input type="radio" name="food" value="chicken" /> Chicken
<input type="radio" name="food" value="beef" /> Beef
```

in an XForm, you would write this:

```
<select1 ref="food">
  <label>Chicken or beef:</label>
  <item>
    <label>Chicken</label><value>chicken</value>
  </item>
  <item>
    <label>Beef</label><value>beef</value>
  </item>
</select1>
```

Notice there are a few new elements and attributes: the ref attribute replaces the name attribute, while each possible option is represented by an `<item>` element. The `<item>` element contains both a `<label>` (which would act the same as the (X)HTML equivalent, except there's no need for the for attribute) and a `<value>`, which would most likely be invisible by default.

How this would render depends on what device is doing the rendering; it might *not* be rendered as radio buttons—it could render as radio buttons, or as a drop-down list, or a fixed menu. The author can provide a suggestion as to how the markup should render by including an appearance attribute on <select1>, with possible values of full, compact, or minimal, but ultimately the decision is left up to the rendering device; if it decides there's not enough screen space for a full appearance, it might select the minimal alternative instead.

If you wanted to allow for more than one selection—maybe your users like chicken *and* beef—you just replace <select1> with <select>, and everything just said remains the same.

Other changes from (X)HTML forms include the following:

- The <form> element is replaced by the <model> element.
- The action and method attributes now apply to a new <submission> element.
- <legend> is retired in favor of <label>.
- <fieldset> is replaced by <group>.
- <optgroup> is replaced by <choices>.
- File inputs are now included with an <upload> element.
- Password inputs are now included with the charmingly named <secret> element.

There's more; entirely new to XForms are the <range> and <output> elements. <range> is similar to the proprietary range input type described in Chapter 4, with user agents possibly rendering this as a slider:

```
<range start="1" end="100" step="10" />
```

The <output> element allows users to preview the values they're submitting and can also be used to calculate values—all without anything being submitted back to the server. For instance:

```
<output value="totalprice - discount" />
```

would display the sum of a previous form control named totalprice minus the value of another form control known as discount, allowing the user to see changes on the fly, without Ajax or any other scripting techniques.

A complete description of XForms is beyond the scope of this book, particularly as the specification has not yet been finalized, so I suggest reading "XForms for HTML Authors" by Steve Pemberton (www.w3.org/MarkUp/Forms/2003/xforms-for-html-authors.html) for a detailed tutorial on the subject, and also have a look at "XForms—The Next Generation of Web Forms" (www.w3.org/MarkUp/Forms/).

Preparing for XHTML 2.0

As the XHTML 2.0 specification has not been finalized and major browsers do not yet support any of it, using it in a real website is not feasible. According to the W3C's roadmap, it is not due to become an official W3C recommendation until at least 2007, and from there it must still go through several additional phases before it can be used in the field. Nevertheless, if you want to be ahead of the game, there are still several ways you can start preparing:

- Go all the way in separating your presentational and behavioral markup from your content. Make sure you're writing strict, well-formed XHTML 1.1.

- Start including metadata within your pages by using microformats, e.g., use hCard for marking up your contact details.

- Start serving your XHTML with the MIME type of application/xhtml+xml to prepare you for the extra strictness of XML—XHTML 2.0 will require you to do this.

- Learn more about XML and about XForms.

- Start experimenting with XHTML 2.0 with the X-Smiles browser (www.xsmiles.org/), which offers support for both XHTML 2.0 and XForms, among other technologies.

Next, in the green corner, Web Applications 1.0.

Web Applications 1.0

So, if the W3C is all about XHTML, who is behind Web Applications? Step forward, Web Hypertext Application Technology Working Group (WHATWG to its friends). WHATWG is a "loose unofficial collaboration of web browser manufacturers [Apple, Mozilla, and Opera are all involved] and interested parties who wish to develop new technologies designed to allow authors to write and deploy applications over the World Wide Web" (www.whatwg.org/).

Web Applications 1.0 is designed to be backwardly compatible with both HTML 4.01 and XHTML 1.0. The objective, as just stated, is to allow easier development of web applications by solving some of the problems in existing versions of (X)HTML (such as the limited form controls). As with XHTML 2.0, work on Web Applications is still in progress and subject to change.

> *A Web Application is defined by WHATWG as an application accessed over the Web via a web browser, such as eBay or Amazon.*

New tags and attributes in Web Applications 1.0

A criticism that WHATWG has of XHTML 2.0 is that it is stuck using the same "document" metaphor of previous versions of HTML—suitable for literary works or technical manuals, but less suitable for, say, auction sites, search engines, and personal homepages. Thus, Web Applications brings us several new section elements with self-explanatory meanings— <section>, <nav>, <article>, <aside>, <header>, and <footer>.

At the time of writing, the Web Applications 1.0 specification (www.whatwg.org/specs/ web-apps/current-work/) also includes a new <t> tag for indicating the time, a <meter> tag for representing scalar measurement within a known range (such as hard disk usage), and a <progress> tag for indicating the competition progress of a task. The <table> tag and all associated tags are supplemented by the new, more flexible <datagrid> tag.

Also included is the <canvas> element, originally introduced by Apple in Safari for the implementation of the Mac OSX Dashboard but now also found in Mozilla (and other browsers using the same engine) and Opera 9. It is essentially an image element that supports programmatic drawing (http://weblogs.mozillazine.org/hyatt/archives/2004_07.html#005913).

Web Forms 2.0

The scope of Web Forms 2.0 is not as ambitious as that of XForms, focusing on improving the form controls available in the browser. Included in Web Forms is client-side validation, control over auto-completion, an autofocus attribute to control which form element gains keyboard focus when the page has loaded, improvements on file upload controls (such as specifying the expected file type and controls on the file size), new types of input controls such as datetime, number, range, email, url, and more (some of which have already gained support—see Chapter 4).

Preparing for Web Applications 1.0

As with XHTML 2.0, the Web Applications specification is still very much a work in progress, and it's hard to predict when the browser support for it will be at such a level to allow for practical use rather than theoretical discussion. As noted previously, though, the <canvas> element is already implemented in Safari, Mozilla, and Opera 9, and Opera 9 also includes some support for Web Forms 2.0, so the support is trickling in despite the advice of the WHATWG to avoid implementing these features until the specifications have been finalized. If you wish to try and prepare yourself, simply continue what you're doing—this suite of technologies is intended to be backwardly compatible with both HTML 4.01 and XHTML 1.0, so adoption should be simpler than that of XHTML 2.0.

Summary

Should you be worried about any of this? At the moment, I would describe the two preceding technologies as "points of interest." They're certainly going to go through many revisions before being completed, and then the decision on whether to use them should be based on a *need* to use them, and whether your audience is actually using a browsing device capable of displaying these new toys.

Also, remember that browsers are probably not going to simply stop understanding any previous version of (X)HTML when these new versions are available, so even if you don't find what's to come appealing, you can still use what you already know. Furthermore, the issue of Internet Explorer will continue to be a factor—with versions 5 through 6 making up roughly 80–90% of the browser usage share, using any new features from either new technologies could prove problematic. However, although Internet Explorer 7 will not be implementing of these new features, Microsoft has suggested that future updates to its browser will not be as slow to arrive as version 7 was, so by the time XHTML 2.0 and Web Applications 1.0 are ready to use, the browser support may be there as well—fingers crossed.

APPENDIX A **XHTML AS XML**

XML Parsing Error
Location: http://ht
Line Number 8, Co

```
<body>&
-------^
```

Unhandled

Internet Explorer doesn'
of file you have selecte

You can choose to save
can configure a Helper

MIME Type: application
File Name: xhtml.xhtm

(Cancel) (Save File As...)

is Ruby

is is Ruby

When we all started writing XHTML instead of HTML, it was the cool new thing: it would replace HTML, browser's would "accord it special treatment," we would be able to work easily with other XML applications, and it would be more accessible and work better on a wider variety of devices and browsers.

A few years on, and that's mostly turned out to be incorrect, or related more to the style of authoring than the markup language used. Because the truth is that XHTML sent across the tubes with a MIME type of text/html is HTML, or at least is *treated* like HTML. Browsers accord it no special treatment, you can't include XML applications in it, and it's no more or less accessible than HTML.

There are no inherent advantages in serving XHTML as HTML. There aren't really any *disadvantages*, either; if there were, we'd have heard about it by now, given the large number of people now authoring in XHTML. So, as I said in Chapter 1, use XHTML or use HTML—just make sure you write it *well*.

But what if you *do* want to take advantage of XHTML's XML features? Well, that's different—XHTML served with a MIME type of application/xhtml+xml (i.e., served as *XML*) *does* have advantages (and some disadvantages as well). In fact, a lot of those advantages are the advantages we all thought we were getting originally anyway—a draconian strictness and formality in the language, and integration with other XML-based applications. The disadvantages are that you have to work a bit harder to ensure your markup is flawless, and you lose some browser support, most noticeably the support of Internet Explorer.

The purpose of this appendix is to explain how to serve your XHTML as XML and what you can expect to gain (and lose) from that. We'll also take a look at XHTML 1.1 (which is supposed to be served as XML, always), and we'll take a quick look at Ruby markup.

Serving XHTML as XML

Serving XHTML as XML is actually quite simple and can apply to all of your files or on a file-by-file basis, depending upon your need. The following examples assume that you're running Apache web server.

Let's imagine for the moment that you want to serve any file with an extension of .xhtml as XML. You don't *have* to call it .xhtml, but this will at least help to differentiate between your XHTML as XML and your (X)HTML as HTML. All you need to do is open up your .htaccess file that's stored in the root of your website (or create one if it doesn't exist) and add this line to it:

```
AddType application/xhtml+xml xhtml
```

And that's all you need to do. Easy, eh? You can all go home now if you like.

Ah, but what if you want nonsupportive browsers (Internet Explorer) to be able to view your pages? Well, that can be done as well, with these lines:

```
RewriteEngine On
RewriteBase /
RewriteCond %{HTTP_ACCEPT} !application/xhtml\+xml
RewriteCond %{HTTP_ACCEPT} (text/html|\*/\*)
RewriteCond %{REQUEST_FILENAME} .*\.xhtml
RewriteRule ^.*$ - "[T=text/html,L]"
```

What this is doing is simply serving the .xhtml file as HTML (that's with a MIME type of text/html) if the browser can't accept it when it's sent with a MIME type of application/xhtml+xml. So, most modern browsers get XML, all others get HTML—best of both worlds, and it's acceptable to do this so long as you're talking about XHTML 1.0 (XHTML 1.1 is treated differently, as discussed further in its own section later in this appendix).

But what if you don't want to apply this to all of your files, or don't have access to your .htaccess file? Well, you can do it on a per-page basis as well by including a script at the start of your file that sets the header information. In PHP, this can be as simple as this:

```php
<?php if (strpos($_SERVER['HTTP_ACCEPT'],'application/xhtml+xml'))
  {
   header('Content-type: application/xhtml+xml; charset=UTF-8');
  } else {
     header('Content-type: text/html; charset=UTF-8'); }
?>
```

This is pretty much the same as what was going on in the .htaccess file. If the browser requesting the file can accept an HTTP header of application/xhtml+xml, that's how it will be served; if not, it'll be served as text/html.

The advantage of this sort of content negotiation is that you get to serve XML to those browsers that can handle it, but you can still provide the page content to those that can't. However, it's also a disadvantage, as you won't be able to include any XML-based applications within your pages, such as MathML (www.w3.org/Math/)—or rather, you can, but a browser receiving the HTML version won't know what to do with it, and the meaning will be lost.

So that your markup is compatible with both XML-capable agents and noncapable agents, you have to write it in a specific way; some things that are acceptable in XML can cause problems when HTML parsers attempt to rendering, and vice versa. For instance, although
</br> is legal XML, in HTML some browsers can interpret that as two line breaks, or there may be other unforeseen side effects. Other guidelines include the following:

- Don't include the XML declaration, as that will switch Internet Explorer to quirks mode.

- If you have an empty container tag, don't try and make it self-closing (i.e., an empty <div> should still be closed with a separate </div>, and should not be written as <div />).

- Keep all of your CSS and JavaScript in external files and just reference them with a <style>, <link>, or <script> tag.

A

- Avoid line breaks and extraneous whitespace within attribute values.
- When specifying the language of an element, use both the HTML lang attribute and the XML xml:lang attribute (i.e., <i lang="fr" xml:lang="fr">).

For a complete list of guidelines, see the W3C's "HTML Compatibility Guidelines" (www.w3.org/TR/xhtml1/#guidelines).

Things to watch out for

So now that you're serving your content as XML, you need to make sure of a few things. To begin with, all of your markup must be well formed. Not necessarily *valid*. You can place a <p> inside an <em>, and that would be invalid according to any (X)HTML specification (as it's a block-level element within an inline element); but as long as both tags are closed and they're not overlapping, then that's still well-formed markup. Any errors— unencoded entities, overlapping tags, anything that causes the document to no longer be well formed—will prevent the page content from appearing at all; all that will be displayed is an XML parsing error, as shown in Figure A-1.

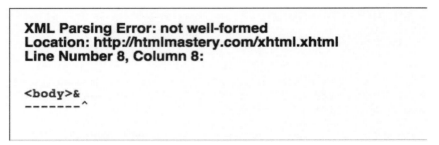

Figure A-1. An XML parsing error

Any user agent that doesn't know what to do with XHTML as XML will try and download the file instead of displaying the contents, as the message in Figure A-2 indicates.

Figure A-2. Internet Explorer tries to download the file instead of displaying it.

If you have any form of commenting facility on your website—most blogs do, for instance—or anything similar that allows people to instantly post markup to your site, you run the risk of anybody being able to break the page (or pages) that the comment appears on. Unless your system can strictly validate the comment input, all it takes is for me to come along and type `<p class="whoops>blah blah</p>` with a missing close quote, and the page will be broken to everybody until you can get online to edit the comment.

CSS selectors will become case sensitive; for example, `#Content {font-style: normal;}` will only target an element with an id value of Content, but not content. In any case, it's good practice for your CSS selectors to accurately tally up with their markup counterparts, whatever version of HTML you're writing.

The `<body>` will no longer be treated in the special way browsers normally treat it; it will be treated just as a `<div>`. This means that any styles that you want to have an effect across the entire viewport must be applied to `<html>` instead.

JavaScript works differently. Any JavaScript that relies on the `document.write` method will no longer work; this is because this method allows you to insert markup that is not well formed. Instead, you need to use the `document.createElement` method. Also, collections such as `document.images`, `document.links`, and `document.forms`—methods that return collections of images, links, and forms, respectively—will not work. The `document.getElementsByTagName` method must be used in place to retrieve the specific elements you want. For example:

```
var elsrc = document.images[0].src;
```

would be expressed as

```
var el = document.getElementsByTagName("img")[0];
var elsrc = el.getAttribute("src");
```

XHTML 1.1

XHTML 1.1 has only a few differences from the strict flavor of XHTML 1.0. The available elements and attributes are the same, though XHTML 1.1 also includes the Ruby module, which I'll talk about more in the section "Ruby" later in this appendix. XHTML 1.1 also has its own doctype:

```
<!DOCTYPE html PUBLIC "-//W3C//DTD XHTML 1.1//EN"
"http://www.w3.org/TR/xhtml11/DTD/xhtml11.dtd">
```

There are no strict, transitional, or frameset varieties here—you're either writing to the XHTML 1.1 DTD or you're not.

XHTML 1.1 *must* be served with a MIME type of application/xhtml+xml (www.w3.org/TR/xhtml-media-types/#summary), and if you're not doing that, then you're not really using XHTML 1.1. Yes, you can slap an XHTML 1.1 doctype on your content and that content can still validate—because validators check that the markup is valid, not the server behavior.

Browsers will also still display it, but they're just treating it as HTML, just as they would with one of the XHTML 1.0 variants, so this is to be expected.

If you're writing XHTML 1.1 but serving it as text/html, don't fool yourself into thinking that you're being more advanced than if you were writing any other version of (X)HTML—you're not. At best, you might be fooling some clients or managers. After all, 1.1 is a higher number than 1.0, so it must be better, right? Sorry, but no, not really—served as HTML, XHTML 1.1 is no better or worse, and it becomes again an issue of how well you write it rather than any inherent strengths and advantages.

Modularization

Anyway, what is XHTML 1.1 and how is it different from XHTML 1.0? Well, the key difference is that it has been *modularized*, which is in no way as painful as it sounds when carried out correctly. What this means is that what you know as XHTML has been broken down into several different modules—for instance, the structure module, which contains the <body>, <head>, <html> and <title> elements, or the list module, which contains the <dl>, <dt>, <dd>, <ol>, <ul> and <li> elements. This then allows people to create subsets (or supersets) of XHTML using only the modules they need, or to integrate other XML applications to create what is known as an **XHTML Family** document type—such as XHTML 1.1 plus MathML.

XHTML Basic (www.w3.org/TR/xhtml-basic) is an example of this modular form of XHTML. It's a stripped-down version of XHTML that's designed for use on devices that may have small screens or very low bandwidth such as mobile phones. It's actually a fairly complete implementation, only leaving out the presentation module (which consists of <b>, <big>, <hr>, <i>, <small>, <sub>, <sup>,[1] and <tt>) and the frames module,[2] but it also only includes the basic XHTML tables module that not only forbids the nesting of tables, but also only includes the <caption>, <table>, <td>, <th>, and <tr> elements. The full tables module contains the same as the basic module but also includes all the other table elements—<col>, <colgroup>, <tbody>, <thead>, and <tfoot> (it also contains a greater number of attributes).

> There also exists XHTML Mobile Profile, or XHTML-MP for short, which is a superset of XHTML Basic developed by the Open Mobile Alliance (an organization consisting of numerous mobile operators and device and network suppliers), which is essentially just XHTML Basic with a few presentational elements such as <b> and <big> thrown in. It's unrelated to the W3C, but if you're interested, I suggest reading the tutorial at http://htmlmastery.com/s/xhtml-mp/. It's uncertain to me at this stage whether there's any real value in developing mobile pages in XHTML-MP over XHTML Basic with CSS—time will tell.

---

1. I disagree that <sup> and <sub> are presentational—when used in mathematical and scientific formulae, they convey as much meaning as they do presentation—but nobody listens to me.

2. For full details on all of the different modules and their contents, see www.w3.org/TR/xhtml-modularization/abstract_modules.html.

Another example is XHTML-Print (www.w3.org/TR/xhtml-print/), which is only a proposed recommendation at the time of writing but appears to be fairly complete. XHTML-Print is based on XHTML Basic, but it is designed to provide a simple page description format where content preservation and reproduction are more important than layout preservation, in environments where it may not be possible to install specific printer drivers. It includes the script module but not the intrinsic events module, it includes the presentation module but not the frames module, and so on.

There's also XHTML 2.0, covered in Chapter 7, which uses modules from XForms (also covered in Chapter 7); XML Events, a module that provides XML languages with the "ability to uniformly integrate event listeners and associated event handlers with Document Object Model (DOM) Level 2 event interfaces" (www.w3.org/TR/xml-events/); and Ruby, which we'll look at now.

Ruby

Ruby refers to a fragment of text that has an association with another fragment of text, known as the **base text**—it is most often used to provide a short annotation of the base text, or a pronunciation guide, and is used frequently in East Asian typography. Typically it can be presented as shown in Figure A-3.

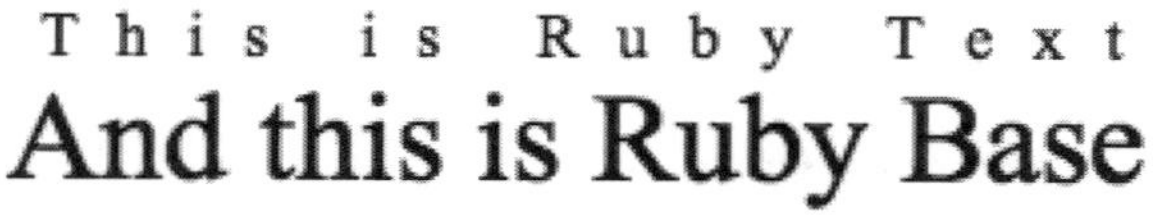

This is Ruby Text
And this is Ruby Base

Figure A-3. Ruby text

The Ruby text is roughly half the size of the base text (the name "Ruby" in this case comes from the name of the 5.5-point font size historically used in British printing, about half the size of the 10-point size used for normal text), and runs beneath it or above it, or alongside it if the language is written vertically instead of horizontally. Using the Ruby elements provides a semantic and structural association between the texts.

So far as browser support goes, it's unfortunately a sorry state of affairs, with only Internet Explorer for both Windows and the Mac offering any native support[3] (and only really for the "simple" variety of Ruby markup, detailed in the next section). There is also a Firefox extension (http://piro.sakura.ne.jp/xul/_rubysupport.html.en) that provides some support, though it comes with a dire warning that you should not use it if you want a stable browser, so use with caution. An alternative is to use the markup anyway, but then trick nonsupportive browsers into displaying it as desired with CSS.

---

3. Somewhat bewilderingly; you need to be writing to the XHTML 1.1 doctype to be using Ruby markup, and XHTML 1.1 must be served as XML—which Internet Explorer doesn't support. So what it's doing offering Ruby support is anybody's guess, though I imagine it has something to do with providing for the Asian market.

A

As noted previously, there are two types of Ruby markup: simple and complex. The former associates just a single fragment of Ruby text with a single fragment of base text, and it also comes with a fallback mechanism so that nonsupportive browsers can make some sense out of things. The latter allows authors to associate up to two Ruby texts with one base text, and it also allows for groups of Ruby and base associations. However, complex Ruby markup provides no fallback mechanism.

Simple Ruby markup

Simple Ruby markup consists of a single <ruby> container, which contains one <rb> element for the base text (Ruby base) and one <rt> element for the Ruby text:

```
<ruby>
  <rb>WWW</rb>
  <rt>World Wide Web</rt>
</ruby>
```

Internet Explorer will display the Ruby element as shown in Figure A-4.

World Wide Web

WWW

Figure A-4. The Ruby text in Internet Explorer

Nonsupportive browsers will display it as shown in Figure A-5.

WWW World Wide Web

Figure A-5. The preceding Ruby text in Firefox

It still makes sense, but it's a bit untidy. Fortunately, the problem of nonsupportive user agents has been dealt with; by using the <rp> element (Ruby parenthesis), we can make the presentation of that Ruby content more appropriate:

```
<ruby>
  <rb>WWW</rb>
  <rp>(</rp><rt>World Wide Web</rt><rp>)</rp>
</ruby>
```

Supportive browsers will ignore the contents of the <rp>, but nonsupportive browsers will display the parentheses, as shown in Figure A-6.

WWW (World Wide Web)

Figure A-6. Firefox shows the parentheses, but Internet Explorer will not.

This is exactly what user agents are supposed to do with tags and elements they don't understand—ignore them, but display their content anyway. It's why you can use an <abbr> but still have the content appear in Internet Explorer 6 and below.

Alternatively, if you're not concerned about those user agents that don't support CSS2, you can use the CSS content property to automatically insert parentheses without having to manually insert them in the markup:

```
rt:before { content: "(" }
rt:after { content: ")" }
```

Complex Ruby markup

More complex Ruby markup is used to associate more than one Ruby text with a base text. To do this, you need to use some Ruby container elements—<rbc> and <rtc> (Ruby base container and Ruby text container). Thus the following:

```
<ruby>
  <rbc>
    <rb>10</rb>
    <rb>31</rb>
    <rb>2002</rb>
  </rbc>
  <rtc>
    <rt>Month</rt>
    <rt>Day</rt>
    <rt>Year</rt>
  </rtc>
  <rtc>
    <rt rbspan="3">Expiration Date</rt>
  </rtc>
</ruby>
```

The contents of each <rb> in the <rbc> element all now have an association with each of the <rt> elements in the <rtc> element. Furthermore, the final <rt> in the second <rtc> is using an rbspan attribute to indicate that it is associated with all three base texts.

The <rp> element cannot be used when you're using complex Ruby markup—you can't place it within either an <rbc> or an <rtc> and remain valid. This is because <rp> was only provided as a fallback mechanism, and trying to come up with a meaningful fallback display and constructing the markup could be difficult, if not impossible.

Summary

Despite the hype, serving XHTML as XML on the Web still appears to largely be a minority interest; at most, web authors appear to be using content negotiation simply because that appears to be the right thing to do according to the XHTML specifications, rather than there being many inherent benefits to it. I suspect that a key reason behind the low adoption of XHTML as XML is the absence of any support from Internet Explorer—even version 7 fails to recognize the application/xhtml+xml MIME type—but it could also be because XHTML as XML demands more from the author, and part of HTML's appeal is that it's relatively simple for people to pick up. Indeed, it's arguable that had the language not been as straightforward, and had browsers been draconian in their handling of poorly written markup, the Web might not have proven to be so popular. This is just theorizing, though.

Seeing as XHTML 1.1 and the forthcoming XHTML 2.0 come with an insistence that they be served as XML, it seems that as far as the W3C is concerned, XHTML as XML is the future. When this future will arrive, however, is anybody's guess.

Some things, I'm afraid, are simply unavoidable, and when you write a book purporting to cover *every* (X)HTML tag that there is, you can't just not mention frames because you don't like them—tempting though that may be. So here they are, but discussed in an appendix rather than in a dedicated chapter, as their use usually contravenes every notion of good practice, and more often than not there's a better, more accessible and usable solution.

That said, we're long past the days when frames were in common use anyway. The many arguments against them—browsers struggled with printing framed pages and with bookmarking them, browsers lacking support for frames, and so on—have since dwindled due to advances in browser technology. Despite these advances, however, problems do still exist:

- The browser's back button can no longer work intuitively.
- You can't easily reference a specific document within a frameset.
- The browser's reload button may reload the entire frameset, resetting the frame contents to their default sources, rather than reloading the specific framed document.
- Search engines can struggle when navigating through framed documents.
- Search engines can index pages outside of the frameset, producing pages lacking in branding or navigation.
- Numerous accessibility issues exist with using frames.

Even discoverability can be a problem if the web designer has set things so that the frames lack borders and scrollbars; you may not even realize you're within a frameset until you try to refresh the page. Some browsers will allow you to right-click a framed page and reload it or bookmark it, but you have to know where it is to be able to manipulate it; it isn't always clear. Frames always were a clunky solution to a problem with serious usability and accessibility issues, and this remains the case today.

Furthermore, the arguments *for* them—mostly related to being able to include persistent and consistent navigation on every page—have also dwindled due to advances in server technology; using server-side includes (SSIs) or PHP server-side include statements (which I'll give an overview of later in this appendix in the section "Alternatives to frames") allows you to include consistent navigation on any page you like while only having to update one file. CSS also allows you to create a frame-like appearance, as you'll see further on in the section "Frame-like behavior with CSS."

So frames in their current incarnation can practically be considered obsolete. For those who want to build their own website, even the cheapest hosting packages these days will at least allow SSI, and the rise of hosted blog services such as LiveJournal, TypePad, and Blogger (where both the website code and markup are all provided alongside the hosting) means that amateur bloggers have much less of a need to build their own system from the ground up.

However, they are still used, albeit rarely—such as in an offline help package distributed with an application. There are also *inline frames*—the `<iframe>`—to consider. This element is used a lot more, mostly to embed third-party ads (for instance, Google's AdSense) on your webpages, but it has been removed from strict XHTML 1.0, so when I get to it, I'll give you a look at what the W3C is planning for us to use instead: XFrames.

So, let's begin by taking a quick look at how frames are currently used in (X)HTML, which should be considered more as a historical footnote than recommended production techniques; if you think you need to use frames, please do consider all the alternatives first. If after that you *still* think you need to use frames, please use them with caution. Frame markup remains valid markup (more or less) to this day, but there are many, many good reasons as to why their use is now practically nonexistent.

(X)HTML frames

To use (X)HTML frames, first of all, you need to make sure you're using the correct doctype (you may remember this from Chapter 1). There is a specific doctype that should be used when, and *only* when, you're using frames. For sites written in HTML, that doctype is

```
<!DOCTYPE HTML PUBLIC "-//W3C//DTD HTML 4.01 Frameset//EN"
    "http://www.w3.org/TR/html4/frameset.dtd">
```

while the XHTML equivalent is similar:

```
<!DOCTYPE html PUBLIC "-//W3C//DTD XHTML 1.0 Frameset//EN"
    "http://www.w3.org/TR/xhtml1/DTD/xhtml1-frameset.dtd">
```

That doctype is to be used on the root document—the one that will contain the frames. The doctypes you use on the files you're loading into the frames do not have to use the frameset doctype.

From there, the document will contain at least one <frameset>, which will define the number of rows and columns within the document, and will in turn contain usually at least two self-closing <frame> elements, which will load in the framed documents. So the markup for a simple two-frame document, in which the navigation frame is to be 80 pixels wide and the content frame is to fill the rest of the available space, would look somewhat like this:

```
<frameset cols="80,*">
  <frame src="nav.html" scrolling="no" noresize="noresize" ➥
name="navFrame" title="Navigation" />
  <frame src="content.html" name="mainFrame" title="Content" />
</frameset>
```

> *There should technically also be a* <noframes> *section that displays content to those user agents lacking support for frames; those that do support frames would not display the contents. This is of less importance these days than it used to be, as all browsers come with frame support—even text browsers such as Lynx come with some support for navigating framed documents. Historically the* <noframes> *content provided by developers has been limited to messages such as "Your browser doesn't support frames." Not especially helpful, and another reason that the use of frames had been criticized in the past.*

Note the few frame-specific attributes in the preceding code. The <frameset> uses the cols attribute, with a comma-separated list of values, to determine the number of columns contained within the frameset, and the sizes of each one (using the * character to indicate that the size should expand to fit—you can also use percentage values that allow the frames to scale with the size of the viewport). If your frameset contains horizontal frames instead of vertical frames (or a combination of both), the rows attribute works in the same way.

The src attribute is used to point to the file to be loaded within the frame; it can be an (X)HTML document, an image, a text file—anything that a browser can display. Because it allows for both relative and absolute URLs, it is possible to load another website's content into your own frameset—a nefarious practice referred to as **framejacking**.

The noresize attribute used on the <frame> element prevents the frame from being resized—fairly obvious that one. If left out, users can drag the border between the two frames (if it's visible) and change the width of the columns as they please.

There are some presentational attributes—scrolling (yes | no | auto) frameborder, marginwidth, marginheight—these can all be better controlled with the CSS overflow, border, and margin properties.

Finally, there exists here a longdesc attribute, which you may remember turned up in the discussion of images in Chapter 2. The principle is similar here: the value of a longdesc is a URL that points to a page giving a long description of the *purpose* of the frame, rather than its content—as the content of the frame can change, a hard-coded description of that content could cease very quickly to be accurate. The browser support, however, is the same as for the <img> variety—effectively zero.

Targeting links within frames

A link in one frame will always open within that frame, unless told otherwise; this can lead to another problem from the frames era, where websites could get stuck in somebody else's frameset.

To get a link in one frame to open in another, you need to use the deprecated target attribute on the link, and make sure each frame has a unique name. Thus, a link like this:

```
<a href="about.html" target="mainFrame">About</a>
```

will open up the page about.html not in its own frame, but in the frame named mainFrame. Adding target attributes on every link could get quite laborious, so you can save a bit of time by using the <base> element. This is a self-closing element that sits in the <head>, and it must be placed before any <style>, <script>, or <link> elements that are pointing to external sources. Its purpose is to define the root URL that all relative links should use as their base:

```
<head>
  <base href="http://unfortunatelypaul.com" />
  ...
```

So in the preceding example, when you click the About link, the browser would read that URL as http://unfortunatelypaul.com/about.html—even if the site domain was different.

Why is this relevant here? Because you can also include a target attribute within the <base>:

```
<head>
  <base target="mainFrame" />
  ...
```

By including this in the markup of your navigation page, each link will gain the target attribute value without your needing to type it in on each <a>. To solve the problem of new sites opening within a frameset, you can use a target value of _top on any external hyperlinks, which will replace the entire frameset.

Inline frames

An inline frame does not require the use of a frameset doctype. It is used to create a fixed-width box[1] into which another document can be loaded, and it can be placed into a web page in exactly the same way as you would place a <div> or a <table> or any other element. It loads its content via the src attribute just like a regular frame, and its noframes content is actually stored within the content of the tag itself:

```
<iframe src="frame.html"><a href="frame.html">➥
View the content of this frame</a></iframe>
```

A browser that supported the <iframe> element would ignore its content and display the contents of frame.html within the frame boundaries; a browser that lacked <iframe> support would instead display the link to the document.

B

There are several presentational attributes that can be used, all of which can be better controlled with CSS; the scrolling attribute mentioned earlier that determines whether a scrollbar will ever be visible on the frame can be controlled with the CSS overflow property (overflow: hidden, overflow: scroll, and overflow: auto). The frameborder, marginwidth, and marginheight attributes can all be reproduced with border and margin.

Alternatives to frames

Server-side technologies allow for a lot of the functionality of frames to be reproduced. A classic reason for using frames was to create consistent navigation; by including the navigation menu in a frame, you could ensure it remained the same on every page. These days, unless you're creating a website that is to be run entirely from the client side, you can use

---

1. Although you can give an <iframe> a width or height value in percentages, the frame won't scale when you resize your viewport. For instance, an <iframe> with a width of 60% will remain fixed at 60% of whatever the width of the viewport was when the document was first loaded.

server-side includes that piece together your files on the web server before sending the completed pages down the pipe to the user. I'm going to take a very brief look at two ways of doing this: with SSI and PHP.

First, SSIs. To use these, your files must usually end with an `.shtml` file extension rather than `.html` or `.htm`, though this can be dependent on how your web server is set up. An SSI looks like this:

```
<!--#include file="nav.html" -->
```

By placing that line in your web page, the server will insert the contents of nav.html into the document in its place (assuming that nav.html is contained within the same directory as the file you place this include in); then when you need to change your navigation, you just have to change the contents of nav.html. You can find detailed instructions on all you can do with SSIs in "Introduction to Server Side Includes" (http://httpd.apache.org/docs/1.3/howto/ssi.html).

If PHP is available on your server, you can use that instead. Again, you will most likely need to ensure your files all end with a `.php` extension, but servers can be set up to parse files with an extension of `.html` or `.htm` as PHP, so check with your system administrator. A typical PHP include looks like this:

```
<?php include 'nav.html'; ?>
```

Also available is the `require` function, which will cause the page to stop loading if nav.html is not available, and `require_once`, which acts in the same way as `require`, but will not include nav.html more than once. PHP errors will be generated and displayed to the user if there's a problem, but these error messages can be suppressed by prefixing the function with an ampersand, like this:

```
<?php @include 'nav.html'; ?>
```

More information on PHP includes can be found in the PHP manual (http://uk2.php.net/manual/en/function.include.php).

Frame-like behavior with CSS

If you've previously used frames because of their distinct visual nature—a combination of fixed and scrollable divisions—advances in server technology won't be of much use to you. However, advances in CSS (or, more accurately, advances in CSS support from the browsers) allow you to reproduce these effects to some extent, though sometimes not without a certain amount of cross-browser hackery.

At its most basic, use of the CSS `overflow` property can reproduce a frame-like effect; by applying `overflow:scroll` to an element and constraining its width or height, a scrollbar will appear, as shown in Figure B-1.

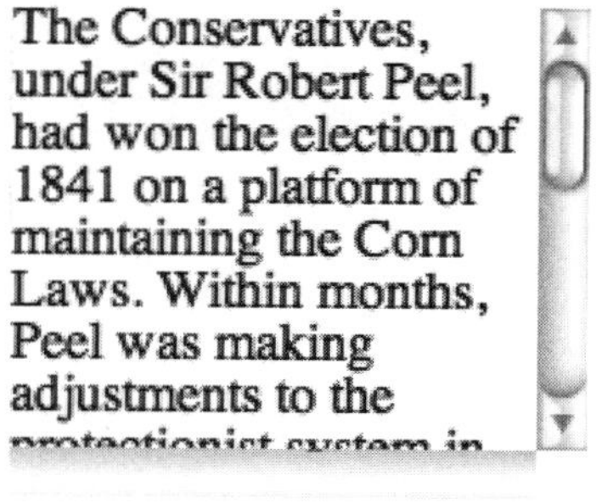

The Conservatives,
under Sir Robert Peel,
had won the election of
1841 on a platform of
maintaining the Corn
Laws. Within months,
Peel was making
adjustments to the
protectionist system in

Figure B-1. A paragraph with a fixed width and height and overflow:scroll forcing a scrollbar; the default is for the paragraph contents to spill out across the boundaries of the paragraph.

You can be even more specific by using the overflow-x and overflow-y properties, which control the nature of the overflow in either the horizontal or vertical axis. These properties will cause your CSS to fail validation, however, as they were originally created by Microsoft (though they are now supported in Mozilla browsers, as well as the very latest bleeding-edge builds of Safari, and thus will probably be in a released version by the time this book is in your hands). The two properties are being included as part of the CSS3 box-model module (www.w3.org/TR/2002/WD-css3-box-20021024/#the-overflow-x), so they will eventually be considered standard CSS, and the support is already there in the real world.

Also of use is the position property with a value of fixed, which allows you to position an element within the viewport and force it to remain in place while the rest of the content scrolls. For instance, in Figures B-2 and B-3, the heading (an <h1>) remains visible while the rest of the page content scrolls behind it.

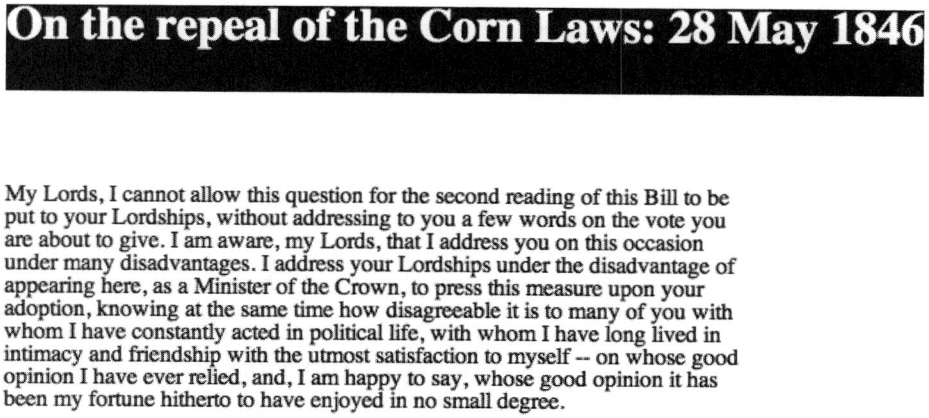

On the repeal of the Corn Laws: 28 May 1846

My Lords, I cannot allow this question for the second reading of this Bill to be put to your Lordships, without addressing to you a few words on the vote you are about to give. I am aware, my Lords, that I address you on this occasion under many disadvantages. I address your Lordships under the disadvantage of appearing here, as a Minister of the Crown, to press this measure upon your adoption, knowing at the same time how disagreeable it is to many of you with whom I have constantly acted in political life, with whom I have long lived in intimacy and friendship with the utmost satisfaction to myself -- on whose good opinion I have ever relied, and, I am happy to say, whose good opinion it has been my fortune hitherto to have enjoyed in no small degree.

Figure B-2. The header will remain in place as the content scrolls underneath it . . .

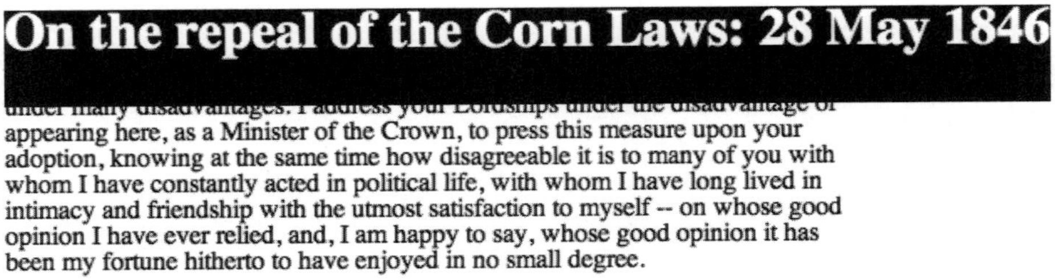

On the repeal of the Corn Laws: 28 May 1846

under many disadvantages. I address your Lordships under the disadvantage of appearing here, as a Minister of the Crown, to press this measure upon your adoption, knowing at the same time how disagreeable it is to many of you with whom I have constantly acted in political life, with whom I have long lived in intimacy and friendship with the utmost satisfaction to myself -- on whose good opinion I have ever relied, and, I am happy to say, whose good opinion it has been my fortune hitherto to have enjoyed in no small degree.

Figure B-3. . . . like so.

The CSS for this is simple:

```
h1 { position: fixed;}
```

This isn't supported in Internet Explorer 6 and below (support has been introduced in IE7), but there are various hacks and scripts available that can trick the browser and fake the effect. I've had good results using a JavaScript solution provided by Doxdesk (www.doxdesk.com/software/js/fixed.html), but you can also try the various CSS solutions around. (There are several. Stu Nicholl's, available at www.cssplay.co.uk/layouts/fixed.html, is one I've used in the past to good effect.) A word of warning about this style of displaying your content though: if your users use their Page Down button to scroll the content, they can end up having to use their cursor keys to go back up a few lines as the content scrolls underneath the fixed element, so use with caution.

Roger Johansson has an exhaustive frame-like effect with support for multiple browsers, detailed in "CSS Frames, v2, full-height (www.456bereastreet.com/archive/200609/css_frames_v2_fullheight/). This sees the creation of a page with a fixed-height header, a fixed-height footer that stays glued to the bottom of the browser viewport, and a scrollable middle section. Also of interest is Emil Stenström's "Frames or Iframes with CSS" (http://friendlybit.com/css/frames-or-iframes-with-css/).

Future frames: XFrames

The forthcoming XHTML 2.0 recommendation doesn't include any frame markup; that functionality will instead be available as an XML application named XFrames (not part of any (X)HTML specification but sharing the syntax and some common elements), which is being created to overcome many of the problems the current (X)HTML implementation of frames suffer from. At the time of writing, no browser has any support for XFrames aside from the X-Smiles browser mentioned in Chapter 7, so all of what's to follow is largely theoretical and also subject to change, as the specification has not yet been finalized.

XFrame markup is a lot like the current (X)HTML frame markup. Replacing the <frameset> is the <frames> tag, not to be confused with <frame>, which is more or less the same as its (X)HTML equivalent. Also the same are the <head>, <title>, and <style> elements—these all act exactly as you would expect them to. Finally, there's a <group> element, which replaces the notion of nested framesets. Here's an example of a simple XFrames document—this is a trimmed down example from the current XFrames working draft:

```
<frames xmlns="http://www.w3.org/2002/06/xframes/">
  <head>
    <title>Home page</title>
  </head>
  <group compose="vertical">
    <frame xml:id="banner" source="banner.html" />
    <group compose="horizontal">
            <frame xml:id="atoz" source="atoz.html" />
            <frame xml:id="main" source="news.html" />
            <frame xml:id="nav" source="nav.html" />
    </group>
    <frame xml:id="footer" source="copyright.html" />
  </group>
</frames>
```

This describes a three-column layout topped and tailed with a horizontal header and a horizontal footer that both span the widths of the three central columns. You can see that the src attribute has been replaced by the source attribute—it still does the same thing, though its value can be overridden by values in the URL, discussed in a moment. I'll talk about the compose attribute in a moment, but first let's look at all those xml:id attributes.

The xml:id attribute is the same as the (X)HTML id attribute and follows the same rules. It's used for identifying the framed documents, but can also be used to populate the contents of the frames via a reference in the URL. For example, if you had a document with the file name example.xframes, and the markup was

```
<group compose="horizontal">
  <group compose="vertical">
    <frame xml:id="one" />
    <frame xml:id="two" />
  </group>
  <frame xml:id="three" source="default.html" />
</group>
```

you could populate all of those frames with a URL like this:

```
http://example.com/example.xframes#frames➡
(one=one.html,two=two.html,three=three.html)
```

It's a bit messy, but this way the URL is always representative of the contents of the frameset, changing in relation to the activities of the user, making it possible to bookmark and reference specific frameset configurations. The value provided in the URL for the frame named three will override the value set in the source attribute; if not set in the URL, it will display default.html instead. In the absence of any values supplied, the frames simply remain empty.

Regarding the presentation of XFrames, there's more flexibility, and they follow the same ethos of separating style from content that's seen in the XHTML 2.0 working draft—where all the markup can do is "suggest" to the rendering device how the markup should be dealt with. This is from the current XFrames working draft (www.w3.org/TR/xframes/):

B

"An XFrames document is a specification for composing several documents, potentially of different types, together in a view. The frames element forms the container for the composed document. The individual sub-documents ('frames') may be composed together in a rectangular space by placing them next to, or above, each other in rows and columns, or they may be displayed as separate movable window-like panes, or as tabbed panes, or in any other suitable manner."

So there's more flexibility in terms of displaying the framed content—traditionally, or as movable windows, or as tabbed panes, and so on; this allows for a greater level of device independence, with the user agent selecting a display method suitable to the display device. A "suggestion" as to the preferred way of presenting an XFrame document can be included within the XFrame markup—the compose attribute, used on the <group> tag. It accepts values of

- vertical: Frames within the group should be tiled vertically, one above the other. This would also be the default value if the user agent didn't understand the supplied value.

- horizontal: Frames within the group should be tiled horizontally, all along the same row.

- single: Only one frame at a time should be visible, but the user should be able to see that other frames are selectable, so this is similar to a tabbed interface.

- free: The frames are available as movable, overlapping windows within the frames container.

So that's XFrames in a nutshell: more powerful, flexible, and accessible than (X)HTML frames, but probably not usable in a production environment for a good few years yet—for the time being, merely another point of interest.

Summary

That covers frames—a collection of elements that were pretty horrible when first introduced, continued to be horrible during their heyday, and remain horrible in obscurity today. But, as the existence of XFrames demonstrates, they're here to stay, in one form or another, and when used appropriately and with an awareness of the many usability and accessibility issues they can cause, they *can* be useful. Apart from <iframe>, though, it would be a rare situation that leads the modern web designer to needing to use frames, and until XFrames is finalized and has enough browser support to be usable, frames should be considered a historical curiosity more than anything else.

INDEX